Francis Bacon, philosopher, essayist, scientist, statesman and jurist, was one of the great Renaissance men. One of his proudest boasts, "I have taken all knowledge to be my province," is not simply a grandiose comment; it clearly reflects Bacon's all-encompassing genius.

Bacon's niche in the history of thought rests on his studies of the modern inductive method in science and his logical systemization of scientific procedures. He contributed passionately and vigorously to the improvement and development of man's concepts in moral as well as scientific areas. His was one of the outstanding minds of the mighty English Renaissance.

Henry LeRoy Finch, Ph.D., author of the Introduction, has taught Philosophy at Sarah Lawrence College since 1953. He has written extensively on philosophical subjects for the professional journals and is a regular book reviewer for *Bibliography of Philosophy*. He also conducts a program called "Philosophy Forum" over radio station WBAI-FM, New York.

THE COMPLETE
ESSAYS OF
FRANCIS BACON

Including
THE NEW ATLANTIS
and
NOVUM ORGANUM

With an Introduction by
HENRY LeROY FINCH

WASHINGTON SQUARE PRESS, INC. • NEW YORK

THE COMPLETE ESSAYS OF FRANCIS BACON
Including THE NEW ATLANTIS
and NOVUM ORGANUM

A *Washington Square Press* edition
1st printing.......................August, 1963

Published by
Washington Square Press, Inc., 630 Fifth Avenue, New York, N.Y.

L

WASHINGTON SQUARE PRESS editions are distributed in
the U.S. by Affiliated Publishers, a division of Pocket
Books, Inc., 630 Fifth Avenue, New York 20, N.Y.

Contents

Introduction

FRANCIS BACON stands out for us today as one of the major prophets of technology and organized science. At the doorway to our age, more than 300 years ago, he caught the utopian spirit of modern science and proclaimed the possibility of science transforming the earth for human benefit. In the statement "knowledge is power" [1] he epitomized a fundamental modern attitude and need that has come to have an even more startling significance for us with the release of nuclear energy and the awareness of the even greater power implicit in the discovery of antimatter.

But Bacon is important also for a more profound and subtler reason. In his own life he embodied the torturous problem of the relation between science and morality. As a statesman and holder of high public office he found himself subject to forces and rules that his temperament and philosophy ill-fitted him to deal with, and his career ended in the disgrace of conviction for bribery while serving as Lord Chancellor. We cannot study his life without wondering about the differences between human dealings with nature and human dealings with other men.

Like so many of his Elizabethan contemporaries, Bacon remains fascinating and enigmatic—still the subject of controversy and speculation—because of the many conflicts and contradictions of his personality, the mixture of old and new in his ideas and the scope and daring of his imagination. The ambitious statesman and extravagant courtier combine with the cool observer of human frailties; the passionate encyclopedist and composer of endless tables and classifications with the astute student of physical nature. And all is flavored with just a touch—so characteristically Renaissance—of the charlatan, or, to give it another name, of the self-glorifying. Philosopher or publicist? Statesman or self-seeker? We are as far from having solved the riddle of Francis Bacon as we are from having solved the riddle of modern science itself.

It is doubtful whether Bacon deserves to be called a scientist. He made no important scientific discoveries himself, and, more serious, failed to appreciate the most significant scientific discoveries of his own day. In his many writings he made no mention of Kepler or Napier's logarithms; he rejected Copernicus's theory and failed to understand Harvey's work on the blood; reviewing mechanics, he did not mention Galileo, although Galileo's studies of falling bodies had been made thirty years before (he also failed to mention Archimedes!).[2] These omissions cannot be explained on the grounds that knowledge of these things was not common intellectual currency. Rather, to a certain extent, they reflect Bacon's faulty conception of scientific methodology, just that on which he himself set perhaps the greatest store.

Bacon inherited the Renaissance passion to encompass all knowledge, but, unlike his encyclopedist predecessors, he saw the importance—indeed the supreme importance—for science of methodology.[3] He believed that the use of the right method in science could compensate for all the failings of men's senses and reason, which—probably it was not unconnected with his Calvinist upbringing—he never chose to ignore. Method was to be the open-sesame to all benefits and future glories, the means by which inventions and discoveries might proliferate to blanket the earth.

Bacon's conception of the scientific method, furthermore, rightly emphasized the importance of induction, anticipating the inductive methods of John Stuart Mill, which, acknowledged or unacknowledged, are essential to science. Although he was far from being the first to do so (his tone might suggest this), he rejected what he regarded as the unproductive Aristotelian-Scholastic overemphasis on deductive logic. (He was, in fact, a relative latecomer to the denunciation of Aristotle, since the Aristotelian authority had been waning for a long time.) But, equally important, he also rejected the mere collection or piling up of facts. Facts had to be assembled according to definite inductive criteria, listed at tedious length in his many tables.[4]

Bacon's idea of the scientific method was conspicuously inadequate, in the light of what has happened since, in its failure to recognize the constant interaction of fact and theory in science. The Baconian method has never been, and probably never can be, applied for it is based upon a faulty premise—the premise that, in science, facts and theories can be isolated from each other. Today it is no longer a merely academic point (if it ever was) that every experiment and every use of instruments is already impregnated with definition and theory.[5] Except at the level of natural history, which is where Bacon's method remained, there is in science no such thing as pure observation, free from all theory. Constantly changing methods of observation and description themselves introduce theoretical components, and this was already implicitly recognized by Galileo, who, far more than Bacon, deserves to be called the father of modern scientific method.

It was, in a sense, Bacon's "encyclopedism" that betrayed him. He held what the British logician, John Venn, called "the alphabetical view of the universe"; that is, the view that the facts of nature, however complex (and he did not underrate their complexity) could be broken up, organized and labeled, once and for all.[6] Although he saw the "progressive" character of science, he did not see the "progressive" character of facts. For him the necessary distinctions between facts were all there to be catalogued at the outset as part of a universal dictionary of nature. That the important point was that new methods of experiment and observation would constantly require new distinctions of facts to be made ever afresh escaped him.

It is perhaps the most serious charge against Bacon as an exponent of science that he is, in part, responsible for the myth that science begins by observing and collecting facts and then goes on to make theories. This is not and cannot be the scientific method, and the notion that it is has only worked harm. The relation between observation and theory is both subtler and more fruitful than this, and it is never broken at any level.

What Bacon failed to emphasize, or perhaps even to recognize, was that it is not desirable, even if it were possible, to approach facts in science without hypotheses or preconceptions. On the contrary, as Morris Cohen observed:

> Fruitful observation depends not as Bacon thought upon the absence of bias or anticipatory ideas, but rather on the logical multiplication of them so that having many possibilities in mind, we are better prepared to direct our attention to what others have never thought of as within the field of possibility.[7]

Bacon seriously underestimated—not at every point, but at *almost* every point—the speculative and hypothetical factor in science. Science progresses by what Karl Popper calls "bold ideas, unjustified anticipations and speculative thought, [which] are our only means for interpreting nature: our only organon, our only instrument for grasping her." [8] These are just the "anticipations, rash and premature" that Bacon rejected, but now put as *questions* to nature rather than as the dogmatic *conclusions* to which he really objected. Bacon wanted to guard against hasty and empty generalizations. What he could not foresee was that no method of collecting, comparing or organizing already evident facts could replace daring and imaginative hypotheses.

Similarly, his failure to appreciate the importance of mathematics, which he regarded as simply an "auxiliary" or "handmaiden" to inductive science, damaged his understanding of scientific method.[9] Here again Galileo, for whom the book of nature was written in the "language of mathematics," was more prescient, and he anticipated the future direction of science more correctly than did Bacon.[10]

Yet when all this is said, Bacon remains still perhaps *the* major prophet of modern science, not for his conception of scientific method, but for his insistence upon the practical significance of science. In an almost uncanny way he foresaw the practical benefits to be expected, and he proclaimed that these benefits were a worthy, and indeed the worthiest, goal of science.

> It is not possible to run a course aright when the goal itself has not been rightly placed. Now the true and lawful goal of the sciences is none other than this: that human life be endowed with new discoveries and powers.[11]

Bacon proclaimed, in other words, "the empire of man over things" and "the power and dominion of the human race itself over the universe." [12] What counted for him is what he states as his own purpose: to extend "the power and greatness of man." [13]

No fear of hybris constrains this Promethean vision. On the contrary, Bacon sees it as having a religious sanction, since God has given man "dominion over nature." It is, he believes, the mission of science to repair the damage done by the Fall of Man and to restore man to his original glory. Nature is to be conquered, commanded, subdued. It must no longer be thought that such great powers and achievements are impossible for men because of human weakness. If only the right method is used, nothing is impossible, for "human knowledge and human power meet in one." [14]

There can be no doubt that this outburst of confidence and enthusiasm was greatly stimulated by the voyages of discovery that fanned the Elizabethan imagination. Bacon's own imagination was caught by the discovery of America, as well as by his reflections on the inventions of printing, gunpowder and the magnet. He compared himself to Columbus and spoke of "the breath of hope which blows on us from that New Continent." [15] (And indeed it was on "that New Continent" that the practical science he envisaged was to make its greatest headway.)

In a characteristic juxtaposition of ideas, he saw in the prophecy of Daniel that "Many shall run to and fro, and knowledge shall be increased" something

> clearly intimating that the thorough passage of the world (which now by so many distant voyages seems to be accomplished, or in the course of accomplishment), and the advancement of the sciences, are destined by fate, that is, by Divine Providence, to meet in the same age.[16]

It is characteristic of Bacon that he placed his vision of the future scientific society on an island even beyond America in the South Seas, and that this society combined both Christian virtues and science. Bacon saw that something truly new was starting (what we would call the "technological world"); that it would depend upon collective organized science; and that, to be successful, it would have to unite moral and religious virtues with scientific research. The *New Atlantis* has been called the "fullest and clearest expression of his ideal of organized scientific research." [17] Bacon's famous House of Salomon became the inspiration for the founding of the Royal Society of London by men all deeply influenced by his teachings.[18]

Standing today at the beginning of a new age of voyages—this time voyages into space—we can feel some of the enthusiasm that Bacon felt during the Elizabethan age of voyages. But perhaps today we are not so confident as he was about the relations of science and morality. After Buchenwald and Hiroshima, science may not have, as some physicists have said, "tasted sin," but it has certainly been forced to raise the question of to what uses scientific discoveries will be put, and how men are to deal with each other. And this brings us to the problem raised by Bacon's own life.

Bacon was born in London in 1561, three years before Galileo, to a titled and powerful family close to the court of Elizabeth. His father was a prominent statesman, his mother an accomplished and educated woman, passionately religious, who brought up her children in an atmosphere of learning and Puritanism. Bacon was sent to Cambridge at the age of twelve, where he remained for three years. Reading for the law was interrupted by the chance to go abroad on diplomatic work, and it was while he was in France that he learned of his father's death. By mischance his father had failed to make provision for him, the youngest son, and this event colored Bacon's whole life. At the age of eighteen he found himself without the funds or parental influence so important to the style of life and advancement of a courtier. For the rest of his life he was seldom out of debt and seldom ceased importuning those he thought might be able to advance him.

Unlike Descartes in the next generation, who withdrew from the world to meditate and write, Bacon, though occasionally tempted by this alternative, longed for a public career and high office. If his first aim was to found a new science, his second and equally intense aim was to gain official advancement. While the two aims may have been linked in his mind by the thought that only in power could his scientific plans be carried out, it was not always apparent that this was so. On some occasions they appeared to Bacon himself, as we know from his papers, to be in conflict.

He entered the House of Commons as a young man, but all attempts to gain appointments through the influence of his uncle, Lord Burghley, the Queen's chief adviser, and others, failed. It was not until 1607, after the death of Elizabeth, and when Bacon was well along in his forties, that his ambitions began to be realized, and he was appointed Solicitor-General by James I. In 1613 he became Attorney-General and in 1618, Lord Chancellor, the highest appointive office in the land. After only three years in this last post he was convicted of bribery and removed from office, retiring to the country, where he died in 1626. It was during this final retirement that he wrote the *New Atlantis* and completed the *Essays* in the form that we have them today. (The first edition of the *Essays*, containing only ten of them, was his first published work and was brought out in 1597.)

The two events that shadowed Bacon's life and that contain part of the key to his character were his role in the prosecution of the Earl of Essex for high treason and his admitted taking of bribes, which led to his final downfall.

Essex had been a friend and patron of Bacon. He became involved in a foolish and ill-conceived rebellion, which conjured up visions of the "popish plots" of the day. There is no reasonable doubt about Essex's guilt (though there may be of his mental stability). In any case, Bacon, acting for the Queen, was largely instrumental in obtaining a conviction and death penalty against him. It is fashionable today to put duty to the state above duty to friends, and recent biographers have tried to exonerate Bacon from the charge of betraying a friend.[19] But it is hard to escape the impression that Bacon's zeal in the matter went beyond the needs of public duty, and this view is not incompatible with the impression of coldness and detachment in human affairs that Bacon's life often suggests.[20]

In the matter of taking bribes Bacon admitted his guilt and failed to offer any defense. Again, recent biographers have pointed to the prevalence of "gifts" to public officials in this period, measuring Bacon's conduct by the common practice of the day. Yet the best moral opinion of the time condemned the practice, and Bacon himself in the *New Atlantis* speaks against people being "twice paid." This episode seems better understood as a culminating example of a certain "compliancy" or "moral pliability" that runs like a never-broken thread through Bacon's career.

If there was a flaw in Bacon's character, it was that he sought to deal with people in somewhat the same way that he recommended dealing with nature: he sought to manipulate them by bending to them. He had said: "Nature to be commanded must be obeyed." [21] This same principle, when applied to human beings, produced a lack of moral resistance. In his letters to the great and powerful a note of obsequiousness and flattery constantly crept in. As one of his biographers has written:

> He prided himself upon his capacity for becoming *all things to all men;* but when he applied this maxim to his intercourse with the great, it always resulted in his becoming nothing but a flatterer or an obsequious adviser. As he bowed to Nature in the certainty of overcoming her by obedience, so he bowed to kings and favorites; but with the opposite result, that he became not their master but their servant.[22]

Bacon's *Essays,* looked at from one point of view, are a revealing self-portrait. They make up what is in many respects a compendium of worldly wisdom—a guide to how to navigate through the intrigues of life— not unlike the handbooks for princes and courtiers of the period. It is not surprising that one of the authors Bacon refers to most frequently in all his writings is Machiavelli. And Bacon has learned the lesson of Machiavelli well: to view the affairs of human life with a dispassionate eye. In one place he writes:

> We are much beholden to Machiavelli and other writers of that class, who openly and unfeignedly declare or describe what men do, and not what they ought to do. For it is not possible to join the wisdom of the serpent with the innocence of the dove, except man be perfectly acquainted with the nature of evil itself. . . .[23]

In the *Essays* Bacon is well aware of the extent to which self-love, passion, "vain imaginations," custom and lies determine human behavior. He tells us: "There is in human nature generally more of the fool than of the wise," [24] and "there is rarely any rising, but by a commixture of good and evil arts." [25] With his Puritan training and observation of life he is free from any false optimism about human behavior. He has studied men and knows what moves them.

> If you would work any man, you must either know
> his nature and fashions and so lead him; or his ends,
> and so persuade him; or his weakness and disadvan-
> tages, and so awe him; or those that have interest in
> him, and so govern him.[26]

He has read men and knows their ways. But to what use
is this knowledge to be put? Is it to be used to manipulate and control?

Yet the *Essays* are more than a "guide to power";
there is a deeper reflection on life in them also, an awareness of the wider dimensions in which men are concerned
with such things as truth, death, beauty, youth and age.
And it is for his comments on these aspects of life that
Bacon's *Essays* are most memorable and have furnished
more near-proverbial wisdom than probably any other
book in the English language, outside of Shakespeare's
plays. We have only to run through the many striking
first lines of the *Essays*—and Bacon was a master of the
opening line—to realize the extent to which Baconian
thoughts, as well as the Baconian style, with its terseness
and hammerlike quality, have penetrated into English
literature.

Never far in the background of all Bacon's writings
is his religion, affecting his attitude toward human per-
versities (and the tendency to take advantage of them)
and lifting his idea of the uses of science above any
crude utilitarianism. He rejects what he calls the "evil
arts," as, for example, the principle of Machiavelli that
only the appearance, and not the substance, of virtue
matters, commenting that "the shortest way is commonly
the foulest and muddiest. . . ." [27] And he recognizes, not
least in the *New Atlantis*, the need for pity and compassion in human affairs. Even more than philosophy (the
"love of wisdom"), it is philanthropy (the "love of man")
that moves him. But this love, as he expresses it in both
his writings and his life, has a generalized and impersonal
quality. Love in a personal sense he seems to distrust.
More than once in speaking of personal life, he quotes
approvingly the cold and detached precept: "Love as if

you were sometime to hate, and hate as if you were some-time to love." [28] It is as if in this sphere he could not reach to that particularity around which, in the realm of knowledge, his whole conception of science was built.

Today, when we are much concerned about the rela-tions between science and politics and science and hu-manities, it is a matter for serious reflection that some of the qualities that may make a man most suited for think-ing about nature may also make him least suited for deal-ings with human beings. Such appears to have been the case with Bacon. His disinterestedness as a student of nature looked remote and calculating in the human realm. His flexibility and versatility, so apt in natural philosophy, appeared, when they operated in human affairs, as a certain unreliability and attachment to expediency.

In its uses, science itself exemplifies the same flexibility and amoralism. Practically it is all things to all men, indis-criminately serving whatever appears to be needed, or whatever those in power say is needed. The equation of knowledge and power in the study of nature leads on to the same equation in human affairs, but with the terms reversed. Knowledge leads to power, but political power dictates to the uses of knowledge, and practical science, like the perfect courtier, obeys. Science in its applica-tions is no better and no worse than those who call the tune.

Bacon, prescient as he was, anticipated this, for he wrote:

Only let the human race recover that right over na-ture which belongs to it by divine bequest and let power be given it; the exercise thereof will be gov-erned by sound reason and true religion.[29]

In the shadow today of a nuclear holocaust we would not be so likely to take for granted what is expressed in the second half of that sentence. To us it is more like a hope than a certainty. For we know what Bacon did not: that science without conscience can destroy mankind. And we also know that, if we are to survive, the equation of knowledge and power, which we have accepted, will someday have to be matched in the human world by the medieval equation of knowledge and love, which we have rejected.

HENRY LE ROY FINCH
Sarah Lawrence College

Notes

1. This actual phrase appears only as a parenthesis in a discussion of God. Bacon wrote: *"nam et ipsa scientia potestas est"* ("for knowledge itself is power"). "De Haeresibus," *Meditationes Sacrae*.

2. This matter is discussed by Bacon's editor, James Spedding, in a Preface to the *De Interpretatione Naturae Proemium* in the Spedding, Ellis and Heath edition.

3. *See* Virgil K. Whitaker, *Francis Bacon's Intellectual Milieu*. William Andrews Clark Memorial Library publication. (Los Angeles: University of California Press, 1962.)

4. *Novum Organum*, II. (*See also* I, cxvi.)

5. "Experiment is planned action in which every step is governed by theory." Karl R. Popper, *The Logic of Scientific Discovery* (New York: Basic Books, 1959), p. 280. *See also* Pierre Duhem, *The Aim and Structure of Physical Theory*, II, v. (Reprinted in Arthur Danto and Sidney Morgenbesser, *Philosophy of Science* [New York: Meridian Books, 1960], pp. 182-97.)

6. John Venn, *Principles of Empirical or Inductive Logic* (London: Macmillan & Co., 1907), p. 358. Bacon's "alphabetical view" has something in common with the *"signatura rerum"* of the alchemists and occultists, as found, for example, in his contemporary, Jacob Boehme.

7. Morris R. Cohen, *Reason and Nature* (Glencoe, Ill.: Free Press of Glencoe, 1953), p. 17. (*See also* the same author's *Preface to Logic* [New York: Meridian Books, 1944], pp. 135 and 157.)

8. Popper, *op. cit.*, p. 280.

9. *De Augmentis*, III, vi. "Mathematics was beginning to be the great instrument of exact inquiry: Bacon threw the science aside, from ignorance, just at the time when his enormous sagacity, applied to knowledge, would have made him see the part it was to play. If Newton had taken Bacon for his master, not he, but somebody else, would have been

Newton." Augustus De Morgan, *Budget of Paradoxes* (London, 1872), pp. 53-54.

10. Galileo, *The Assayer*. Excerpted in Stillman Drake, *Discoveries and Opinions of Galileo* (Garden City, N.Y.: Doubleday & Co., 1957), p. 238.

11. *Novum Organum,* I, lxxxi.

12. *Ibid.,* I, cxxix.

13. *Ibid.,* I, cxvi.

14. *Ibid.,* I, xcii. I, iii.

15. *Ibid.,* I, xcii and cxiv. *See* E. J. Payne, "The New World," in *Cambridge Modern History,* I (Cambridge, 1902), pp. 37-66.

16. *Ibid.,* I, xciii.

17. Benjamin Farrington, *Francis Bacon* (New York: H. Schuman, 1949), p. 17.

18. Martha Ornstein, *Role of Scientific Societies in the Seventeenth Century* (Chicago: University of Chicago Press, 1928), pp. 39ff. and 92ff. Bacon's conception of the House of Salomon also serves to link him with Freemasonry and Rosicrucianism, in both of which Solomon's Temple plays an important part, and both of which were beginning to flourish in Bacon's day. One authority on Freemasonry, James Hughan, wrote: "The *New Atlantis* seems to be, and probably is, the key to the modern rituals of Freemasonry." Quoted in Alfred Dodd, *Francis Bacon's Personal Life-Story* (London, n.d., p. 158.)

19. Farrington, *op. cit.* and J. G. Crowther, *Francis Bacon* (London, 1960).

20. *See* R. W. Church, *Bacon* (New York: Harper & Row, 1902). Israel Levine, *Francis Bacon* (London, 1925). E. A. Abbott, *Francis Bacon* (London, 1885).

21. *Novum Organum,* I, iii.

22. Abbott, *op. cit.,* p. 327. *See Advancement of Learning,* II. "The mind of a wise man is compared to a glass, wherein the images of all diversity of natures and customs are represented. . . ."

23. *De Augmentis,* VII, 2.

24. *Essays,* 12.

25. *Ibid.,* 14.

26. *Ibid.,* 47.

27. *De Augmentis,* VIII, 2.

28. *Ibid.*

29. *Novum Organum,* I, cxxix.

Bibliography

Abbott, E. A. *Francis Bacon: An Account of His Life and Works*. London: Macmillan & Co., 1885.

Crowther, J. G. *Francis Bacon: The First Statesman of Science*. London: Cresset, 1960.

Ducasse, C. J. "Francis Bacon's Philosophy of Science," *Structure, Method and Meaning*. Henle, Kallen, Langer (eds.). New York: Liberal Arts Press, 1951, pp. 115-44.

Eisley, Loren. *Francis Bacon and the Modern Dilemma*. Lincoln, Neb.: University of Nebraska Press, 1961.

Farrington, Benjamin. *Francis Bacon: Philosopher of Industrial Science*. New York: H. Schuman, 1949.

Fischer, Kuno. *Francis Bacon of Verulam*. Translated by John Oxenford. London: Longmans, Green & Co., 1857.

Green, A. W. *Sir Francis Bacon*. Denver: A. Swallow, 1952.

Jones, R. F. *The Seventeenth Century: Studies in the History of English Thought and Literature from Bacon to Pope*. Stanford, Calif.: Stanford University Press, 1951.

Levine, Israel. *Francis Bacon (1561–1626)*. London: L. Parsons, 1925.

Ornstein, Martha. *The Role of Scientific Societies in the Seventeenth Century*. Chicago: University of Chicago Press, 1928.

Spedding, James. *Letters and Life of Francis Bacon*. 7 vols. London: Longmans, Green & Co., 1874.

———, R. L. Ellis, D. D. Heath (eds.). *Works of Francis Bacon*. 14 vols. London: Longmans, Green & Co., 1857. 15 vols. Boston: Houghton, Mifflin & Co., n.d.

Wallace, Karl R. *Francis Bacon on Communication and Rhetoric*. Chapel Hill, N. C.: University of North Carolina Press, 1943.

Whitaker, V. K. *Francis Bacon's Intellectual Milieu*. William Andrews Clark Memorial Library publication. Los Angeles: University of California Press, 1962.

Wiener, P. P., Aaron Noland (eds.). *Roots of Scientific Thought: A Cultural Perspective*. New York: Basic Books, 1957. *See* essays by M. E. Prior, R. McRae, Marie Boas, pp. 382-411, 458-460.

Willey, Basil. *The Seventeenth Century Background*. London: Chatto & Windus, 1946, chaps. 1 and 2.

THE COMPLETE ESSAYS
OF FRANCIS BACON

INCLUDING

THE NEW ATLANTIS
AND
NOVUM ORGANUM

LETTER

TO MY

LORD TREASURER BURGHLEY

[1592]

LETTER TO MY LORD TREASURER BURGHLEY (1592)

My Lord,

With as much confidence as mine own honest and faithful devotion unto your service and your honourable correspondence unto me and my poor estate can breed in a man, do I commend myself unto your Lordship. I wax now somewhat ancient; one and thirty years is a great deal of sand in the hour-glass. My health, I thank God, I find confirmed; and I do not fear that action shall impair it, because I account my ordinary course of study and meditation to be more painful than most parts of action are. I ever bare a mind (in some middle place that I could discharge) to serve her Majesty; not as a man born under Sol, that loveth honour; nor under Jupiter, that loveth business (for the contemplative planet carrieth me away wholly); but as a man born under an excellent Sovereign, that deserveth the dedication of all men's abilities. Besides, I do not find in myself so much self-love, but that the greater parts of my thoughts are

1

to deserve well (if I were able) of my friends, and namely of your Lordship; who being the Atlas of this commonwealth, the honour of my house, and the second founder of my poor estate, I am tied by all duties, both of a good patriot, and of an unworthy kinsman, and of an obliged servant, to employ whatsoever I am to do you service. Again, the meanness of my estate doth somewhat move me: for though I cannot accuse myself that I am either prodigal or slothful, yet my health is not to spend, nor my course to get. Lastly, I confess that I have as vast contemplative ends, as I have moderate civil ends: for I have taken all knowledge to be my province; and if I could purge it of two sorts of rovers, whereof the one with frivolous disputations, confutations, and verbosities, the other with blind experiments and auricular traditions and impostures, hath committed so many spoils, I hope I should bring in industrious observations, grounded conclusions, and profitable inventions and discoveries; the best state of that province. This, whether it be curiosity, or vain-glory, or nature, or (if one take it favourably) *philanthropia,* is so fixed in my mind as it cannot be removed. And I do easily see, that place of any reasonable countenance doth bring commandment of more wits than of a man's own; which is the thing I greatly affect. And for your Lordship, perhaps you shall not find more strength and less encounter in any other. And if your Lordship shall find now, or at any time, that I do seek or affect any place whereunto any that is nearer unto your Lordship shall be concurrent, say then that I am a most dishonest man. And if your Lordship will not carry me on, I will not do as Anaxagoras did, who reduced himself with contemplation unto voluntary poverty: but this I will do; I will sell the inheritance that I have, and purchase some lease of quick revenue, or some office of gain that shall be executed by deputy, and so give over all care of service, and become some sorry bookmaker, or a true pioneer in that mine of truth, which (he said) lay so deep. This which I have writ unto your Lordship is rather thoughts than words, being set down without all art, disguising, or reservation. Wherein I have done honour both to your Lordship's wisdom, in judging that that will be best believed of your Lordship which is truest, and to your Lordship's good nature, in retaining nothing from you. And even so I wish your Lordship all happiness, and to myself means and occasion to be added to my faithful desire to do you service. From my lodging at Gray's Inn.

THE

ESSAYES OR COUNSELS

CIVILL AND MORALL

OF

FRANCIS LO. VERULAM,

VISCOUNT ST. ALBAN

NEWLY ENLARGED

To THE MOST HIGH AND EXCELLENT PRINCE, HENRY,
PRINCE OF WALES, DUKE OF CORNWALL, AND EARL
OF CHESTER.

It may please your Highness,

Having divided my life into the contemplative and
active part, I am desirous to give his Majesty and your
Highness of the fruits of both, simple though they be.
To write just treatises requireth leisure in the writer,
and leisure in the reader, and therefore are not so fit,
neither in regard of your Highness's princely affairs, nor
in regard of my continual services; which is the cause
that hath made me choose to write certain brief notes,
set down rather significantly than curiously, which I
have called *Essays*. The word is late, but the thing is
ancient. For Seneca's epistles to Lucilius, if one mark
them well, are but *Essays*, that is, dispersed meditations,
though conveyed in the form of epistles. These labours
of mine I know cannot be worthy of your Highness, for
what can be worthy of you? But my hope is, they may

be as grains of salt, that will rather give you an appetite than offend you with satiety. And although they handle those things wherein both men's lives and their pens are most conversant, yet (what I have attained I know not) but I have endeavoured to make them not vulgar, but of a nature whereof a man shall find much in experience, and little in books; so as they are neither repetitions nor fancies. But howsoever, I shall most humbly desire your Highness to accept them in gracious part, and to conceive, that if I cannot rest, but must shew my dutiful and devoted affection to your Highness in these things which proceed from myself, I shall be much more ready to do it in performance of any of your princely commandments. And so wishing your Highness all princely felicity, I rest,

Your Highness's most humble servant.

ESSAYS OR COUNSELS

CIVIL AND MORAL

[1625]

· 1 ·

OF TRUTH

What is Truth? said jesting Pilate; and would not stay for
an answer. Certainly there be that delight in giddiness,
and count it a bondage to fix a belief; affecting free-will
in thinking, as well as in acting. And though the sects of
philosophers of that kind be gone, yet there remain certain
discoursing wits which are of the same veins, though
there be not so much blood in them as was in those of
the ancients. But it is not only the difficulty and labour
which men take in finding out of truth; nor again that
when it is found it imposeth upon men's thoughts; that
doth bring lies in favour; but a natural though corrupt
love of the lie itself. One of the later school of the Grecians examineth the matter, and is at a stand to think
what should be in it, that men should love lies, where
neither they make for pleasure, as with poets, nor for
advantage, as with the merchant; but for the lie's sake.
But I cannot tell: this same truth is a naked and open
day-light, that doth not shew the masks and mummeries
and triumphs of the world, half so stately and daintily as
candle-lights. Truth may perhaps come to the price of a
pearl, that sheweth best by day; but it will not rise to
the price of a diamond or carbuncle, that sheweth best
in varied lights. A mixture of a lie doth ever add pleasure.
Doth any man doubt, that if there were taken out of
men's minds vain opinions, flattering hopes, false valua-
tions, imaginations as one would, and the like, but it
would leave the minds of a number of men poor shrunken

6

things, full of melancholy and indisposition, and unpleasing to themselves? One of the Fathers, in great severity, called poesy *vinum dæmonum* [devil's-wine], because it filleth the imagination; and yet it is but with the shadow of a lie. But it is not the lie that passeth through the mind, but the lie that sinketh in and settleth in it, that doth the hurt; such as we spake of before. But howsoever these things are thus in men's depraved judgments and affections, yet truth, which only doth judge itself, teacheth that the inquiry of truth, which is the love-making or wooing of it, the knowledge of truth, which is the presence of it, and the belief of truth, which is the enjoying of it, is the sovereign good of human nature. The first creature of God, in the works of the days, was the light of the sense; the last was the light of reason; and his sabbath work ever since, is the illumination of his Spirit. First he breathed light upon the face of the matter or chaos; then he breathed light into the face of man; and still he breatheth and inspireth light into the face of his chosen. The poet that beautified the sect that was otherwise inferior to the rest, saith yet excellently well: *It is a pleasure to stand upon the shore, and to see ships tossed upon the sea; a pleasure to stand in the window of a castle, and to see a battle and the adventures thereof below: but no pleasure is comparable to the standing upon the vantage ground of Truth,* (a hill not to be commanded, and where the air is always clear and serene,) *and to see the errors, and wanderings, and mists, and tempests, in the vale below;* so always that this prospect be with pity, and not with swelling or pride. Certainly, it is heaven upon earth, to have a man's mind move in charity, rest in providence, and turn upon the poles of truth.

To pass from theological and philosophical truth, to the truth of civil business; it will be acknowledged even by those that practise it not, that clear and round dealing is the honour of man's nature; and that mixture of falsehood is like allay in coin of gold and silver, which may make the metal work the better, but it embaseth it. For these winding and crooked courses are the goings of the serpent; which goeth basely upon the belly, and not upon the feet. There is no vice that doth so cover a man with shame as to be found false and perfidious. And therefore Montaigne saith prettily, when he inquired the reason, why the word of the lie should be such a disgrace and such an odious charge? Saith he, *If it be well weighed, to say that a man lieth, is as much to say, as that he is brave towards God and a coward towards men.* For a lie faces God, and shrinks from man. Surely the wickedness of falsehood and breach of faith cannot possibly be so highly expressed, as in that it shall be the last peal to call the judgments of God upon the generations of men; it being foretold, that when Christ cometh, *he shall not find faith upon the earth.*

· 2 ·

OF DEATH

MEN fear Death, as children fear to go in the dark; and as that natural fear in children is increased with tales, so is the other. Certainly, the contemplation of death, as the wages of sin and passage to another world, is holy and religious; but the fear of it, as a tribute due unto nature, is weak. Yet in religious meditations there is sometimes mixture of vanity and of superstition. You shall read in some of the friars' books of mortification, that a man should think with himself what the pain is if he have but his finger's end pressed or tortured, and thereby imagine what the pains of death are, when the whole body is corrupted and dissolved; when many times death passeth with less pain than the torture of a limb: for the most vital parts are not the quickest of sense. And by him that spake only as a philosopher and natural man, it was well said, *Pompa mortis magis terret, quam mors ipsa* [it is the accompaniments of death that are frightful rather than death itself]. Groans and convulsions, and a discoloured face, and friends weeping, and blacks, and obsequies, and the like, shew death terrible. It is worthy

the observing, that there is no passion in the mind of man
so weak, but it mates and masters the fear of death;
and therefore death is no such terrible enemy when a
man hath so many attendants about him that can win the
combat of him. Revenge triumphs over death; Love
slights it; Honour aspireth to it; Grief flieth to it; Fear
pre-occupateth it; nay we read, after Otho the emperor
had slain himself, Pity (which is the tenderest of affections) provoked many to die, out of mere compassion
to their sovereign, and as the truest sort of followers.
Nay Seneca adds niceness and satiety: *Cogita quamdiu
eadem feceris; mori velle, non tantum fortis, aut miser, sed
etiam fastidiosus potest.* A man would die, though he
were neither valiant nor miserable, only upon a weariness
to do the same thing so oft over and over. It is no less
worthy to observe, how little alteration in good spirits the
approaches of death make; for they appear to be the
same men till the last instant. Augustus Cæsar died in a
compliment; *Livia, conjugii nostri memor, vive et vale*
[farewell, Livia; and forget not the days of our marriage].
Tiberius in dissimulation; as Tacitus saith of him, *Jam
Tiberium vires et corpus, non dissimulatio, deserebant*
[his powers of body were gone, but his power of dissimulation still remained]. Vespasian in a jest; sitting upon
the stool, *Ut puto Deus fio:* [I think I am becoming a
god]. Galba with a sentence; *Feri, si ex re sit populi
Romani:* [strike, if it be for the good of Rome;] holding
forth his neck. Septimius Severus in despatch; *Adeste si
quid mihi restat agendum* [make haste, if there is anything more for me to do]. And the like. Certainly the
Stoics bestowed too much cost upon death, and by their
great preparations made it appear more fearful. Better
saith he, *qui finem vitæ extremum inter munera ponat
naturæ* [who accounts the close of life as one of the
benefits of nature]. It is as natural to die as to be born;
and to a little infant, perhaps, the one is as painful as the
other. He that dies in an earnest pursuit, is like one that
is wounded in hot blood; who, for the time, scarce feels
the hurt; and therefore a mind fixed and bent upon somewhat that is good doth avert the dolours of death. But

above all, believe it, the sweetest canticle is, *Nunc dimittis;* when a man hath obtained worthy ends and expectations. Death hath this also; that it openeth the gate to good fame, and extinguisheth envy. *Extinctus amabitur idem* [the same man that was envied while he lived, shall be loved when he is gone].

· 3 ·

OF UNITY IN RELIGION

RELIGION being the chief band of human society, it is a happy thing when itself is well contained within the true band of Unity. The quarrels and divisions about religion were evils unknown to the heathen. The reason was, because the religion of the heathen consisted rather in rites and ceremonies, than in any constant belief. For you may imagine what kind of faith theirs was, when the chief doctors and fathers of their church were the poets. But the true God hath this attribute, that he is a *jealous God;* and therefore his worship and religion will endure no mixture nor partner. We shall therefore speak a few words concerning the Unity of the Church; what are the Fruits thereof; what the Bounds; and what the Means.

The Fruits of Unity (next unto the well pleasing of God, which is all in all) are two; the one towards those that are without the church, the other towards those that are within. For the former; it is certain that heresies and schisms are of all others the greatest scandals; yea, more than corruption of manners. For as in the natural body a wound or solution of continuity is worse than corrupt humour; so in the spiritual. So that nothing doth so much keep men out of the church, and drive men out of the church, as breach of unity. And therefore, whensoever it cometh to that pass, that one saith *Ecce in deserto* [Behold! in the desert], another saith *Ecce in penetralibus* [Behold! in the sanctuary]; that is, when some men seek Christ in the conventicles of heretics, and others in an outward face of a church, that voice had need continually to sound in men's ears, *Nolite exire,—Go not out*. The Doctor of the Gentiles (the propriety of whose vocation drew him to have a special care of those without) saith, *If an heathen come in, and hear you speak with several tongues, will he not say that you are mad?* And certainly it is little better, when atheists and profane persons do hear of so many discordant and contrary opinions in religion; it doth avert them from the church, and maketh them *to sit down in the chair of the scorners*. It is but a light thing to be vouched in so serious a matter, but yet it expresseth well the deformity. There is a master of scoffing, that in his catalogue of books of a feigned library sets down this title of a book, *The morris-dance of Heretics*. For indeed every sect of them hath a diverse posture or cringe by themselves, which cannot but move derision in worldlings and depraved politics, who are apt to contemn holy things.

As for the fruit towards those that are within; it is peace; which containeth infinite blessings. It establisheth faith. It kindleth charity. The outward peace of the church distilleth into peace of conscience. And it turneth the labours of writing and reading of controversies into treatises of mortification and devotion.

Concerning the Bounds of Unity; the true placing of them importeth exceedingly. There appear to be two extremes. For to certain zelants all speech of pacification is odious. *Is it peace, Jehu? What hast thou to do with peace? turn thee behind me*. Peace is not the matter, but following and party. Contrariwise, certain Laodiceans and lukewarm persons think they may accommodate points of religion by middle ways, and taking part of both, and witty reconcilements; as if they would make an arbitrement between God and man. Both these extremes are to be avoided; which will be done, if the league of Christians penned by our Saviour himself were in the two cross clauses thereof soundly and plainly expounded: *He that is not with us is against us;* and again, *He that is not against us is with us;* that is, if the points fundamental and of substance in religion were truly discerned and distinguished from points not merely of faith, but of opinion, order, or good intention. This is a thing may seem to many a matter trivial, and done already. But if it were done less partially, it would be embraced more generally.

Of this I may give only this advice, according to my small model. Men ought to take heed of rending God's church by two kinds of controversies. The one is, when the matter of the point controverted is too small and light, not worth the heat and strife about it, kindled only by contradiction. For as it is noted by one of the fathers, *Christ's coat indeed had no seam, but the church's vesture was of divers colours;* whereupon he saith, *In veste varietas sit, scissura non sit,* [let there be variety in the garment, but let there be no division:] they be two things, Unity and Uniformity. The other is, when the matter of the point controverted is great, but it is driven to an over-great subtilty and obscurity; so that it becometh a thing rather ingenious than substantial. A man that is of judgment and understanding shall sometimes hear ignorant men differ, and know well within himself that those which so differ mean one thing, and yet they themselves would never agree. And if it come so to pass in that distance of judgment which is between man and man, shall we not think that God above, that knows the heart, doth not discern that frail men in some of their contradictions intend the same thing; and accepteth of both? The nature of such controversies is excellently expressed by St. Paul in the warning and precept that he giveth concerning the same, *Devita profanas vocum novitates, et oppositiones falsi nominis scientiæ* [Avoid profane novelties of terms, and oppositions of science falsely so called]. Men create oppositions which are not; and put them into new terms so fixed, as whereas the meaning ought to govern the term, the term in effect governeth the meaning. There be also two false peaces or unities: the one, when the peace is grounded but upon an implicit ignorance; for all colours will agree in the dark: the other, when it is pieced up upon a direct admission of contraries in fundamental points. For truth and falsehood, in such things, are like the iron and clay in the toes of Nabuchadnezzar's image; they may cleave, but they will not incorporate.

Concerning the Means of procuring Unity; men must beware, that in the procuring or muniting of religious unity they do not dissolve and deface the laws of charity and of human society. There be two swords amongst Christians, the spiritual and temporal; and both have their due office and place in the maintenance of religion. But we may not take up the third sword, which is Mahomet's sword, or like unto it; that is, to propagate religion by wars or by sanguinary persecutions to force consciences; except it be in cases of overt scandal, blasphemy, or intermixture of practice against the state; much less to nourish seditions; to authorise conspiracies and rebellions; to put the sword into the people's hands; and the like; tending to the subversion of all government, which is the ordinance of God. For this is but to dash the first table against the second; and so to consider men as Christians, as we forget that they are men. Lucretius the poet, when he beheld the act of Agamemnon, that could endure the sacrificing of his own daughter, exclaimed:

Tantum Relligio potuit suadere malorum:

[to such ill actions Religion could persuade a man]. What would he have said, if he had known of the massacre in France, or the powder treason of England? He would have been seven times more Epicure and atheist than he was. For as the temporal sword is to be drawn with great circumspection in cases of religion; so it is a thing monstrous to put it into the hands of the common people. Let that be left unto the Anabaptists, and other furies. It was great blasphemy when the devil said, *I will ascend and be like the Highest;* but it is greater blasphemy to personate God, and bring him in saying, *I will descend, and be like the prince of darkness:* and what is it better, to make the cause of religion to descend to the cruel and execrable actions of murthering princes, butchery of people, and subversion of states and governments? Surely this is to bring down the Holy Ghost, instead of the likeness of a dove, in the shape of a vulture or raven; and set out of the bark of a Christian church a flag of a bark of pirates and Assassins. Therefore it is most necessary that the church by doctrine and decree, princes by their sword, and all learnings, both Christian and moral, as by their Mercury rod, do damn and send to hell for ever those facts and opinions tending to the support of the same; as hath been already in good part done. Surely in counsels concerning religion, that counsel of the apostle would be prefixed, *Ira hominis non implet justitiam Dei* [The wrath of man worketh not the righteousness of God]. And it was a notable observation of a wise father, and no less ingenuously confessed; *that those which held and persuaded pressure of consciences, were commonly interested therein themselves for their own ends.*

· 4 ·

Of Revenge

REVENGE is a kind of wild justice; which the more man's nature runs to, the more ought law to weed it out. For as for the first wrong, it doth but offend the law; but the revenge of that wrong putteth the law out of office. Certainly, in taking revenge, a man is but even with his enemy; but in passing it over, he is superior; for it is a prince's part to pardon. And Salomon, I am sure, saith, *It is the glory of a man to pass by an offence.* That which is past is gone, and irrevocable; and wise men have enough to do with things present and to come; therefore they do but trifle with themselves, that labour in past matters. There is no man doth a wrong for the wrong's sake; but thereby to purchase himself profit, or pleasure, or honour, or the like. Therefore why should I be angry with a man for loving himself better than me? And if any man should do wrong merely out of ill-nature, why, yet it is but like the thorn or briar, which prick and scratch, because they can do no other. The most tolerable sort of revenge is for those wrongs which there is no law to remedy; but then let a man take heed the revenge be such as there is no law to punish; else a man's enemy is still

before hand, and it is two for one. Some, when they take
revenge, are desirous the party should know whence it
cometh. This the more generous. For the delight seemeth
to be not so much in doing the hurt as in making the party
repent. But base and crafty cowards are like the arrow
that flieth in the dark. Cosmus, duke of Florence, had a
desperate saying against perfidious or neglecting friends,
as if those wrongs were unpardonable; *You shall read*
(saith he) *that we are commanded to forgive our ene-*
mies; but you never read that we are commanded to for-
give our friends. But yet the spirit of Job was in a better
tune: *Shall we* (saith he) *take good at God's hands, and*
not be content to take evil also? And so of friends in a
proportion. This is certain, that a man that studieth revenge keeps his own wounds green, which otherwise
would heal and do well. Public revenges are for the most
part fortunate; as that for the death of Cæsar; for the
death of Pertinax; for the death of Henry the Third of
France; and many more. But in private revenges it is not
so. Nay rather, vindictive persons live the life of witches;
who, as they are mischievous, so end they infortunate.

· 5 ·

OF ADVERSITY

IT was a high speech of Seneca (after the manner of the
Stoics), *that the good things which belong to prosperity*
are to be wished; but the good things that belong to ad-
versity are to be admired. Bona rerum secundarum op-
tabilia; adversarum mirabilia. Certainly if miracles be the
command over nature, they appear most in adversity. It
is yet a higher speech of his than the other (much too
high for a heathen), *It is true greatness to have in one the*
frailty of a man, and the security of a God. Vere magnum
habere fragilitatem hominis, securitatem Dei. This would
have done better in poesy, where transcendences are more
allowed. And the poets indeed have been busy with it;
for it is in effect the thing which is figured in that strange

fiction of the ancient poets, which seemeth not to be without mystery; nay, and to have some approach to the state of a Christian; that *Hercules, when he went to unbind Prometheus* (by whom human nature is represented), *sailed the length of the great ocean in an earthen pot or pitcher;* lively describing Christian resolution, that saileth in the frail bark of the flesh through the waves of the world. But to speak in a mean. The virtue of Prosperity is temperance, the virtue of Adversity is fortitude; which in morals is the more heroical virtue. Prosperity is the blessing of the Old Testament; Adversity is the blessing of the New; which carrieth the greater benediction, and the clearer revelation of God's favour. Yet even in the Old Testament, if you listen to David's harp, you shall hear as many hearse-like airs as carols; and the pencil of the Holy Ghost hath laboured more in describing the afflictions of Job than the felicities of Salomon. Prosperity is not without many fears and distastes; and Adversity is not without comforts and hopes. We see in needle-works and embroideries, it is more pleasing to have a lively work upon a sad and solemn ground, than to have a dark and melancholy work upon a lightsome ground: judge therefore of the pleasure of the heart by the pleasure of the eye. Certainly virtue is like precious odours, most fragrant when they are incensed or crushed: for Prosperity doth best discover vice, but Adversity doth best discover virtue.

· 6 ·

OF SIMULATION AND DISSIMULATION

DISSIMULATION is but a faint kind of policy or wisdom; for it asketh a strong wit and a strong heart to know when to tell truth, and to do it. Therefore it is the weaker sort of politics that are the great dissemblers.

Tacitus saith, *Livia sorted well with the arts of her husband and dissimulation of her son;* attributing arts or policy to Augustus, and dissimulation to Tiberius. And

again, when Mucianus encourageth Vespasian to take
arms against Vitellius, he saith, *We rise not against the
piercing judgment of Augustus, nor the extreme caution
or closeness of Tiberius.* These properties, of arts or policy
and dissimulation or closeness, are indeed habits and
faculties several, and to be distinguished. For if a man
have that penetration of judgment as he can discern what
things are to be laid open, and what to be secreted, and
what to be shewed at half lights, and to whom and when,
(which indeed are arts of state and arts of life, as Tacitus
well calleth them,) to him a habit of dissimulation is a
hinderance and a poorness. But if a man cannot obtain to
that judgment, then it is left to him generally to be close,
and a dissembler. For where a man cannot choose or vary
in particulars, there it is good to take the safest and wari-
est way in general; like the going softly, by one that cannot well see. Certainly the ablest men that ever were have
had all an openness and frankness of dealing; and a name
of certainty and veracity; but then they were like horses
well managed; for they could tell passing well when to
stop or turn; and at such times when they thought the
case indeed required dissimulation, if then they used it,
it came to pass that the former opinion spread abroad of
their good faith and clearness of dealing made them almost invisible.

There be three degrees of this hiding and veiling of a
man's self. The first, Closeness, Reservation, and Secrecy;
when a man leaveth himself without observation, or without hold to be taken, what he is. The second, Dissimulation, in the negative; when a man lets fall signs and arguments, that he is not that he is. And the third, Simulation,
in the affirmative; when a man industriously and expressly
feigns and pretends to be that he is not.

For the first of these, Secrecy; it is indeed the virtue of
a confessor. And assuredly the secret man heareth many
confessions. For who will open himself to a blab or bab-
bler? But if a man be thought secret, it inviteth discovery;
as the more close air sucketh in the more open; and as in
confession the revealing is not for worldly use, but for the
ease of a man's heart, so secret men come to the knowl-

edge of many things in that kind; while men rather discharge their minds than impart their minds. In few words,
mysteries are due to secrecy. Besides (to say truth)
nakedness is uncomely, as well in mind as body; and it
addeth no small reverence to men's manners and actions,
if they be not altogether open. As for talkers and futile
persons, they are commonly vain and credulous withal.
For he that talketh what he knoweth, will also talk what
he knoweth not. Therefore set it down, *that an habit of
secrecy is both politic and moral*. And in this part, it is
good that a man's face give his tongue leave to speak.
For the discovery of a man's self by the tracts of his
countenance is a great weakness and betraying; by how
much it is many times more marked and believed than a
man's words.

For the second, which is Dissimulation; it followeth
many times upon secrecy by a necessity; so that he that
will be secret must be a dissembler in some degree. For
men are too cunning to suffer a man to keep an indifferent carriage between both, and to be secret, without
swaying the balance on either side. They will so beset
a man with questions, and draw him on, and pick it out
of him, that, without an absurd silence, he must shew an
inclination one way; or if he do not, they will gather as
much by his silence as by his speech. As for equivoca-
tions, or oraculous speeches, they cannot hold out long.
So that no man can be secret, except he give himself a
little scope of dissimulation; which is, as it were, but the
skirts or train of secrecy.

But for the third degree, which is Simulation and false
profession; that I hold more culpable, and less politic; except it be in great and rare matters. And therefore a general custom of simulation (which is this last degree) is
a vice, rising either of a natural falseness or fearfulness,
or of a mind that hath some main faults, which because
a man must needs disguise, it maketh him practise simulation in other things, lest his hand should be out of ure.

The great advantages of simulation and dissimulation
are three. First, to lay asleep opposition, and to surprise.
For where a man's intentions are published, it is an

alarum to call up all that are against them. The second is, to reserve to a man's self a fair retreat. For if a man engage himself by a manifest declaration, he must go through or take a fall. The third is, the better to discover the mind of another. For to him that opens himself men will hardly shew themselves adverse; but will (fair) let him go on, and turn their freedom of speech to freedom of thought. And therefore it is a good shrewd proverb of the Spaniard, *Tell a lie and find a troth.* As if there were no way of discovery but by simulation. There be also three disadvantages, to set it even. The first, that simulation and dissimulation commonly carry with them a shew of fearfulness, which in any business doth spoil the feathers of round flying up to the mark. The second, that it puzzleth and perplexeth the conceits of many, that perhaps would otherwise co-operate with him; and makes a man walk almost alone to his own ends. The third and greatest, is, that it depriveth a man of one of the most principal instruments for action; which is trust and belief. The best composition and temperature is to have openness in fame and opinion; secrecy in habit; dissimulation in seasonable use; and a power to feign, if there be no remedy.

· 7 ·

OF PARENTS AND CHILDREN

THE joys of parents are secret; and so are their griefs and fears. They cannot utter the one; nor they will not utter the other. Children sweeten labours; but they make misfortunes more bitter. They increase the cares of life; but they mitigate the remembrance of death. The perpetuity by generation is common to beasts; but memory, merit, and noble works, are proper to men. And surely a man shall see the noblest works and foundations have proceeded from childless men; which have sought to express the images of their minds, where those of their bodies have failed. So the care of posterity is most in them that have no posterity. They that are the first raisers of their houses are most indulgent towards their children; beholding them as the continuance not only of their kind but of their work; and so both children and creatures.

The difference in affection of parents towards their several children is many times unequal; and sometimes unworthy; especially in the mother; as Salomon saith, *A wise son rejoiceth the father, but an ungracious son shames the mother.* A man shall see, where there is a house full of children, one or two of the eldest respected, and the youngest made wantons; but in the midst some that are as it were forgotten, who many times nevertheless prove the best. The illiberality of parents in allowance towards their children is an harmful error; makes them base; acquaints them with shifts; makes them sort with mean company; and makes them surfeit more when they come to plenty. And therefore the proof is best, when men keep their authority towards their children, but not their purse. Men have a foolish manner (both parents and schoolmasters and servants) in creating and breeding an emulation between brothers during childhood, which many times sorteth to discord when they are men, and disturbeth families. The Italians make little difference between children and nephews or near kinsfolks; but so they be of the lump, they care not though they pass not through their own body. And, to say truth, in nature it is much a like matter; insomuch that we see a nephew sometimes resembleth an uncle or a kinsman more than his own parent; as the blood happens. Let parents choose betimes the vocations and courses they mean their children should take; for then they are most flexible; and let them not too much apply themselves to the disposition of their children, as thinking they will take best to that which they have most mind to. It is true, that if the affection or aptness of the children be extraordinary, then it is good not to cross it; but generally the precept is good, *optimum elige, suave et facile illud faciet consuetudo* [choose the best—custom will make it pleasant and easy]. Younger brothers are commonly fortunate, but seldom or never where the elder are disinherited.

OF MARRIAGE AND SINGLE LIFE

HE that hath wife and children hath given hostages to fortune; for they are impediments to great enterprises, either of virtue or mischief. Certainly the best works, and of greatest merit for the public, have proceeded from the unmarried or childless men; which both in affection and means have married and endowed the public. Yet it were great reason that those that have children should have greatest care of future times; unto which they know they must transmit their dearest pledges. Some there are, who though they lead a single life, yet their thoughts do end with themselves, and account future times impertinences. Nay, there are some other that account wife and children but as bills of charges. Nay more, there are some foolish rich covetous men, that take a pride in having no children, because they may be thought so much the richer. For perhaps they have heard some talk, *Such an one is a great rich man,* and another except to it, *Yea, but he hath a great charge of children;* as if it were an abatement to his riches. But the most ordinary cause of a single life is liberty, especially in certain self-pleasing and humorous minds, which are so sensible of every restraint, as they will go near to think their girdles and garters to be bonds and shackles. Unmarried men are best friends, best masters, best servants; but not always best subjects; for they are light to run away; and almost all fugitives are of that condition. A single life doth well with churchmen; for charity will hardly water the ground where it must first fill a pool. It is indifferent for judges and magistrates; for if they be facile and corrupt, you shall have a servant five times worse than a wife. For soldiers, I find the generals commonly in their hortatives put men in mind of their wives and children; and I think the despising of marriage amongst the Turks maketh the vulgar soldier more base. Certainly wife and children are a kind of discipline of

humanity; and single men, though they may be many
times more charitable, because their means are less exhaust, yet, on the other side, they are more cruel and
hardhearted (good to make severe inquisitors,) because
their tenderness is not so oft called upon. Grave natures,
led by custom, and therefore constant, are commonly loving husbands; as was said of Ulysses, *vetulam suam præ-
tulit immortalitati* [he preferred his old wife to immor-
tality]. Chaste women are often proud and froward, as
presuming upon the merit of their chastity. It is one of
the best bonds both of chastity and obedience in the wife,
if she think her husband wise; which she will never do if
she find him jealous. Wives are young men's mistresses;
companions for middle age; and old men's nurses. So as
a man may have a quarrel to marry when he will. But yet
he was reputed one of the wise men, that made answer
to the question, when a man should marry?—*A young
man not yet, an elder man not at all*. It is often seen that
bad husbands have very good wives; whether it be that
it raiseth the price of their husband's kindness when it
comes; or that the wives take a pride in their patience.
But this never fails, if the bad husbands were of their own
choosing, against their friends' consent; for then they will
be sure to make good their own folly.

· 9 ·

Of Envy

THERE be none of the affections which have been noted
to fascinate or bewitch, but love and envy. They both
have vehement wishes; they frame themselves readily
into imaginations and suggestions; and they come easily
into the eye, especially upon the presence of the objects;
which are the points that conduce to fascination, if any
such thing there be. We see likewise the scripture calleth
envy an *evil eye;* and the astrologers call the evil influences of the stars *evil aspects;* so that still there seemeth
to be acknowledged, in the act of envy, an ejaculation or

irradiation of the eye. Nay some have been so curious as to note, that the times when the stroke or percussion of an envious eye doth most hurt, are when the party envied is beheld in glory or triumph; for that sets an edge upon envy: and besides, at such times the spirits of the person envied do come forth most into the outward parts, and so meet the blow.

But leaving these curiosities, (though not unworthy to be thought on in fit place,) we will handle, what persons are apt to envy others; what persons are most subject to be envied themselves; and what is the difference between public and private envy.

A man that hath no virtue in himself, ever envieth virtue in others. For men's minds will either feed upon their own good or upon others' evil; and who wanteth the one will prey upon the other; and whoso is out of hope to attain to another's virtue, will seek to come at even hand by depressing another's fortune.

A man that is busy and inquisitive is commonly envious. For to know much of other men's matters cannot be because all that ado may concern his own estate; therefore it must needs be that he taketh a kind of play-pleasure in looking upon the fortunes of others. Neither can he that mindeth but his own business find much matter for envy. For envy is a gadding passion, and walketh the streets, and doth not keep home: *Non est curiosus, quin idem sit malevolus* [There is no curious man but has some malevolence to quicken his curiosity].

Men of noble birth are noted to be envious towards new men when they rise. For the distance is altered; and it is like a deceit of the eye, that when others come on they think themselves go back.

Deformed persons, and eunuchs, and old men, and bastards, are envious. For he that cannot possibly mend his own case will do what he can to impair another's; except these defects light upon a very brave and heroical nature, which thinketh to make his natural wants part of his honour; in that it should be said, that an eunuch, or a lame man, did such great matters; affecting the honour of a miracle; as it was in Narses the eunuch, and Agesilaus and Tamberlanes, that were lame men.

The same is the case of men that rise after calamities and misfortunes. For they are as men fallen out with the times; and think other men's harms a redemption of their own sufferings.

They that desire to excel in too many matters, out of levity and vain-glory, are ever envious. For they cannot want work; it being impossible but many in some one of those things should surpass them. Which was the character of Adrian the Emperor; that mortally envied poets and painters and artificers, in works wherein he had a vein to excel.

Lastly, near kinsfolks, and fellows in office, and those that have been bred together, are more apt to envy their equals when they are raised. For it doth upbraid unto them their own fortunes, and pointeth at them, and cometh oftener into their remembrance, and incurreth likewise more into the note of others; and envy ever redoubleth from speech and fame. Cain's envy was the more vile and malignant towards his brother Abel, because when his sacrifice was better accepted there was no body to look on. Thus much for those that are apt to envy.

Concerning those that are more or less subject to envy: First, persons of eminent virtue, when they are advanced, are less envied. For their fortune seemeth but due unto them; and no man envieth the payment of a debt, but rewards and liberality rather. Again, envy is ever joined with the comparing of a man's self; and where there is no comparison, no envy; and therefore kings are not envied but by kings. Nevertheless it is to be noted that unworthy persons are most envied at their first coming in, and afterwards overcome it better; whereas contrariwise, persons of worth and merit are most envied when their fortune continueth long. For by that time, though their virtue be the same, yet it hath not the same lustre; for fresh men grow up that darken it.

Persons of noble blood are less envied in their rising. For it seemeth but right done to their birth. Besides,

there seemeth not much added to their fortune; and envy
is as the sunbeams, that beat hotter upon a bank or steep
rising ground than upon a flat. And for the same reason
those that are advanced by degrees are less envied
than those that are advanced suddenly and *per saltum*
[by a leap].

Those that have joined with their honour great travels,
cares, or perils, are less subject to envy. For men think
that they earn their honours hardly, and pity them sometimes; and pity ever healeth envy. Wherefore you shall
observe that the more deep and sober sort of politic persons, in their greatness, are ever bemoaning themselves,
what a life they lead; chanting a *quanta patimur* [how
we suffer!]. Not that they feel it so, but only to abate the
edge of envy. But this is to be understood of business
that is laid upon men, and not such as they call unto
themselves. For nothing increaseth envy more than an un-
necessary and ambitious engrossing of business. And
nothing doth extinguish envy more than for a great person to preserve all other inferior officers in their full rights
and pre-eminences of their places. For by that means
there be so many screens between him and envy.

Above all, those are most subject to envy, which carry
the greatness of their fortunes in an insolent and proud
manner; being never well but while they are shewing how
great they are, either by outward pomp, or by triumphing
over all opposition or competition; whereas wise men will
rather do sacrifice to envy, in suffering themselves sometimes of purpose to be crossed and overborne in things
that do not much concern them. Notwithstanding so
much is true, that the carriage of greatness in a plain and
open manner (so it be without arrogancy and vain-glory)
doth draw less envy than if it be in a more crafty and
cunning fashion. For in that course a man doth but disavow fortune; and seemeth to be conscious of his own
want in worth; and doth but teach others to envy him.

Lastly, to conclude this part; as we said in the beginning that the act of envy had somewhat in it of witchcraft,
so there is no other cure of envy but the cure of witchcraft; and that is, to remove the *lot* (as they call it) and

to lay it upon another. For which purpose, the wiser sort of great persons bring in ever upon the stage somebody upon whom to derive the envy that would come upon themselves; sometimes upon ministers and servants; sometimes upon colleagues and associates; and the like; and for that turn there are never wanting some persons of violent and undertaking natures, who, so they may have power and business, will take it at any cost.

Now, to speak of public envy. There is yet some good in public envy, whereas in private there is none. For public envy is as an ostracism, that eclipseth men when they grow too great. And therefore it is a bridle also to great ones, to keep them within bounds.

This envy, being in the Latin word *invidia*, goeth in the modern languages by the name of *discontentment;* of which we shall speak in handling Sedition. It is a disease in a state like to infection. For as infection spreadeth upon that which is sound, and tainteth it; so when envy is gotten once into a state, it traduceth even the best actions thereof, and turneth them into an ill odour. And therefore there is little won by intermingling of plausible actions. For that doth argue but a weakness and fear of envy, which hurteth so much the more; as it is likewise usual in infections; which if you fear them, you call them upon you.

This public envy seemeth to beat chiefly upon principal officers or ministers, rather than upon kings and estates themselves. But this is a sure rule, that if the envy upon the minister be great, when the cause of it in him is small; or if the envy be general in a manner upon all the ministers of an estate; then the envy (though hidden) is truly upon the state itself. And so much of public envy or discontentment, and the difference thereof from private envy, which was handled in the first place.

We will add this in general, touching the affection of envy; that of all other affections it is the most importune and continual. For of other affections there is occasion given but now and then; and therefore it was well said, *Invidia festos dies non agit:* [Envy keeps no holidays:] for it is ever working upon some or other. And it is also noted that love and envy do make a man pine, which other affections do not, because they are not so continual. It is also the vilest affection, and the most depraved; for which cause it is the proper attribute of the devil, who is called *The envious man, that soweth tares amongst the wheat by night;* as it always cometh to pass, that envy worketh subtilly, and in the dark; and to the prejudice of good things, such as is the wheat.

· 10 ·

OF LOVE

THE stage is more beholding to Love, than the life of man. For as to the stage, love is ever matter of comedies, and now and then of tragedies; but in life it doth much mischief; sometimes like a syren, sometimes like a fury. You may observe, that amongst all the great and worthy persons (whereof the memory remaineth, either ancient or recent,) there is not one that hath been transported to the mad degree of love: which shews that great spirits and great business do keep out this weak passion. You must except nevertheless Marcus Antonius, the half part-ner of the empire of Rome, and Appius Claudius, the de-cemvir and lawgiver; whereof the former was indeed a voluptuous man, and inordinate; but the latter was an austere and wise man: and therefore it seems (though rarely) that love can find entrance not only into an open heart, but also into a heart well fortified, if watch be not well kept. It is a poor saying of Epicurus, *Satis magnum alter alteri theatrum sumus* [Each is to other a theatre large enough]; as if man, made for the contemplation of heaven and all noble objects, should do nothing but kneel before a little idol, and make himself a subject, though not of the mouth (as beasts are), yet of the eye; which was given him for higher purposes. It is a strange thing to note the excess of this passion, and how it braves the nature and value of things, by this; that the speaking in a perpetual hyperbole is comely in nothing but in love.

Neither is it merely in the phrase; for whereas it hath been well said that the arch-flatterer, with whom all the petty flatterers have intelligence, is a man's self; certainly the lover is more. For there was never proud man thought so absurdly well of himself as the lover doth of the person loved; and therefore it was well said, *That it is impossible to love and to be wise.* Neither doth this weakness appear to others only, and not to the party loved; but to the loved most of all, except the love be reciproque. For it is a true rule, that love is ever rewarded either with the reciproque or with an inward and secret contempt. By how much the more men ought to beware of this passion, which loseth not only other things, but itself. As for the other losses, the poet's relation doth well figure them. That he that preferred Helena, quitted the gifts of Juno and Pallas. For whosoever esteemeth too much of amorous affection quitteth both riches and wisdom. This passion hath his floods in the very times of weakness; which are great prosperity and great adversity; though this latter hath been less observed: both which times kindle love, and make it more fervent, and therefore shew it to be the child of folly. They do best, who if they cannot but admit love, yet make it keep quarter; and sever it wholly from their serious affairs and actions of life; for if it check once with business, it troubleth men's fortunes, and maketh men that they can no ways be true to their own ends. I know not how, but martial men are given to love: I think it is but as they are given to wine; for perils commonly ask to be paid in pleasures. There is in man's nature a secret inclination and motion towards love of others, which if it be not spent upon some one or a few, doth naturally spread itself towards many, and maketh men become humane and charitable; as it is seen sometime in friars. Nuptial love maketh mankind; friendly love perfecteth it; but wanton love corrupteth and embaseth it.

OF GREAT PLACE

MEN in great place are thrice servants: servants of the sovereign or state; servants of fame; and servants of business. So as they have no freedom; neither in their persons, nor in their actions, nor in their times. It is a strange desire, to seek power and to lose liberty: or to seek power over others and to lose power over a man's self. The rising unto place is laborious; and by pains men come to greater pains; and it is sometimes base; and by indignities men come to dignities. The standing is slippery, and the regress is either a downfall, or at least an eclipse, which is a melancholy thing. *Cum non sis qui fueris, non esse cur velis vivere* [When a man feels that he is no longer what he was, he loses all his interest in life]. Nay, retire men cannot when they would, neither will they when it were reason; but are impatient of privateness, even in age and sickness, which require the shadow; like old townsmen, that will be still sitting at their street door, though thereby they offer age to scorn. Certainly great persons had need to borrow other men's opinions, to think themselves happy; for if they judge by their own feeling, they cannot find it: but if they think with themselves what other men think of them, and that other men would fain be as they are, then they are happy as it were by report; when perhaps they find the contrary within. For they are the first that find their own griefs, though they be the last that find their own faults. Certainly men in great fortunes are strangers to themselves, and while they are in the puzzle of business they have no time to tend their health either of body or mind. *Illi mors gravis incubat, qui notus nimis omnibus, ignotus moritur sibi* [It is a sad fate for a man to die too well known to everybody else, and still unknown to himself]. In place there is licence to do good and evil; whereof the latter is a curse: for in evil the best condition is not to will; the second not to can. But power to do good is the true and lawful end of aspiring. For good thoughts (though God accept them) yet towards men are little better than good dreams, except they be put in act; and that cannot be without power and place, as the vantage and commanding ground. Merit and good works is the end of man's motion; and conscience of the same is the accomplishment of man's rest. For if a man can be partaker of God's theatre, he shall likewise be partaker of God's rest. *Et conversus Deus, ut aspiceret opera quæ fecerunt manus suæ, vidit quod omnia essent bona nimis;* [And God turned to look upon the works which his hands had made, and saw that all were very good;] and then the sabbath. In the discharge of thy place set before thee the best examples; for imitation is a globe of precepts. And after a time set before thee thine own example; and examine thyself strictly whether thou didst not best at first. Neglect not also the examples of those that have carried themselves ill in the same place; not to set off thyself by taxing their memory, but to direct thyself what to avoid. Reform therefore, without bravery or scandal of former times and persons; but yet set it down to thyself as well to create good precedents as to follow them. Reduce things to the first institution, and observe wherein and how they have degenerate; but yet ask counsel of both times; of the ancient time, what is best; and of the latter time, what is fittest. Seek to make thy course regular, that men may know beforehand what they may expect; but be not too positive and peremptory; and express thyself well when thou digressest from thy rule. Preserve the right of thy place; but stir not questions of jurisdiction: and rather assume thy right in silence and *de facto* [as an accepted fact], than voice it with claims and challenges. Preserve likewise the rights of inferior places; and think it more honour to direct in chief than to be busy in all. Embrace and invite helps and advices touching the execution of thy place; and do not drive away such as bring thee information, as meddlers; but accept of them in good part. The vices of authority are chiefly four; delays, corruption, roughness, and facility. For delays; give easy access; keep times appointed; go through with that which is in hand, and interlace not business but of necessity. For corruption; do not only bind thine own hands or thy servants' hands from taking, but bind the hands of suitors also from offering. For integrity used doth the one; but integrity professed, and with a manifest detestation of bribery, doth the other. And avoid not only the fault, but the suspicion. Whosoever is found variable, and changeth manifestly without manifest cause, giveth suspicion of corruption. Therefore always when thou changest thine opinion or course, profess it plainly, and declare it, together with the reasons that move thee to change; and do not think to steal it. A servant or a favourite, if he be inward, and no other apparent cause of esteem, is commonly thought but a by-way to close corruption. For roughness; it is a needless cause of discontent: severity breedeth fear, but roughness breedeth hate. Even reproofs from authority ought to be grave, and not taunting. As for facility; it is worse than bribery. For bribes come but now and then; but if importunity or idle respects lead a man, he shall never be without. As Salomon saith, *To respect persons is not good; for such a man will transgress for a piece of bread.* It is most true that was anciently spoken, *A place sheweth the man.* And it sheweth some to the better, and some to the worse. *Omnium consensu capax imperii, nisi imperasset,* [a man whom every body would have thought fit for empire if he had not been emperor,] saith Tacitus of Galba; but of Vespasian he saith, *Solus imperantium, Vespasianus mutatus in melius:* [He was the only emperor whom the possession of power changed for the better;] though the one was meant of sufficiency, the other of manners and affection. It is an assured sign of a worthy and generous spirit, whom honour amends. For honour is, or should be, the place of virtue; and as in nature things move violently to their place and calmly in their place, so virtue in ambition is violent, in authority settled and calm. All rising to great place is by a winding stair; and if there be factions, it is good to side a man's self whilst he is in the rising, and to balance himself when he is placed. Use the memory of thy predecessor fairly and tenderly; for if thou dost not, it is a debt will sure be paid when thou art gone. If thou have colleagues, respect them, and rather call them when they look not for it, than exclude them when they have reason to look to be called. Be not too sensible or too remembering of thy place in conversation and private answers to suitors; but let rather be said, *When he sits in place he is another man.*

· 12 ·

Of Boldness

It is a trivial grammar-school text, but yet worthy a wise man's consideration. Question was asked of Demosthenes, *what was the chief part of an orator?* he answered, *action:* what next? *action.* what next again? *action.* He said it that knew it best, and had by nature himself no advantage in that he commended. A strange thing, that that part of an orator which is but superficial, and rather the virtue of a player, should be placed so high, above those other noble parts of invention, elocution, and the rest; nay almost alone, as if it were all in all. But the reason is plain. There is in human nature generally more of the fool than of the wise; and therefore those faculties by which the foolish part of men's minds is taken are most potent. Wonderful like is the case of Boldness, in civil business; what first? Boldness: what second and third? Boldness. And yet boldness is a child of ignorance and baseness, far inferior to other parts. But nevertheless it doth fascinate and bind hand and foot those that are either shallow in judgment or weak in courage, which are the greatest part; yea and prevaileth with wise men at weak times. Therefore we see it hath done wonders in popular states; but with senates and princes less; and more ever upon the first entrance of bold persons into action than soon after; for boldness is an ill keeper of promise. Surely as there are mountebanks for the natural body, so are there mountebanks for the politic body; men that undertake great cures, and perhaps have been lucky in two or three experiments, but want the grounds of science, and therefore cannot hold out. Nay you shall see a bold fellow many times do Mahomet's miracle. Mahomet made the people believe that he would call an hill to him, and from the top of it offer up his prayers for the observers of his law. The people assembled; Mahomet called the hill to come to him, again and again; and when the hill stood still, he was never a whit abashed, but said, *If the hill will not come to Mahomet, Mahomet will go to the hill.* So these men, when they have promised great matters and failed most shamefully, yet (if they have the perfection of boldness) they will but slight it over, and make a turn, and no more ado. Certainly to men of great judgment, bold persons are a sport to behold; nay and to the vulgar also, boldness has somewhat of the ridiculous. For if absurdity be the subject of laughter, doubt you not but great boldness is seldom without some absurdity. Especially it is a sport to see, when a bold fellow is out of countenance; for that puts his face into a most shrunken and wooden posture; as needs it must; for in bashfulness the spirits do a little go and come; but with bold men, upon like occasion, they stand at a stay; like a stale at chess, where it is no mate, but yet the game cannot stir. But this last were fitter for a satire than for a serious observation. This is well to be weighed; that boldness is ever blind; for it seeth not dangers and inconveniences. Therefore it is ill in counsel, good in execution; so that the right use of bold persons is, that they never command in chief, but be seconds, and under the direction of others. For in counsel it is good to see dangers; and in execution not to see them, except they be very great.

· 13 ·

Of Goodness and Goodness of Nature

I TAKE Goodness in this sense, the affecting of the weal of men, which is that the Grecians call *Philanthropia;* and the word *humanity* (as it is used) is a little too light to express it. Goodness I call the habit, and Goodness of Nature the inclination. This of all virtues and dignities of the mind is the greatest; being the character of the Deity: and without it man is a busy, mischievous, wretched thing; no better than a kind of vermin. Goodness answers to the theological virtue Charity, and admits no excess, but error. The desire of power in excess caused the angels to fall; the desire of knowledge in excess caused man to fall: but in charity there is no excess; neither can angel or man come in danger by it. The inclination to goodness is imprinted deeply in the nature of man; insomuch that if it issue not towards men, it will take unto other living creatures; as it is seen in the Turks, a cruel people, who nevertheless are kind to beasts, and give alms to dogs and birds; insomuch as Busbechius reporteth, a Christian boy in Constantinople had like to have been stoned for gagging in a waggishness a long-billed fowl. Errors indeed in this virtue of goodness or charity may be committed. The Italians have an ungracious proverb, *Tanto buon che val niente; So good, that he is good for nothing.* And one of the doctors of Italy, Nicholas Machiavel, had the confidence to put in writing, almost in plain terms, *That the Christian faith had given up good men in prey to those that are tyrannical and unjust.* Which he spake, because indeed there was never law, or sect, or opinion, did so much magnify goodness, as the Christian religion doth. Therefore, to avoid the scandal and the danger both, it is good to take knowledge of the errors of an habit so excellent. Seek the good of other men, but be not in bondage to their faces or fancies; for that is but facility or softness; which taketh an honest mind prisoner. Neither give thou Æsop's cock a gem, who would be better pleased and happier if he had a barley-corn. The example of God teacheth the lesson truly; *He sendeth his rain, and maketh his sun to shine, upon the just and unjust;* but he doth not rain wealth, nor shine honour and virtues, upon men equally. Common benefits are to be communicate with all; but peculiar benefits with choice. And beware how in making the portraiture thou breakest the pattern.

For divinity maketh the love of ourselves the pattern; the love of our neighbours but the portraiture. *Sell all thou hast, and give it to the poor, and follow me:* but sell not all thou hast, except thou come and follow me; that is, except thou have a vocation wherein thou mayest do as much good with little means as with great; for otherwise in feeding the streams thou driest the fountain. Neither is there only a habit of goodness, directed by right reason; but there is in some men, even in nature, a disposition towards it; as on the other side there is a natural malignity. For there be that in their nature do not affect the good of others. The lighter sort of malignity turneth but to a crossness, or frowardness, or aptness to oppose, or difficilness, or the like; but the deeper sort to envy and mere mischief. Such men in other men's calamities are, as it were, in season, and are ever on the loading part: not so good as the dogs that licked Lazarus' sores; but like flies that are still buzzing upon any thing that is raw; *misanthropi*, that make it their practice to bring men to the bough, and yet have never a tree for the purpose in their gardens, as Timon had. Such dispositions are the very errours of human nature; and yet they are the fittest timber to make great politiques of; like to knee timber, that is good for ships, that are ordained to be tossed; but not for building houses, that shall stand firm. The parts and signs of goodness are many. If a man be gracious and courteous to strangers, it shews he is a citizen of the world, and that his heart is no island cut off from other lands, but a continent that joins to them. If he be compassionate towards the afflictions of others, it shews that his heart is like the noble tree that is wounded itself when it gives the balm. If he easily pardons and remits offences, it shews that his mind is planted above injuries; so that he cannot be shot. If he be thankful for small benefits, it shews that he weighs men's minds, and not their trash. But above all, if he have St. Paul's perfection, that he would wish to be an *anathema* from Christ for the salvation of his brethren, it shews much of a divine nature, and a kind of conformity with Christ himself.

OF NOBILITY

WE will speak of Nobility first as a portion of an estate; then as a condition of particular persons. A monarchy where there is no nobility at all, is ever a pure and absolute tyranny; as that of the Turks. For nobility attempers sovereignty, and draws the eyes of the people somewhat aside from the line royal. But for democracies, they need it not; and they are commonly more quiet and less subject to sedition, than where there are stirps of nobles. For men's eyes are upon the business, and not upon the persons; or if upon the persons, it is for the business sake, as fittest, and not for flags and pedigree. We see the Switzers last well, notwithstanding their diversity of religion and of cantons. For utility is their bond, and not respects. The united provinces of the Low Countries in their government excel; for where there is an equality, the consultations are more indifferent, and the payments and tributes more cheerful. A great and potent nobility addeth majesty to a monarch, but diminisheth power; and putteth life and spirit into the people, but presseth their fortune. It is well when nobles are not too great for sovereignty nor for justice; and yet maintained in that height, as the insolency of inferiors may be broken upon them before it come on too fast upon the majesty of kings. A numerous nobility causeth poverty and inconvenience in a state; for it is a surcharge of expense; and besides, it being of necessity that many of the nobility fall in time to be weak in fortune, it maketh a kind of disproportion between honour and means.

As for nobility in particular persons; it is a reverend thing to see an ancient castle or building not in decay; or to see a fair timber tree sound and perfect. How much more to behold an ancient noble family, which hath stood against the waves and weathers of time. For new nobility is but the act of power, but ancient nobility is the act of time. Those that are first raised to nobility are commonly more virtuous, but less innocent, than their descendants; for there is rarely any rising but by a commixture of good and evil arts. But it is reason the memory of their virtues remain to their posterity, and their faults die with themselves. Nobility of birth commonly abateth industry; and he that is not industrious, envieth him that is. Besides, noble persons cannot go much higher: and he that standeth at a stay when others rise, can hardly avoid motions of envy. On the other side, nobility extinguisheth the passive envy from others towards them; because they are in possession of honour. Certainly, kings that have able men of their nobility shall find ease in employing them, and a better slide into their business; for people naturally bend to them, as born in some sort to command.

· 15 ·

OF SEDITIONS AND TROUBLES

SHEPHERDS of people had need know the calendars of tempests in state; which are commonly greatest when things grow to equality; as natural tempests are greatest about the *Equinoctia*. And as there are certain hollow blasts of wind and secret swellings of seas before a tempest, so are there in states:

—— Ille etiam cæcos instare tumultus
Sæpe monet, fraudesque et operta tumescere bella.
[Of troubles imminent and treasons dark
Thence warning comes, and wars in secret gathering.]

Libels and licentious discourses against the state, when they are frequent and open; and in like sort, false news often running up and down to the disadvantage of the state, and hastily embraced; are amongst the signs of troubles. Virgil giving the pedigree of Fame, saith *she was sister to the Giants:*

Illam Terra parens, irâ irritata Deorum,
Extremam (ut perhibent) Cœo Enceladoque sororem
Progenuit.

As if fames were the relics of seditions past; but they are
no less indeed the preludes of seditions to come. Howsoever he noteth it right, that seditious tumults and seditious fames differ no more but as brother and sister, masculine and feminine; especially if it come to that, that the
best actions of a state, and the most plausible, and which
ought to give greatest contentment, are taken in ill sense,
and traduced: for that shews the envy great, as Tacitus
saith, *conflata magna invidia, seu bene seu male gesta
premunt* [when dislike prevails against the government,
good actions and bad offend alike]. Neither doth it follow, that because these fames are a sign of troubles, that
the suppressing of them with too much severity should
be a remedy of troubles. For the despising of them many
times checks them best; and the going about to stop them
doth make a wonder long-lived. Also that kind of obedience which Tacitus speaketh of, is to be held suspected:
*Erant in officio, sed tamen qui mallent mandata imperanti-
um interpretari quam exequi;* [ready to serve, and yet
more disposed to construe commands than execute them;]
disputing, excusing, cavilling upon mandates and directions, is a kind of shaking off the yoke, and assay of dis-
obedience; especially if in those disputings they which
are for the direction speak fearfully and tenderly, and
those that are against it audaciously.

Also, as Machiavel noteth well, when princes, that
ought to be common parents, make themselves as a party,
and lean to a side, it is as a boat that is overthrown by
uneven weight on the one side; as was well seen in the
time of Henry the Third of France; for first himself entered league for the extirpation of the Protestants; and
presently after the same league was turned upon himself.
For when the authority of princes is made but an accessary to a cause, and that there be other bands that tie
faster than the band of sovereignty, kings begin to be
put almost out of possession.

Also, when discords, and quarrels, and factions, are carried openly and audaciously, it is a sign the reverence of government is lost. For the motions of the greatest persons in a government ought to be as the motions of the planets under *primum mobile;* (according to the old opinion,) which is, that every of them is carried swiftly by the highest motion, and softly in their own motion. And therefore, when great ones in their own particular motion move violently, and, as Tacitus expresseth it well, *liberius quam ut imperantium meminissent,* [unrestrained by reverence for the government], it is a sign the orbs are out of frame. For reverence is that wherewith princes are girt from God; who threateneth the dissolving thereof; *Solvam cingula regum* [I will unbind the girdles of kings].

So when any of the four pillars of government are mainly shaken or weakened (which are Religion, Justice, Counsel, and Treasure), men had need to pray for fair weather. But let us pass from this part of predictions (concerning which, nevertheless, more light may be taken from that which followeth); and let us speak first of the Materials of seditions; then of the Motives of them; and thirdly of the Remedies.

Concerning the Materials of seditions. It is a thing well to be considered; for the surest way to prevent seditions (if the times do bear it) is to take away the matter of them. For if there be fuel prepared, it is hard to tell whence the spark shall come that shall set it on fire. The matter of seditions is of two kinds; much poverty and much discontentment. It is certain, so many overthrown estates, so many votes for troubles. Lucan noteth well the state of Rome before the civil war,

> Hinc usura vorax, rapidumque in tempore fœnus,
> Hinc concussa fides, et multis utile bellum:

[estates eaten up by usurious rates of interest, credit shaken, war a gain to many].

This same *multis utile bellum* [war a gain to many], is an assured and infallible sign of a state disposed to seditions and troubles. And if this poverty and broken estate in the better sort be joined with a want and necessity in the mean people, the danger is imminent and great. For the rebellions of the belly are the worst. As for discontentments, they are in the politic body like to humours in the natural, which are apt to gather a preternatural heat and to inflame. And let no prince measure the danger of them by this, whether they be just or unjust: for that were to imagine people to be too reasonable; who do often spurn at their own good: nor yet by this, whether the griefs whereupon they rise be in fact great or small: for they are the most dangerous discontentments where the fear is greater than the feeling: *Dolendi modus, timendi non item* [Suffering has its limit, but fears are endless]. Besides, in great oppressions, the same things that provoke the patience, do withal mate the courage; but in fears it is not so. Neither let any prince or state be secure concerning discontentments, because they have been often, or have been long, and yet no peril hath ensued: for as it is true that every vapour or fume doth not turn into a storm; so it is nevertheless true that storms, though they blow over divers times, yet may fall at last; and, as the Spanish proverb noteth well, *The cord breaketh at the last by the weakest pull.*

The Causes and Motives of seditions are, innovation in religion; taxes; alteration of laws and customs; breaking of privileges; general oppression; advancement of unworthy persons; strangers; dearths; disbanded soldiers; factions grown desperate; and whatsoever, in offending people, joineth and knitteth them in a common cause.

For the Remedies; there may be some general preservatives, whereof we will speak: as for the just cure, it must answer to the particular disease; and so be left to counsel rather than rule.

The first remedy or prevention is to remove by all means possible that material cause of sedition whereof we spake; which is, want and poverty in the estate. To which purpose serveth, the opening and well-balancing of trade; the cherishing of manufactures; the banishing of idleness; the repressing of waste and excess by sumptuary laws; the improvement and husbanding of the soil; the regulating of prices of things vendible; the moderating of taxes and tributes, and the like. Generally, it is to be foreseen that the population of a kingdom (especially if it be not mown down by wars) do not exceed the stock of the kingdom which should maintain them. Neither is the population to be reckoned only by number; for a smaller number that spend more and earn less, do wear out an estate sooner than a greater number that live lower and gather more. Therefore the multiplying of nobility and other degrees of quality in an over proportion to the common people, doth speedily bring a state to necessity; and so doth likewise an overgrown clergy; for they bring nothing to the stock; and in like manner, when more are bred scholars than preferments can take off.

It is likewise to be remembered, that forasmuch as the increase of any estate must be upon the foreigner (for whatsoever is somewhere gotten is somewhere lost), there be but three things which one nation selleth unto another; the commodity as nature yieldeth it; the manufacture; and the vecture, or carriage. So that if these three wheels go, wealth will flow as in a spring tide. And it cometh many times to pass, that *materiam superabit opus;* that the work and carriage is more worth than the material, and enricheth a state more; as is notably seen in the Low-Countrymen, who have the best mines above ground in the world.

Above all things, good policy is to be used that the treasure and monies in a state be not gathered into few hands. For otherwise a state may have a great stock, and yet starve. And money is like muck, not good except it be spread. This is done chiefly by suppressing, or at the least keeping a strait hand upon the devouring trades of usury, ingrossing, great pasturages, and the like.

For removing discontentments, or at least the danger of them; there is in every state (as we know) two portions of subjects; the nobless and the commonalty. When one of these is discontent, the danger is not great; for common people are of slow motion, if they be not excited by the greater sort; and the greater sort are of small strength, except the multitude be apt and ready to move of themselves. Then is the danger, when the greater sort do but wait for the troubling of the waters amongst the meaner, that then they may declare themselves. The poets feign, that the rest of the gods would have bound Jupiter; which he hearing of, by the counsel of Pallas, sent for Briareus, with his hundred hands, to come in to his aid. An emblem, no doubt, to show how safe it is for monarchs to make sure of the good will of common people.

To give moderate liberty for griefs and discontentments to evaporate (so it be without too great insolency or bravery), is a safe way. For he that turneth the humours back, and maketh the wound bleed inwards, endangereth malign ulcers and pernicious imposthumations.

The part of Epimetheus mought well become Prometheus, in the case of discontentments; for there is not a better provision against them. Epimetheus, when griefs and evils flew abroad, at last shut the lid, and kept hope in the bottom of the vessel. Certainly, the politic and artificial nourishing and entertaining of hopes, and carrying men from hopes to hopes, is one of the best antidotes against the poison of discontentments. And it is a certain sign of a wise government and proceeding, when it can hold men's hearts by hopes, when it cannot by satisfaction; and when it can handle things in such manner, as no evil shall appear so peremptory but that it hath some outlet of hope: which is the less hard to do, because both particular persons and factions are apt enough to flatter themselves, or at least to brave that they believe not.

Also the foresight and prevention, that there be no likely or fit head whereunto discontented persons may resort, and under whom they may join, is a known, but an excellent point of caution. I understand a fit head to be one that hath greatness and reputation; that hath confidence with the discontented party, and upon whom they turn their eyes; and that is thought discontented in his own particular: which kind of persons are either to be won and reconciled to the state, and that in a fast and true manner; or to be fronted with some other of the same party, that may oppose them, and so divide the reputation. Generally, the dividing and breaking of all factions and combinations that are adverse to the state, and setting them at distance, or at least distrust, amongst themselves, is not one of the worst remedies. For it is a desperate case, if those that hold with the proceeding of the state be full of discord and faction, and those that are against it be entire and united.

I have noted that some witty and sharp speeches which have fallen from princes have given fire to seditions. Cæsar did himself infinite hurt in that speech, *Sylla nescivit literas, non potuit dictare:* [Scylla was no scholar, he could not dictate:] for it did utterly cut off that hope which men had entertained, that he would at one time or other give over his dictatorship. Galba undid himself by that speech, *legi a se militem, non emi;* [that he did not buy his soldiers, but levied them:] for it put the soldiers out of hope of the donative. Probus likewise, by that speech, *si vixero, non opus erit amplius Romano imperio militibus;* [if I live, the Roman empire shall have no more need of soldiers:] a speech of great despair for the soldiers. And many the like. Surely princes had need, in tender matters and ticklish times, to beware what they say; especially in these short speeches, which fly abroad like darts, and are thought to be shot out of their secret intentions. For as for large discourses, they are flat things, and not so much noted.

Lastly, let princes, against all events, not be without some great person, one or rather more, of military valour, near unto them, for the repressing of seditions in their beginnings. For without that, there useth to be more trepidation in court upon the first breaking out of troubles than were fit. And the state runneth the danger of that which Tacitus saith; *Atque is habitus animorum fuit, ut pessimum facinus auderent pauci, plures vellent, omnes paterentur* [A few were in a humour to attempt mischief, more to desire, all to allow it]. But let such military persons be assured, and well reputed of, rather than factious and popular; holding also good correspondence with the other great men in the state; or else the remedy is worse than the disease.

16

OF ATHEISM

I HAD rather believe all the fables in the Legend, and the Talmud, and the Alcoran, than that this universal frame is without a mind. And therefore God never wrought miracle to convince atheism, because his ordinary works convince it. It is true, that a little philosophy inclineth man's mind to atheism; but depth in philosophy bringeth men's minds about to religion. For while the mind of man looketh upon second causes scattered, it may sometimes rest in them, and go no further; but when it beholdeth the chain of them, confederate and linked together, it must needs fly to Providence and Deity. Nay, even that school which is most accused of atheism doth most demonstrate religion; that is, the school of Leucippus and Democritus and Epicurus. For it is a thousand times more credible, that four mutable elements, and one immutable fifth essence, duly and eternally placed, need no God, than that an army of infinite small portions or seeds unplaced, should have produced this order and beauty without a divine marshal. The scripture saith, *The fool hath said in his heart, there is no God;* it is not said, *The fool hath thought in his heart;* so as he rather saith it by rote to himself, as that he would have, than that he can throughly believe it, or be persuaded of it. For none deny there is a God, but those for whom it maketh that there were no God. It appeareth in nothing more, that atheism is rather in the lip than in the heart of man, than by this; that atheists will ever be talking of that their opinion, as if they fainted in it within themselves, and would be glad to be strengthened by the consent of others. Nay more, you shall have atheists strive to get disciples, as it fareth with other sects. And, which is most of all, you shall have of them that will suffer for atheism, and not recant; whereas if they did truly think that there were no such thing as God, why should they trouble themselves? Epicurus is charged that he did but dissemble for his credit's sake, when he affirmed there were blessed natures, but such as enjoyed themselves without having respect to the government of the world. Wherein they say he did temporize; though in secret he thought there was no God. But certainly he is traduced; for his words are noble and divine: *Non Deos vulgi negare profanum; sed vulgi opiniones Diis applicare profanum* [There is no profanity in refusing to believe in the Gods of the vulgar: the profanity is in believing of the Gods what the vulgar believe of them]. Plato could have said no more. And although he had the confidence to deny the administration, he had not the power to deny the nature. The Indians of the west have names for their particular gods, though they have no name for God: as if the heathens should have had the names Jupiter, Apollo, Mars, &c. but not the words *Deus;* which shews that even those barbarous people have the notion, though they have not the latitude and extent of it. So that against atheists the very savages take part with the very subtlest philosophers. The contemplative atheist is rare: a Diagoras, a Bion, a Lucian perhaps, and some others; and yet they seem to be more than they are; for that all that impugn a received religion or superstition are by the adverse part branded with the name of atheists. But the great atheists indeed are hypocrites; which are ever handling holy things, but without feeling; so as they must needs be cauterized in the end. The causes of atheism are; divisions in religion, if they be many; for any one main division addeth zeal to both sides; but many divisions introduce atheism. Another is, scandal of priests; when it is come to that which St. Bernard saith, *Non est jam dicere, ut populus sic sacerdos; quia nec sic populus ut sacerdos* [One cannot now say, the priest is as the people, for the truth is that the people are not so bad as the priest]. A third is, custom of profane scoffing in holy matters; which doth by little and little deface the reverence of religion. And lastly, learned times, specially with peace and prosperity; for troubles and adversities do more bow men's minds to religion. They that deny a God destroy man's nobility; for certainly

man is of kin to the beasts by his body; and, if he be not
of kin to God by his spirit, he is a base and ignoble
creature. It destroys likewise magnanimity, and the raising of human nature; for take an example of a dog, and
mark what a generosity and courage he will put on when
he finds himself maintained by a man; who to him is instead of a God, or *melior natura;* which courage is manifestly such as that creature, without that confidence of a
better nature than his own, could never attain. So man,
when he resteth and assureth himself upon divine protection and favour, gathereth a force and faith which
human nature in itself could not obtain. Therefore, as
atheism is in all respects hateful, so in this, that it depriveth human nature of the means to exalt itself above
human frailty. As it is in particular persons, so it is in
nations. Never was there such a state for magnanimity as
Rome. Of this state hear what Cicero saith: *Quam volu-
mus licet, patres conscripti, nos amemus, tamen nec nu-
mero Hispanos, nec robore Gallos, nec calliditate Pœnos,
nec artibus Græcos, nec denique hoc ipso hujus gentis et
terræ domestico nativoque sensu Italos ipsos et Latinos;
sed pietate, ac religione, atque hac una sapientia, quod
Deorum immortalium numine omnia regi gubernarique
perspeximus, omnes gentes nationesque superavimus*
[Pride ourselves as we may upon our country, yet are
we not in number superior to the Spaniards, nor in
strength to the Gauls, nor in cunning to the Carthaginians,
nor to the Greeks in arts, nor to the Italians and Latins
themselves in the homely and native sense which belongs
to this nation and land; it is in piety only and religion, and
the wisdom of regarding the providence of the Immortal
Gods as that which rules and governs all things, that we
have surpassed all nations and peoples].

17

OF SUPERSTITION

IT were better to have no opinion of God at all, than such an opinion as is unworthy of him. For the one is unbelief, and other is contumely: and certainly superstition is the reproach of the Deity. Plutarch saith well to that purpose: *Surely* (saith he) *I had rather a great deal men should say there was no such man at all as Plutarch, than that they should say that there was one Plutarch that would eat his children as soon as they were born;* as the poets speak of Saturn. And as the contumely is greater towards God, so the danger is greater towards men. Atheism leaves a man to sense, to philosophy, to natural piety, to laws, to reputation; all which may be guides to an outward moral virtue, though religion were not; but superstition dismounts all these, and erecteth an absolute monarchy in the minds of men. Therefore atheism did never perturb states; for it makes men wary of themselves, as looking no further: and we see the times inclined to atheism (as the time of Augustus Cæsar) were civil times. But superstition hath been the confusion of many states, and bringeth in a new *primum mobile,* that ravisheth all the spheres of government. The master of superstition is the people; and in all superstition wise men follow fools; and arguments are fitted to practice, in a reversed order. It was gravely said by some of the prelates in the council of Trent, where the doctrine of the schoolmen bare great sway, *that the schoolmen were like astronomers, which did feign eccentrics and epicycles, and such engines of orbs, to save the phænomena; though they knew there were no such things;* and in like manner, that the schoolmen had framed a number of subtle and intricate axioms and theorems, to save the practice of the church. The causes of superstition are, pleasing and sensual rites and ceremonies; excess of outward and pharisaical holiness; over-great reverence of traditions, which cannot but load the church; the stratagems of prelates for their own ambition and lucre; the favouring too much of good intentions, which openeth the gate to conceits and novelties; the taking an aim at divine matters by human, which cannot but breed mixture of imaginations: and, lastly, barbarous times, especially joined with calamities and disasters. Superstition, without a veil, is a deformed thing; for as it addeth deformity to an ape to be so like a man, so the similitude of superstition to religion makes it the more deformed. And as wholesome meat corrupteth to little worms, so good forms and orders corrupt into a number of petty observances. There is a superstition in avoiding superstition, when men think to do best if they go furthest from the superstition formerly received; therefore care would be had that (as it fareth in ill purgings) the good be not taken away with the bad; which commonly is done when the people is the reformer.

· 18 ·

OF TRAVEL

TRAVEL, in the younger sort, is a part of education; in the elder, a part of experience. He that travelleth into a country before he hath some entrance into the language, goeth to school, and not to travel. That young men travel under some tutor, or grave servant, I allow well; so that he be such a one that hath the language, and hath been in the country before; whereby he may be able to tell them what things are worthy to be seen in the country where they go; what acquaintances they are to seek; what exercises or discipline the place yieldeth. For else young men shall go hooded, and look abroad little. It is a strange thing, that in sea voyages, where there is nothing to be seen but sky and sea, men should make diaries; but in land-travel, wherein so much is to be observed, for the most part they omit it; as if chance were fitter to be registered than observation. Let diaries therefore be brought in use. The things to be seen and ob-

served are, the courts of princes, specially when they give
audience to ambassadors; the courts of justice, while they
sit and hear causes; and so of consistories ecclesiastic; the
churches and monasteries, with the monuments which are
therein extant; the walls and fortifications of cities and
towns, and so the havens and harbours; antiquities and
ruins; libraries; colleges, disputations, and lectures, where
any are; shipping and navies; houses and gardens of state
and pleasure, near great cities; armories; arsenals; maga-
zines; exchanges; burses; warehouses; exercises of horse-
manship, fencing, training of soldiers, and the like; comedies, such whereunto the better sort of persons do resort;
treasuries of jewels and robes; cabinets and rarities; and,
to conclude, whatsoever is memorable in the places where
they go. After all which the tutors or servants ought to
make diligent inquiry. As for triumphs, masks, feasts,
weddings, funerals, capital executions, and such shows,
men need not to be put in mind of them; yet are they not
to be neglected. If you will have a young man to put his
travel into a little room, and in short time to gather
much, this you must do. First as was said, he must have
some entrance into the language before he goeth. Then he
must have such a servant or tutor as knoweth the country, as was likewise said. Let him carry with him also
some card or book describing the country where he
travelleth; which will be a good key to his inquiry. Let
him keep also a diary. Let him not stay long in one city
or town; more or less as the place deserveth, but not long;
nay, when he stayeth in one city or town, let him
change his lodging from one end and part of the town to
another; which is a great adamant of acquaintance. Let
him sequester himself from the company of his country-
men, and diet in such places where there is good company
of the nation where he travelleth. Let him upon his removes from one place to another, procure recommendation to some person of quality residing in the place
whither he removeth; that he may use his favour in
those things he desireth to see or know. Thus he may
abridge his travel with much profit. As for the acquaintance which is to be sought in travel; that which is most of

all profitable, is acquaintance with the secretaries and employed men of ambassadors: for so in travelling in one country he shall suck the experience of many. Let him also see and visit eminent persons in all kinds, which are of great name abroad; that he may be able to tell how the life agreeth with the fame. For quarrels, they are with care and discretion to be avoided. They are commonly for mistresses, healths, place, and words. And let a man beware how he keepeth company with choleric and quarrelsome persons; for they will engage him into their own quarrels. When a traveller returneth home, let him not leave the countries where he hath travelled altogether behind him; but maintain a correspondence by letters with those of his acquaintance which are of most worth. And let his travel appear rather in his discourse than in his apparel or gesture; and in his discourse let him be rather advised in his answers, than forward to tell stories; and let it appear that he doth not change his country manners for those of foreign parts; but only prick in some flowers of that he hath learned abroad into the customs of his own country.

· 19 ·

OF EMPIRE

IT is a miserable state of mind to have few things to desire, and many things to fear; and yet that commonly is the case of kings; who, being at the highest, want matter of desire, which makes their minds more languishing; and have many representations of perils and shadows, which makes their minds the less clear. And this is one reason also of that effect which the Scripture speaketh of, *That the king's heart is inscrutable.* For multitude of jealousies, and lack of some predominant desire that should marshal and put in order all the rest, maketh any man's heart hard to find or sound. Hence it comes likewise, that princes many times make themselves desires, and set their hearts upon toys; sometimes upon a building; sometimes upon erecting of an order; sometimes upon the advancing of a person; sometimes upon obtaining excellency in some art or feat of the hand; as Nero for playing on the harp, Domitian for certainty of the hand with the arrow, Commodus for playing at fence, Caracalla for driving chariots, and the like. This seemeth incredible unto those that know not the principle *that the mind of man is more cheered and refreshed by profiting in small things, than by standing at a stay in great.* We see also that kings that have been fortunate conquerors in their first years, it being not possible for them to go forward infinitely, but that they must have some check or arrest in their fortunes, turn in their latter years to be superstitious and melancholy; as did Alexander the Great; Dioclesian; and in our memory, Charles the Fifth; and others: for he that is used to go forward, and findeth a stop, falleth out of his own favour, and is not the thing he was.

To speak now of the true temper of empire; it is a thing rare and hard to keep; for both temper and distemper consist of contraries. But it is one thing to mingle contraries, another to interchange them. The answer of Apollonius to Vespasian is full of excellent instruction. Vespanian asked him, *what was Nero's overthrow?* He answered, *Nero could touch and tune the harp well; but in government sometimes he used to wind the pins too high, sometimes to let them down too low.* And certain it is that nothing destroyeth authority so much as the unequal and untimely interchange of power pressed too far, and relaxed too much.

This is true, that the wisdom of all these latter times in princes' affairs is rather fine deliveries and shiftings of dangers and mischiefs when they are near, than solid and grounded courses to keep them aloof. But this is but to try masteries with fortune. And let men beware how they neglect and suffer matter of trouble to be prepared; for no man can forbid the spark, nor tell whence it may come. The difficulties in princes' business are many and great; but the greatest difficulty is often in their own mind. For it is common with princes (saith Tacitus) to will contradictories, *Sunt plerumque regum voluntates vehementes, et inter se contrariæ* [Their desires are commonly vehement and incompatible one with another]. For it is the solecism of power, to think to command the end, and yet not to endure the mean.

Kings have to deal with their neighbours, their wives, their children, their prelates or clergy, their nobles, their second-nobles or gentlemen, their merchants, their commons, and their men of war; and from all these arise dangers, if care and circumspection be not used.

First for their neighbours; there can no general rule be given (the occasions are so variable,) save one, which ever holdeth; which is, that princes do keep due sentinel, that none of their neighbours do overgrow so (by increase of territory, by embracing of trade, by approaches, or the like), as they become more able to annoy them than they were. And this is generally the work of standing counsels to foresee and to hinder it. During that triumvirate of kings, King Henry the Eighth of England, Francis the First King of France, and Charles the Fifth Emperor, there was such a watch kept, that none of the three could win a palm of ground, but the other two would straightways balance it, either by confederation, or, if need were, by a war; and would not in any wise take up peace at interest. And the like was done by that league (which Guicciardine saith was the security of Italy) made between Ferdinando King of Naples, Lorenzius Medices, and Ludovicus Sforza, potentates, the one of Florence, the other of Milan. Neither is the opinion of some of the schoolmen to be received, *that a war cannot justly be made but upon a precedent injury or provocation.* For there is no question but a just fear of an imminent danger, though there be no blow given, is a lawful cause of a war.

For their wives; there are cruel examples of them. Livia is infamed for the poisoning of her husband; Roxalana, Solyman's wife, was the destruction of that renowned prince Sultan Mustapha, and otherwise troubled his house and succession; Edward the Second of England his queen had the principal hand in the deposing and murther of her husband. This kind of danger is then to be feared chiefly, when the wives have plots for the raising of their own children; or else that they be advoutresses.

For their children; the tragedies likewise of dangers from them have been many. And generally, the entering of fathers into suspicion of their children hath been ever unfortunate. The destruction of Mustapha (that we named before) was so fatal to Solyman's line, as the succession of the Turks from Solyman until this day is suspected to be untrue, and of strange blood; for that Selymus the Second was thought to be supposititious. The destruction of Crispus, a young prince of rare towardness, by Constantinus the Great, his father, was in like manner fatal to his house; for both Constantinus and Constance, his sons, died violent deaths; and Constantius, his other son, did little better, who died indeed of sickness, but after that Julianus had taken arms against him. The destruction of Demetrius, son to Philip the Second of Macedon, turned upon the father, who died of repentance. And many like examples there are; but few or none where the fathers had good by such distrust; except it were where the sons were up in open arms against them; as was Selymus the First against Bajazet; and the three sons of Henry the Second, King of England.

For their prelates; when they are proud and great, there is also danger from them; as it was in the times of Anselmus and Thomas Becket, Archbishops of Canterbury; who with their crosiers did almost try it with the king's sword; and yet they had to deal with stout and haughty kings; William Rufus, Henry the First, and Henry the Second. The danger is not from that state, but where it hath a dependance of foreign authority; or where the churchmen come in and are elected, not by the collation of the king, or particular patrons, but by the people.

For their nobles; to keep them at a distance, it is not amiss; but to depress them, may make a king more absolute, but less safe; and less able to perform any thing that he desires. I have noted it in my History of King Henry the Seventh of England, who depressed his nobility; whereupon it came to pass that his times were full of difficulties and troubles; for the nobility, though they continued loyal unto him, yet did they not co-operate with him in his business. So that in effect he was fain to do all things himself.

For their second-nobles; there is not much danger from them, being a body dispersed. They may sometimes discourse high, but that doth little hurt; besides, they are a counterpoise to the higher nobility, that they grow not too potent; and, lastly, being the most immediate in authority with the common people, they do best temper popular commotions.

For their merchants; they are *vena porta;* and if they flourish not, a kingdom may have good limbs, but will have empty veins, and nourish little. Taxes and imposts upon them do seldom good to the king's revenue; for that that he wins in the hundred he leeseth in the shire; the particular rates being increased, but the total bulk of trading rather decreased.

For their commons; there is little danger from them, except it be where they have great and potent heads; or where you meddle with the point of religion, or their customs, or means of life.

For their men of war; it is a dangerous state where they live and remain in a body, and are used to donatives; whereof we see examples in the janizaries, and pretorian bands of Rome; but trainings of men, and arming them in several places, and under several commanders, and without donatives, are things of defence, and no danger.

Princes are like to heavenly bodies, which cause good or evil times; and which have much veneration, but no rest. All precepts concerning kings are in effect comprehended in those two remembrances; *memento quod es homo;* and *memento quod es Deus,* or *vice Dei;* [Remember that you are a man; and remember that you are a God, or God's lieutenant:] the one bridleth their power, and the other their will.

OF COUNSEL

THE greatest trust between man and man is the trust of giving counsel. For in other confidences men commit the parts of life; their lands, their goods, their child, their credit, some particular affair; but to such as they make their counsellors, they commit the whole: by how much the more they are obliged to all faith and integrity. The wisest princes need not think it any diminution to their greatness, or derogation to their sufficiency to rely upon counsel. God himself is not without, but hath made it one of the great names of his blessed Son; *The Counsellor.* Salomon hath pronounced that *in counsel is stability.* Things will have their first or second agitation: if they be not tossed upon the arguments of counsel, they will be tossed upon the waves of fortune; and be full of inconstancy, doing and undoing, like the reeling of a drunken man. Salomon's son found the force of counsel, as his father saw the necessity of it. For the beloved kingdom of God was first rent and broken by ill counsel; upon which counsel there are set for our instruction the two marks whereby bad counsel is for ever best discerned; that it was young counsel, for the persons; and violent counsel, for the matter.

The ancient times do set forth in figure both the incorporation and inseparable conjunction of counsel with kings, and the wise and politic use of counsel by kings: the one, in that they say Jupiter did marry Metis, which signifieth counsel; whereby they intend that Sovereignty is married to Counsel: the other in that which followeth, which was thus: They say, after Jupiter was married to Metis, she conceived by him and was with child, but Jupiter suffered her not to stay till she brought forth, but eat her up; whereby he became himself with child, and was delivered of Pallas armed, out of his head. Which monstrous fable containeth a secret of empire; how kings are to make use of their counsel of state. That first they ought to refer matters unto them, which is the first begetting or impregnation; but when they are elaborate, moulded, and shaped in the womb of their counsel, and grow ripe and ready to be brought forth, that then they suffer not their counsel to go through with the resolution and direction, as if it depended on them; but take the matter back into their own hands, and make it appear to the world that the decrees and final directions (which, because they come forth with prudence and power, are resembled to Pallas armed) proceeded from themselves; and not only from their authority, but (the more to add reputation to themselves) from their head and device.

Let us now speak of the inconveniences of counsel, and of the remedies. The inconveniences that have been noted in calling and using counsel, are three. First, the revealing of affairs, whereby they become less secret. Secondly, the weakening of the authority of princes, as if they were less of themselves. Thirdly, the danger of being unfaithfully counselled, and more for the good of them that counsel than of him that is counselled. For which inconveniences, the doctrine of Italy, and practice of France, in some kings' times, hath introduced *cabinet* counsels; a remedy worse than the disease.

As to secrecy; princes are not bound to communicate all matters with all counsellors; but may extract and select. Neither is it necessary that he that consulteth what he should do, should declare what he will do. But let princes beware that the unsecreting of their affairs comes not from themselves. And as for cabinet counsels, it may be their motto, *plenus rimarum sum:* [they are full of leaks:] one futile person that maketh it his glory to tell, will do more hurt than many that know it their duty to conceal. It is true there be some affairs which require extreme secrecy, which will hardly go beyond one or two persons besides the king: neither are those counsels unprosperous; for, besides the secrecy, they commonly go on constantly in one spirit of direction, without distraction. But then it must be a prudent king, such as is able to grind with a hand-mill; and those inward counsellors had need also be wise men, and especially true and trusty to the king's ends; as it was with King Henry the Seventh of England, who in his greatest business imparted himself to none, except it were to Morton and Fox.

For weakening of authority; the fable showeth the remedy. Nay, the majesty of kings is rather exalted than diminished when they are in the chair of counsel; neither was there ever prince bereaved of his dependances by his counsel; except where there hath been either an overgreatness in one counsellor or an over-strict combination in divers; which are things soon found and holpen.

For the last inconvenience, that men will counsel with an eye to themselves; certainly, *non inveniet fidem super terram* [he will not find faith on the earth,] is meant of the nature of times, and not of all particular persons. There be that are in nature faithful, and sincere, and plain, and direct; not crafty and involved; let princes, above all, draw to themselves such natures. Besides, counsellors are not commonly so united, but that one counsellor keepeth sentinel over another; so that if any do counsel out of faction or private ends, it commonly comes to the king's ear. But the best remedy is, if princes know their counsellors, as well as their counsellors know them:

Principis est virtus maxima nosse suos.
[The chief virtue of a ruler is to know his own counsellors]

And on the other side, counsellors should not be too speculative into their sovereign's person. The true composition of a counsellor is rather to be skilful in their master's business, than in his nature; for then he is like to advise him, and not feed his humour. It is of singular use to princes if they take the opinions of their counsel both separately and together. For private opinion is more free; but opinion before others is more reverent. In private, men are more bold in their own humours; and in consort, men are more obnoxious to others' humours; therefore it is good to take both; and of the inferior sort rather in private, to preserve freedom; of the greater rather in consort, to preserve respect. It is in vain for princes to take counsel concerning matters, if they take no counsel likewise concerning persons; for all matters are as dead images; and the life of the execution of affairs resteth in the good choice of persons. Neither is it enough to consult concerning persons *secundum genera* [according to types], as in an idea, or mathematical description, what the kind and character of the person should be; for the greatest errors are committed, and the most judgment is shown, in the choice of individuals. It was truly said, *optimi consiliarii mortui:* [the best counsellors are the dead:] books will speak plain when counsellors blanch. Therefore it is good to be conversant in them, specially the books of such as themselves have been actors upon the stage.

The counsels at this day in most places are but familiar meetings, where matters are rather talked on than debated. And they run too swift to the order or act of counsel. It were better that in causes of weight, the matter were propounded one day and not spoken to till the next day; *in nocte consilium* [night is the season for counsel]. So was it done in the Commission of Union between England and Scotland; which was a grave and orderly assembly. I commend set days for petitions; for both it gives the suitors more certainty for their attendance, and it frees the meetings for matters of estate, that they may *hoc agere* [stick to business]. In choice of committees for ripening business for the counsel, it is better to choose indifferent persons, than to make an indifferency by putting in those that are strong on both sides. I commend also standing commissions; as for trade, for treasure, for war, for suits, for some provinces; for where there be divers particular counsels and but one counsel of estate (as it is in Spain), they are, in effect, no more than standing commissions: save that they have greater authority. Let such as are to inform counsels out of their particular professions, (as lawyers, seamen, mintmen, and the like,) be first heard before committees; and then, as occasion serves, before the counsel. And let them not come in multitudes, or in a tribunitious manner; for that is to clamour counsels, not to inform them. A long table and a square table, or seats about the walls, seem things of form, but are things of substance; for at a long table a few at the upper end, in effect, sway all the business; but in the other form there is more use of the counsellors' opinions that sit lower. A king, when he presides in counsel, let him beware how he opens his own inclination too much in that which he propoundeth; for else counsellors will but take the wind of him, and instead of giving free counsel, sing him a song of *placebo*.

· 21 ·

OF DELAYS

FORTUNE is like the market; where many times, if you can stay a little, the price will fall. And again, it is sometimes like Sibylla's offer; which at first offereth the commodity at full, then consumeth part and part, and still holdeth up the price. For occasion (as it is in the common verse) *turneth a bald noddle, after she hath presented her locks in front, and no hold taken;* or at least turneth the handle of the bottle first to be received, and after the belly, which is hard to clasp. There is surely no greater wisdom than well to time the beginnings and onsets of things. Dangers are no more light, if they once seem light; and more dangers have deceived men than forced them. Nay, it were better to meet some dangers half way, though they come nothing near, than to keep too long a watch upon their approaches; for if a man watch too long, it is odds he will fall asleep. On the other side, to be deceived with too long shadows (as some have been when the moon was low and shone on their enemies' back), and so to shoot off before the time; or to teach dangers to come on, by over early buckling towards them; is another extreme. The ripeness or unripeness of the occasion (as we said) must ever be well weighed; and generally it is good to commit the beginnings of all great actions to Argos with his hundred eyes, and the ends to Briareus with his hundred hands; first to watch, and then to speed. For the helmet of Pluto, which maketh the politic man go invisible, is secrecy in the counsel and celerity in the execution. For when things are once come to the execution, there is no secrecy comparable to celerity; like the motion of a bullet in the air, which flieth so swift as it outruns the eye.

· 22 ·

OF CUNNING

WE take Cunning for a sinister or crooked wisdom. And certainly there is a great difference between a cunning man and a wise man; not only in point of honesty, but in point of ability. There be that can pack the cards, and yet cannot play well; so there are some that are good in canvasses and factions, that are otherwise weak men. Again, it is one thing to understand persons, and another thing to understand matters; for many are perfect in men's humours, that are not greatly capable of the real part of business; which is the constitution of one that hath studied men more than books. Such men are fitter for practice than for counsel; and they are good but in their own alley: turn them to new men, and they have lost their aim; so as the old rule to know a fool from a wise man, *Mitte ambos nudos ad ignotos, et videbis,* [Send them both naked to those they know not,] doth scarce hold for them. And because these cunning men are like haberdashers of small wares, it is not amiss to set forth their shop.

It is a point of cunning, to wait upon him with whom you speak, with your eye; as the Jesuits give it in precept: for there be many wise men that have secret hearts and transparent countenances. Yet this would be done with a demure abasing of your eye sometimes, as the Jesuits also do use.

Another is, that when you have any thing to obtain of present despatch, you entertain and amuse the party with whom you deal with some other discourse; that he be not too much awake to make objections. I knew a counsellor and secretary, that never came to Queen Elizabeth of England with bills to sign, but he would always first put her into some discourse of estate, that she mought the less mind the bills.

The like surprise may be made by moving things when the party is in haste, and cannot stay to consider advisedly of that is moved.

If a man would cross a business that he doubts some other would handsomely and effectually move, let him pretend to wish it well, and move it himself in such sort as may foil it.

The breaking off in the midst of that one was about to say, as if he took himself up, breeds a greater appetite in him with whom you confer to know more.

And because it works better when any thing seemeth to be gotten from you by question, than if you offer it of yourself, you may lay a bait for a question, by showing another visage and countenance than you are wont; to the end to give occasion for the party to ask what the matter is of the change? As Nehemias did; *And I had not before that time been sad before the king.*

In things that are tender and unpleasing, it is good to break the ice by some whose words are of less weight, and to reserve the more weighty voice to come in as by chance, so that he may be asked the question upon the other's speech; as Narcissus did, in relating to Claudius the marriage of Messalina and Silius.

In things that a man would not be seen in himself, it is a point of cunning to borrow the name of the world; as to say, *The world says*, or *There is a speech abroad.*

I knew one that, when he wrote a letter, he would put that which was most material in the postscript, as if it had been a bye-matter.

I knew another that, when he came to have speech, he would pass over that that he intended most; and go forth, and come back again, and speak of it as of a thing that he had almost forgot.

Some procure themselves to be surprised at such times as it is like the party that they work upon will suddenly come upon them; and to be found with a letter in their hand, or doing somewhat which they are not accustomed; to the end they may be apposed of those things which of themselves they are desirous to utter.

It is a point of cunning, to let fall those words in a man's own name, which he would have another man learn and use, and thereupon take advantage. I knew two that were competitors for the secretary's place in Queen Elizabeth's time, and yet kept good quarter between themselves; and would confer one with another upon the business; and the one of them said, That to be a secretary *in the declination of a monarchy* was a ticklish thing, and that he did not affect it: the other straight caught up those words, and discoursed with divers of his friends, that he had no reason to desire to be secretary in the declination of a monarchy. The first man took hold of it, and found means it was told the Queen; who hearing of *a declination of a monarchy*, took it so ill, as she would never after hear of the other's suit.

There is a cunning, which we in England call *The turning of the cat in the pan;* which is, when that which a man says to another, he lays it as if another had said it to him. And to say truth, it is not easy, when such a matter passed between two, to make it appear from which of them it first moved and began.

It is a way that some men have, to glance and dart at others by justifying themselves by negatives; as to say *This I do not;* as Tigellinus did towards Burrhus, *Se non diversas spes, sed incolumitatem imperatoris simpliciter spectare* [That he had not several hopes to rest on, but looked simply to the safety of the Emperor].

Some have in readiness so many tales and stories, as there is nothing they would insinuate, but they can wrap it into a tale; which serveth both to keep themselves more in guard, and to make others carry it with more pleasure.

It is a good point of cunning, for a man to shape the answer he would have in his own words and propositions; for it makes the other party stick the less.

It is strange how long some men will lie in wait to

speak somewhat they desire to say; and how far about they will fetch; and how many other matters they will beat over, to come near it. It is a thing of great patience, but yet of much use.

A sudden, bold, and unexpected question doth many times surprise a man, and lay him open. Like to him that, having changed his name and walking in Paul's, another suddenly came behind him and called him by his true name, whereat straightways he looked back.

But these small wares and petty points of cunning are infinite; and it were a good deed to make a list of them; for that nothing doth more hurt in a state than that cunning men pass for wise.

But certainly some there are that know the resorts and falls of business, that cannot sink into the main of it; like a house that hath convenient stairs and entries, but never a fair room. Therefore you shall see them find out pretty looses in the conclusion, but are no ways able to examine or debate matters. And yet commonly they take advantage of their inability, and would be thought wits of direction. Some build rather upon the abusing of others, and (as we now say) *putting tricks upon them*, than upon soundness of their own proceedings. But Salomon saith, *Prudens advertit ad gressus suos: stultus divertit ad dolos* [The wise man taketh heed to his steps: the fool turneth aside to deceits].

• 23 •

OF WISDOM FOR A MAN'S SELF

AN ant is a wise creature for itself, but it is a shrewd thing in an orchard or garden. And certainly men that are great lovers of themselves waste the public. Divide with reason between self-love and society; and be so true to thyself, as thou be not false to others; specially to thy king and country. It is a poor centre of a man's actions, *himself*. It is right earth. For that only stands fast upon his own centre; whereas all things that have affinity with the heavens, move upon the centre of another, which they benefit. The referring of all to a man's self is more tolerable in a sovereign prince; because themselves are not only themselves, but their good and evil is at the peril of the public fortune. But it is a desperate evil in a servant to a prince, or a citizen in a republic. For whatsoever affairs pass such a man's hands, he crooketh them to his own ends; which must needs be often eccentric to the ends of his master or state. Therefore let princes, or states, choose such servants as have not this mark; except they mean their service should be made but the accessary. That which maketh the effect more pernicious is that all proportion is lost. It were disproportion enough for the servant's good to be preferred before the master's; but yet it is a greater extreme, when a little good of the servant shall carry things against a great good of the master's. And yet that is the case of bad officers, treasurers, ambassadors, generals, and other false and corrupt servants; which set a bias upon their bowl, of their own petty ends and envies, to the overthrow of their master's great and important affairs. And for the most part, the good such servants receive is after the model of their own fortune; but the hurt they sell for that good is after the model of their master's fortune. And certainly it is the nature of extreme self-lovers, as they will set an house on fire, and it were but to roast their eggs; and yet these men many times hold credit with their masters, because their study is but to please them and profit themselves; and for either respect they will abandon the good of their affairs.

Wisdom for a man's self is, in many branches thereof, a depraved thing. It is the wisdom of rats, that will be sure to leave a house somewhat before it fall. It is the wisdom of the fox, that thrusts out the badger, who digged and made room for him. It is the wisdom of crocodiles, that shed tears when they would devour. But that which is specially to be noted is, that those which (as Cicero says of Pompey) are *sui amantes, sine rivali* [lovers of themselves without rival] are many times unfortunate. And whereas they have all their times sacrificed to themselves, they become in the end themselves sacrifices to the inconstancy of fortune; whose wings they thought by their self-wisdom to have pinioned.

· 24 ·

OF INNOVATIONS

As the births of living creatures at first are ill-shapen, so are all Innovations, which are the births of time. Yet notwithstanding, as those that first bring honour into their family are commonly more worthy than most that succeed, so the first precedent (if it be good) is seldom attained by imitation. For Ill, to man's nature as it stands perverted, hath a natural motion, strongest in continuance; but Good, as a forced motion, strongest at first. Surely every medicine is an innovation; and he that will not apply new remedies must expect new evils; for time is the greatest innovator; and if time of course alter things to the worse, and wisdom and counsel shall not alter them to the better, what shall be the end? It is true, that what is settled by custom, though it be not good, yet at least it is fit; and those things which have long gone together, are as it were confederate within themselves; whereas new things piece not so well; but though they help by their utility, yet they trouble by their inconformity. Besides, they are like strangers; more admired and less favoured. All this is true, if time stood still; which contrariwise moveth so round, that a froward retention of custom is as turbulent a thing as an innovation; and they that reverence too much old times, are but a scorn to the new. It were good therefore that men in their innovations would follow the example of time itself; which indeed innovateth greatly, but quietly, and by degrees scarce to be perceived. For otherwise, whatsoever is new is unlooked for; and ever it mends some, and pairs other; and he that is holpen takes it for a fortune, and thanks the time; and he that is hurt, for a wrong, and imputeth it to the author. It is good also not to try experiments in states, except the

necessity be urgent, or the utility evident; and well to beware that it be the reformation that draweth on the
change, and not the desire of change that pretendeth the
reformation. And lastly, that the novelty, though it be
not rejected, yet be held for a suspect; and, as the Scripture saith, *that we make a stand upon the ancient way,
and then look about us, and discover what is the straight
and right way, and so to walk in it.*

· 25 ·

OF DISPATCH

AFFECTED dispatch is one of the most dangerous things to
business that can be. It is like that which the physicians
call *predigestion,* or hasty digestion; which is sure to fill
the body full of crudities and secret seeds of diseases.
Therefore measure not dispatch by the times of sitting,
but by the advancement of the business. And as in races
it is not the large stride or high lift that makes the speed;
so in business, the keeping close to the matter, and not
taking of it too much at once, procureth dispatch. It is
the care of some only to come off speedily for the time; or
to contrive some false periods of business, because they
may seem men of dispatch. But it is one thing to abbre-
viate by contracting, another by cutting off. And business
so handled at several sittings or meetings goeth commonly
backward and forward in an unsteady manner. I knew a
wise man that had it for a by-word, when he saw men
hasten to a conclusion, *Stay a little, that we may make an
end the sooner.*

On the other side, true dispatch is a rich thing. For time
is the measure of business, as money is of wares; and business is bought at a dear hand where there is small dispatch. The Spartans and Spaniards have been noted to be
of small dispatch; *Mi venga la muerte de Spagna; Let my
death come from Spain;* for then it will be sure to be long
in coming.

Give good hearing to those that give the first information in business; and rather direct them in the beginning, than interrupt them in the continuance of their speeches; for he that is put out of his own order will go forward and backward, and be more tedious while he waits upon his memory, than he could have been if he had gone on in his own course. But sometimes it is seen that the moderator is more troublesome than the actor.

Iterations are commonly loss of time. But there is no such gain of time as to iterate often the state of the question; for it chaseth away many a frivolous speech as it is coming forth. Long and curious speeches are as fit for dispatch, as a robe or mantle with a long train is for race. Prefaces and passages, and excusations, and other speeches of reference to the person, are great wastes of time; and though they seem to proceed of modesty, they are bravery. Yet beware of being too material when there is any impediment or obstruction in men's wills; for pre-occupation of mind ever requireth preface of speech; like a fomentation to make the unguent enter.

Above all things, order, and distribution, and singling out of parts, is the life of dispatch; so as the distribution be not too subtle: for he that doth not divide will never enter well into business; and he that divideth too much will never come out of it clearly. To choose time is to save time; and an unseasonable motion is but beating the air. There be three parts of business; the preparation, the debate or examination, and the perfection. Whereof, if you look for dispatch, let the middle only be the work of many, and the first and last the work of few. The proceeding upon somewhat conceived in writing doth for the most part facilitate dispatch: for though it should be wholly rejected, yet that negative is more pregnant of direction than an indefinite; as ashes are more generative than dust.

OF SEEMING WISE

IT hath been an opinion, that the French are wiser than
they seem, and the Spaniards seem wiser than they are.
But howsoever it be between nations, certainly it is so between man and man. For as the Apostle saith of godliness,
*Having a shew of godliness, but denying the power there-
of;* so certainly there are in point of wisdom and sufficiency, that do nothing or little very solemnly: *magno
conatu nugas* [trifles achieved by great effort]. It is a
ridiculous thing and fit for a satire to persons of judgment,
to see what shifts these formalists have, and what pro-
spectives to make *superficies* to seem body that hath
depth and bulk. Some are so close and reserved, as they
will not shew their wares but by a dark light; and seem
always to keep back somewhat; and when they know
within themselves they speak of that they do not well
know, would nevertheless seem to others to know of that
which they may not well speak. Some help themselves
with countenance and gesture, and are wise by signs; as
Cicero saith of Piso, that when he answered him, he
fetched one of his brows up to his forehead, and bent the
other down to his chin; *Respondes, altera ad frontem sub-
lato, altero ad mentum depresso supercilio, crudelitatem
tibi non placere* [You answer, with one brow raised to
your forehead and the other dropped to your chin, that
cruelty does not please you]. Some think to bear it by
speaking a great word, and being peremptory; and go on,
and take by admittance that which they cannot make
good. Some, whatsoever is beyond their reach, will seem
to despise or make light of it as impertinent or curious;
and so would have their ignorance seem judgment. Some
are never without a difference, and commonly by amusing
men with a subtilty, blanch the matter; of whom A. Gel-
lius saith, *Hominem delirum, qui verborum minutiis rerum frangit pondera* [a trifler, that with verbal points and

niceties breaks up the mass of matter]. Of which kind also, Plato in his *Protagoras* bringeth in Prodicus in scorn, and maketh him make a speech that consisteth of distinctions from the beginning to the end. Generally, such men in all deliberations find ease to be of the negative side, and affect a credit to object and foretell difficulties; for when propositions are denied, there is an end of them; but if they be allowed, it requireth a new work; which false point of wisdom is the bane of business. To conclude, there is no decaying merchant, or inward beggar, hath so many tricks to uphold the credit of their wealth, as these empty persons have to maintain the credit of their sufficiency. Seeming wise men may make shift to get opinion; but let no man choose them for employment; for certainly you were better take for business a man somewhat absurd than over-formal.

· 27 ·

OF FRIENDSHIP

IT had been hard for him that spake it to have put more truth and untruth together in few words, than in that speech, *Whosoever is delighted in solitude is either a wild beast or a god.* For it is most true that a natural and secret hatred and aversation towards society in any man, hath somewhat of the savage beast; but it is most untrue that it should have any character at all of the divine nature; except it proceed, not out of a pleasure in solitude, but out of a love and desire to sequester a man's self for a higher conversation: such as is found to have been falsely and feignedly in some of the heathen; as Epimenides the Candian, Numa the Roman, Empedocles the Sicilian, and Apollonius of Tyana; and truly and really in divers of the ancient hermits and holy fathers of the church. But little do men perceive what solitude is, and how far it extendeth. For a crowd is not company; and faces are but a gallery of pictures; and talk but a tinkling cymbal, where there is no love. The Latin adage meeteth with it a little: *Magna civitas, magna solitudo;* [a great town is a great solitude;] because in a great town friends are scattered; so that there is not that fellowship, for the most part, which is in less neighbourhoods. But we may go further, and affirm most truly that it is a mere and miserable solitude to want true friends; without which the world is but a wilderness; and even in this sense also of solitude, whosoever in the frame of his nature and affections is unfit for friendship, he taketh it of the beast, and not from humanity.

A principal fruit of friendship is the ease and discharge of the fulness and swellings of the heart, which passions of all kinds do cause and induce. We know diseases of stoppings and suffocations are the most dangerous in the body; and it is not much otherwise in the mind; you may take sarza to open the liver, steel to open the spleen, flower of sulphur for the lungs, castoreum for the brain; but no receipt openeth the heart, but a true friend; to whom you may impart griefs, joys, fears, hopes, suspicions, counsels, and whatsoever lieth upon the heart to oppress it, in a kind of civil shrift or confession.

It is a strange thing to observe how high a rate great kings and monarchs do set upon this fruit of friendship whereof we speak: so great, as they purchase it many times at the hazard of their own safety and greatness. For princes, in regard of the distance of their fortune from that of their subjects and servants, cannot gather this fruit, except (to make themselves capable thereof) they raise some persons to be as it were companions and almost equals to themselves, which many times sorteth to inconvenience. The modern languages give unto such persons the name of favourites, or privadoes; as if it were matter of grace, or conversation. But the Roman name attaineth the true use and cause thereof, naming them *participes curarum* [sharers of cares]; for it is that which tieth the knot. And we see plainly that this hath been done, not by weak and passionate princes only, but by the wisest and most politic that ever reigned; who have oftentimes joined to themselves some of their servants; whom both themselves have called friends, and allowed others likewise to call them in the same manner; using the word which is received between private men.

L. Sylla, when he commanded Rome, raised Pompey (after surnamed the Great) to that height, that Pompey vaunted himself for Sylla's over-match. For when he had carried the consulship for a friend of his, against the pursuit of Sylla, and that Sylla did a little resent thereat, and began to speak great, Pompey turned upon him again, and in effect bade him be quiet; *for that more men adored the sun rising than the sun setting.* With Julius Cæsar, Decimus Brutus had obtained that interest, as he set him down in his testament for heir in remainder after his nephew. And this was the man that had power with him to draw him forth to his death. For when Cæsar would have discharged the senate, in regard of some ill presages, and specially a dream of Calpurnia; this man lifted him gently by the arm out of his chair, telling him he hoped he would not dismiss the senate till his wife had dreamt a better dream. And it seemeth his favour was so great, as Antonius, in a letter which is recited *verbatim* in one of Cicero's Philippics, calleth him *venefica, witch;* as if he had enchanted Cæsar. Augustus raised Agrippa (though of mean birth) to that height, as when he consulted with Mæcenas about the marriage of his daughter Julia, Mæcenas took the liberty to tell him, *that he must either marry his daughter to Agrippa, or take away his life: there was no third way, he had made him so great.* With Tiberius Cæsar, Sejanus had ascended to that height, as they two were termed and reckoned as a pair of friends. Tiberius in a letter to him saith, *hæc pro amicitiâ nostrâ non occultavi;* [these things, as our friendship required, I have not concealed from you;] and the whole senate dedicated an altar to Friendship, as to a goddess, in respect of the great dearness of friendship between them two. The like or more was between Septimius Severus and Plautianus. For he forced his eldest son to marry the daughter of Plautianus; and would often maintain Plautianus in doing affronts to his son; and did write also in a letter to the senate, by these words: *I love the man so well, as I wish he may over-live me.* Now if these princes had been as a Trajan or a Marcus Aurelius, a man might have thought that this had proceeded of an abundant goodness of nature; but being men so wise, of such strength and severity of mind, and so extreme lovers of themselves, as all these were, it proveth most plainly that they found their own felicity (though as great as ever happened to mortal men) but as an half piece, except they mought have a friend to make it entire; and yet, which is more, they were princes that had wives, sons, nephews; and yet all these could not supply the comfort of friendship.

It is not to be forgotten what Comineus observeth of his first master, Duke Charles the Hardy; namely, that he would communicate his secrets with none; and least of all, those secrets which troubled him most. Whereupon he goeth on and saith that towards his latter time *that closeness did impair and a little perish his understanding.* Surely Comineus mought have made the same judgment also, if it had pleased him, of his second master Lewis the Eleventh, whose closeness was indeed his tormentor. The parable of Pythagoras is dark, but true; *Cor ne edito; Eat not the heart.* Certainly, if a man would give it a hard phrase, those that want friends to open themselves unto are cannibals of their own hearts. But one thing is most admirable (wherewith I will conclude this first fruit of friendship), which is, that this communicating of a man's self to his friend works two contrary effects; for it redoubleth joys, and cutteth griefs in halfs. For there is no man that imparteth his joys to his friend, but he joyeth the more: and no man that imparteth his griefs to his friend, but he grieveth the less. So that it is in truth of operation upon a man's mind, of like virtue as the alchymists use to attribute to their stone for man's body; that it worketh all contrary effects, but still to the good and benefit of nature. But yet without praying in aid of alchymists, there is a manifest image of this in the ordinary course of nature. For in bodies, union strengtheneth and cherisheth any natural action; and on the other side weakeneth and dulleth any violent impression: and even so it is of minds.

The second fruit of friendship is healthful and sovereign for the understanding, as the first is for the affections. For friendship maketh indeed a fair day in the affections, from storm and tempests; but it maketh daylight in the understanding, out of darkness and confusion of thoughts. Neither is this to be understood only of faithful counsel, which a man receiveth from his friend; but before you come to that, certain it is that whosoever hath his mind fraught with many thoughts, his wits and understanding do clarify and break up, in the communicating and discoursing with another; he tosseth his thoughts more easily; he marshalleth them more orderly; he seeth how they look when they are turned into words: finally, he waxeth wiser than himself; and that more by an hour's discourse than by a day's meditation. It was well said by Themistocles to the king of Persia, *That speech was like cloth of Arras, opened and put abroad; whereby the imagery doth appear in figure; whereas in thoughts they lie but as in packs.* Neither is this second fruit of friendship, in opening the understanding, restrained only to such friends as are able to give a man counsel; (they indeed are best;) but even without that, a man learneth of himself, and bringeth his own thoughts to light, and whetteth his wits as against a stone, which itself cuts not. In a word, a man were better relate himself to a statua or picture, than to suffer his thoughts to pass in smother.

Add now, to make this second fruit of friendship complete, that other point which lieth more open and falleth within vulgar observation; which is faithful counsel from a friend. Heraclitus saith well in one of his enigmas, *Dry light is ever the best.* And certain it is, that the light that a man receiveth by counsel from another, is drier and purer than that which cometh from his own understanding and judgment; which is ever infused and drenched in his affections and customs. So as there is as much difference between the counsel that a friend giveth, and that a man giveth himself, as there is between the counsel of a friend and of a flatterer. For there is no such flatterer as is a man's self; and there is no such remedy against flattery of a man's self, as the liberty of a friend. Counsel is of two sorts; the one concerning manners, the other concerning business. For the first, the best preservative to keep the mind in health is the faithful admonition of a friend. The calling of a man's self to a strict account is a medicine, sometime, too piercing and corrosive. Reading good books of morality is a little flat and dead. Observing our faults in others is sometimes improper for our case. But the best receipt (best, I say, to work, and best to take) is the admonition of a friend. It is a strange thing to behold what gross errors and extreme absurdities many (especially of the greater sort) do commit, for want of a friend to tell them of them; to the great damage both of their fame and fortune: for, as St. James saith, they are as men *that look sometimes into a glass, and presently forget their own shape and favour.* As for business, a man may think, if he will, that two eyes see no more than one; or that a gamester seeth always more than a looker-on; or that a man in anger is as wise as he that hath said over the four and twenty letters; or that a musket may be shot off as well upon the arm as upon a rest; and such other fond and high imaginations, to think himself all in all. But when all is done, the help of good counsel is that which setteth business straight. And if any man think that he will take counsel, but it shall be by pieces; asking counsel in one business of one man, and in another business of another man; it is well, (that is to say, better perhaps than if he asked none at all;) but he runneth two dangers; one, that he shall not be faithfully counselled; for it is a rare thing, except it be from a perfect and entire friend, to have counsel given, but such as shall be bowed and crooked to some ends which he hath that giveth it. The other, that he shall have counsel given, hurtful and unsafe, (though with good meaning,) and mixed partly of mischief and partly of remedy; even as if you would call a physician that is thought good for the cure of the disease you complain of, but is unacquainted with your body; and therefore may put you in way for a present cure, but overthroweth your health in some other kind; and so cure the disease and kill the patient. But a friend that is wholly acquainted with a man's estate will beware, by furthering any present business, how he dasheth upon other inconvenience. And therefore rest not upon scattered counsels; they will rather distract and mislead, than settle and direct.

After these two noble fruits of friendship, (peace in the affections, and support of the judgment,) followeth the last fruit; which is like the pomegranate, full of many kernels; I mean aid and bearing a part in all actions and occasions. Here the best way to represent to life the manifold use of friendship, is to cast and see how many things there are which a man cannot do himself; and then it will appear that it was a sparing speech of the ancients, to say, *that a friend is another himself;* for that a friend is far more than himself. Men have their time, and die many times in desire of some things which they principally take to heart; the bestowing of a child, the finishing of a work, or the like. If a man have a true friend, he may rest almost secure that the care of those things will continue after him. So that a man hath, as it were, two lives in his desires. A man hath a body, and that body is confined to a place; but where friendship is, all offices of life are as it were granted to him and his deputy. For he may exercise them by his friend. How many things are there which a man cannot, with any face or comeliness, say or do himself? A man can scarce allege his own merits with modesty, much less extol them; a man cannot sometimes brook to supplicate or beg; and a number of the like. But all these things are graceful in a friend's mouth, which are blushing in a man's own. So again, a man's person hath many proper relations which he cannot put off. A man cannot speak to his son but as a father; to his wife but as a husband; to his enemy but upon terms: whereas a friend may speak as the case requires, and not as it sorteth with the person. But to enumerate these things were endless; I have given the rule, where a man cannot fitly play his own part; if he have not a friend, he may quit the stage.

OF EXPENSE

RICHES are for spending, and spending for honour and good actions. Therefore extraordinary expense must be limited by the worth of the occasion; for voluntary undoing may be as well for a man's country as for the kingdom of heaven. But ordinary expense ought to be limited by a man's estate; and governed with such regard, as it be within his compass; and not subject to deceit and abuse of servants; and ordered to the best shew, that the bills may be less than the estimation abroad. Certainly, if a man will keep but of even hand, his ordinary expenses ought to be but to the half of his receipts; and if he think to wax rich, but to the third part. It is no baseness for the greatest to descend and look into their own estate. Some forbear it, not upon negligence alone, but doubting to bring themselves into melancholy, in respect they shall find it broken. But wounds cannot be cured without searching. He that cannot look into his own estate at all, had need both choose well those whom he employeth, and change them often; for new are more timorous and less subtle. He that can look into his estate but seldom, it behoveth him to turn all to certainties. A man had need, if he be plentiful in some kind of expense, to be as saving again in some other. As if he be plentiful in diet, to be saving in apparel; if he be plentiful in the hall, to be saving in the stable; and the like. For he that is plentiful in expenses of all kinds will hardly be preserved from decay. In clearing of a man's estate, he may as well hurt himself in being too sudden, as in letting it run on too long. For hasty selling is commonly as disadvantageable as interest. Besides, he that clears at once will relapse; for finding himself out of straits, he will revert to his customs: but he that cleareth by degrees induceth a habit of frugality, and gaineth as well upon his mind as upon his estate. Certainly, who hath a state to repair, may not despise small things; and commonly it is less dishonourable to abridge petty charges, than to stoop to petty gettings. A man ought warily to begin charges which once begun will continue: but in matters that return not he may be more magnificent.

• 29 •

OF THE TRUE GREATNESS OF KINGDOMS AND ESTATES

THE speech of Themistocles the Athenian, which was haughty and arrogant in taking so much to himself, had been a grave and wise observation and censure, applied at large to others. Desired at a feast to touch a lute, he said, *He could not fiddle, but yet he could make a small town a great city.* These words (holpen a little with a metaphor) may express two differing abilities in those that deal in business of estate. For if a true survey be taken of counsellors and statesmen, there may be found (though rarely) those which can make a small state great, and yet cannot fiddle: as on the other side, there will be found a great many that can fiddle very cunningly, but yet are so far from being able to make a small state great, as their gift lieth the other way; to bring a great and flourishing estate to ruin and decay. And, certainly those degenerate arts and shifts, whereby many counsellors and governors gain both favour with their masters and estimation with the vulgar, deserve no better name than fiddling; being things rather pleasing for the time, and graceful to themselves only, than tending to the weal and advancement of the state which they serve. There are also (no doubt) counsellors and governors which may be held sufficient (*negotiis pares*), able to manage affairs, and to keep them from precipices and manifest inconveniences; which nevertheless are far from the ability to raise and amplify an estate in power, means, and fortune. But be the workmen what they may be, let us speak of the work; that is, the true Greatness of Kingdoms and Estates, and the means thereof. An argument fit for great and mighty princes to have in their hand; to the end that neither by over-measuring their forces, they leese themselves in vain enterprises; nor on the other side, by undervaluing them, they descend to fearful and pusillanimous counsels.

The greatness of an estate in bulk and territory, doth fall under measure; and the greatness of finances and revenew doth fall under computation. The population may appear by musters; and the number and greatness of cities and towns by cards and maps. But yet there is not any thing amongst civil affairs more subject to error, than the right valuation and true judgment concerning the power and forces of an estate. The kingdom of heaven is compared, not to any great kernel or nut, but to a grain of mustard-seed; which is one of the least grains, but hath in it a property and spirit hastily to get up and spread. So are these states great in territory, and yet not apt to enlarge or command; and some that have but a small dimension of stem, and yet apt to be the foundations of great monarchies.

Walled towns, stored arsenals and armories, goodly races of horse, chariots of war, elephants, ordnance, artillery, and the like; all this is but a sheep in a lion's skin, except the breed and disposition of the people be stout and warlike. Nay, number (itself) in armies importeth not much, where the people is of weak courage; for (as Virgil saith) *It never troubles a wolf how many the sheep be.* The army of the Persians in the plains of Arbela was such a vast sea of people, as it did somewhat astonish the commanders in Alexander's army; who came to him therefore, and wished him to set upon them by night; but he answered, *He would not pilfer the victory.* And the defeat was easy. When Tigranes the Armenian, being encamped upon a hill with four hundred thousand men, discovered the army of the Romans, being not above fourteen thousand, marching towards him, he made himself merry with it, and said, *Yonder men are too many for an ambassage, and too few for a fight.* But, before the sun set, he found them enow to give him the chase with infinite slaughter. Many are the examples of the great odds between number and courage: so that a man may truly make a judgment, that the principal point of greatness in any state is to have a race of military men. Neither is money the sinews of war (as it is trivially said), where the sinews of men's arms, in base and effeminate people, are failing. For Solon said well to Crœsus (when in ostentation he shewed him his gold), *Sir, if any other came that hath better iron than you, he will be master of all this gold.* Therefore let any prince or state think soberly of his forces, except his militia of natives be of good and valiant soldiers. And let princes, on the other side, that have subjects of martial disposition, know their own strength; unless they be otherwise wanting unto themselves. As for mercenary forces (which is the help in this case), all examples show that whatsoever estate or prince doth rest upon them, *he may spread his feathers for a time, but he will mew them soon after.*

The blessing of Judah and Issachar will never meet; *that the same people or nation should be both the lion's whelp and the ass between burthens;* neither will it be, that a people overlaid with taxes should ever become valiant and martial. It is true that taxes levied by consent of the estate do abate men's courage less: as it hath been seen notably in the excises of the Low Countries; and, in some degree, in the subsidies of England. For you must note that we speak now of the heart and not of the purse. So that although the same tribute and tax, laid by consent or by imposing, be all one to the purse, yet it works diversly upon the courage. So that you may conclude, *that no people over-charged with tribute is fit for empire.*

Let states that aim at greatness, take heed how their nobility and gentlemen do multiply too fast. For that maketh the common subject grow to be a peasant and base swain, driven out of heart, and in effect but the gentleman's labourer. Even as you may see in coppice woods; if you leave your staddles too thick, you shall never have clean underwood, but shrubs and bushes. So in countries, if the gentlemen be too many, the commons will be base; and you will bring it to that, that not the hundred poll will be fit for an helmet; especially as to the infantry, which is the nerve of an army; and so there will be great popula-

tion and little strength. This which I speak of hath been
no where better seen than by comparing of England and
France; whereof England, though far less in territory and
population, hath been (nevertheless) an over-match; in
regard the middle people of England make good soldiers,
which the peasants of France do not. And herein the device of king Henry the Seventh (whereof I have spoken
largely in the history of his life) was profound and admirable; in making farms and houses of husbandry of a
standard; that is, maintained with such a proportion of
land unto them, as may breed a subject to live in convenient plenty and no servile condition; and to keep the
plough in the hands of the owners, and not mere hirelings.
And thus indeed you shall attain to Virgil's character
which he gives to ancient Italy:

Terra potens armis atque ubere glebæ:

[A land powerful in arms and in productiveness of soil.]
Neither is that state (which, for any thing I know, is almost peculiar to England, and hardly to be found any
where else, except it be perhaps in Poland) to be passed
over; I mean the state of free servants and attendants
upon noblemen and gentlemen; which are no ways inferior unto the yeomanry for arms. And therefore out of
all question, the splendour and magnificence and great
retinues and hospitality of noblemen and gentlemen, received into custom, doth much conduce unto martial
greatness. Whereas, contrariwise, the close and reserved
living of noblemen and gentlemen causeth a penury of
military forces.

By all means it is to be procured, that the trunk of
Nebuchadnezzar's tree of monarchy be great enough to
bear the branches and the boughs; that is, that the natural
subjects of the crown or state bear a sufficient proportion
to the stranger subjects that they govern. Therefore all
states that are liberal of naturalisation towards strangers
are fit for empire. For to think that an handful of people
can, with the greatest courage and policy in the world,
embrace too large extent of dominion, it may hold for a

time, but it will fail suddenly. The Spartans were a nice people in point of naturalisation; whereby, while they kept their compass, they stood firm; but when they did spread, and their boughs were becomen too great for their stem, they became a windfall upon the sudden. Never any state was in this point so open to receive strangers into their body as were the Romans. Therefore it sorted with them accordingly; for they grew to the greatest monarchy. Their manner was to grant naturalisation (which they called *jus civitatis*), and to grant it in the highest degree; that is, not only *jus commercii, jus connubii, jus hæreditatis;* but also *jus suffragii*, and *jus honorum.* And this not to singular persons alone, but likewise to whole families; yea to cities, and sometimes to nations. Add to this their custom of plantation of colonies; whereby the Roman plant was removed into the soil of other nations. And putting both constitutions together, you will say that it was not the Romans that spread upon the world, but it was the world that spread upon the Romans; and that was the sure way of greatness. I have marvelled sometimes at Spain, how they clasp and contain so large dominions with so few natural Spaniards; but sure the whole compass of Spain is a very great body of a tree; far above Rome and Sparta at the first. And besides, though they have not had that usage to naturalise liberally, yet they have that which is next to it; that is, to employ almost indifferently all nations in their militia of ordinary soldiers; yea and sometimes in their highest commands. Nay it seemeth at this instant they are sensible of this want of natives; as by the Pragmatical Sanction, now published, appeareth.

It is certain, that sedentary and within-door arts, and delicate manufactures (that require rather the finger than the arm), have in their nature a contrariety to a military disposition. And generally, all warlike people are a little idle, and love danger better than travail. Neither must they be too much broken of it, if they shall be preserved in vigour. Therefore it was great advantage in the ancient states of Sparta, Athens, Rome, and others, that they had the use of slaves, which commonly did rid those manufactures. But that is abolished, in greatest part, by the Christian law. That which cometh nearest to it, is to leave those arts chiefly to strangers (which for that purpose are the more easily to be received), and to contain the principal bulk of the vulgar natives within those three kinds,— tillers of the ground; free servants; and handicraftsmen of strong and manly arts, as smiths, masons, carpenters, &c: not reckoning professed soldiers.

.But above all, for empire and greatness, it importeth most, that a nation do profess arms as their principal honour, study, and occupation. For the things which we formerly have spoken of are but habilitations toward arms; and what is habilitation without intention and act? Romulus, after his death (as they report or feign), sent a present to the Romans, that above all they should intend arms; and then they should prove the greatest empire of the world. The fabric of the state of Sparta was wholly (though not wisely) framed and composed to that scope and end. The Persians and Macedonians had it for a flash. The Gauls, Germans, Goths, Saxons, Normans, and others, had it for a time. The Turks have it at this day, though in great declination. Of Christian Europe, they that have it are, in effect, only the Spaniards. But it is so plain *that every man profiteth in that he most intendeth,* that it needeth not to be stood upon. It is enough to point at it; that no nation which doth not directly profess arms, may look to have greatness fall into their mouths. And on the other side, it is a most certain oracle of time, that those states that continue long in that profession (as the Romans and Turks principally have done) do wonders. And those that have professed arms but for an age, have notwithstanding commonly attained that greatness in that age which maintained them long after, when their profession and exercise of arms hath grown to decay.

Incident to this point is, for a state to have those laws or customs which may reach forth unto them just occasions (as may be pretended) of war. For there is that justice imprinted in the nature of men, that they enter not upon wars (whereof so many calamities do ensue) but upon some, at the least specious, grounds and quarrels.

The Turk hath at hand, for cause of war, the propagation of his law or sect; a quarrel that he may always command. The Romans, though they esteemed the extending the limits of their empire to be great honour to their generals when it was done, yet they never rested upon that alone to begin a war. First therefore, let nations that pretend to greatness have this; that they be sensible of wrongs, either upon borderers, merchants, or politic ministers; and that they sit not too long upon a provocation. Secondly, let them be prest and ready to give aids and succours to their confederates; as it ever was with the Romans; insomuch, as if the confederates had leagues defensive with divers other states, and, upon invasion offered, did implore their aids severally, yet the Romans would ever be the foremost, and leave it to none other to have the honour. As for the wars which were anciently made on the behalf of a kind of party, or tacit conformity of estate, I do not see how they may be well justified: as when the Romans made a war for the liberty of Græcia; or when the Lacedæmonians and Athenians made wars to set up or pull down democracies and oligarchies; or when wars were made by foreigners, under the pretence of justice or protection, to deliver the subjects of others from tyranny and oppression; and the like. Let it suffice, that no estate expect to be great, that is not awake upon any just occasion of arming.

No body can be healthful without exercise, neither natural body or politic; and certainly to a kingdom or estate, a just and honourable war is the true exercise. A civil war indeed is like the heat of a fever; but a foreign war is like the heat of exercise, and serveth to keep the body in health; for in a slothful peace, both courages will effeminate and manners corrupt. But howsover it be for happiness, without all question, for greatness it maketh, to be still for the most part in arms; and the strength of a veteran army (though it be a chargeable business) always on foot, is that which commonly giveth the law, or at least the reputation, amongst all neighbour states; as may well be seen in Spain, which hath had, in one part or other, a veteran army almost continually, now by the space of six score years.

To be master of the sea is an abridgment of a monarchy. Cicero, writing to Atticus of Pompey his preparation against Cæsar, saith, *Consilium Pompeii plane Themisto-cleum est; putat enim, qui mari potitur, eum rerum potiri;* [Pompey is going upon the policy of Themistocles; thinking that he who commands the sea commands all.] And, without doubt, Pompey had tired out Cæsar, if upon vain confidence he had not left that way. We see the great effects of battles by sea. The battle of Actium decided the empire of the world. The battle of Lepanto arrested the greatness of the Turk. There be many examples where sea-fights have been final to the war; but this is when princes or states have set up their rest upon the battles. But thus much is certain, that he that commands the sea is at great liberty, and may take as much and as little of the war as he will. Whereas those that be strongest by land are many times nevertheless in great straits. Surely, at this day, with us of Europe, the vantage of strength at sea (which is one of the principal dowries of this kingdom of Great Britain) is great; both because most of the kingdoms of Europe are not merely inland, but girt with the sea most part of their compass; and because the wealth of both Indies seems in great part but an accessary to the command of the seas.

The wars of latter ages seem to be made in the dark, in respect of the glory and honour which reflected upon men from the wars in ancient time. There be now, for martial encouragement, some degrees and orders of chivlary; which nevertheless are conferred promiscuously upon soldiers and no soldiers; and some remembrance perhaps upon the scutcheon; and some hospitals for maimed soldiers; and such like things. But in ancient times, the trophies erected upon the place of the victory; the funeral laudatives and monuments for those that died in the wars; the crowns and garlands personal; the style of Emperor, which the great kings of the world after borrowed; the triumphs of the generals upon their return; the great donatives and largesses upon the disbanding of the armies;

were things able to inflame all men's courages. But above all, that of the Triumph, amongst the Romans, was not pageants or gaudery, but one of the wisest and noblest institutions that ever was. For it contained three things; honour to the general; riches to the treasury out of the spoils; and donatives to the army. But that honour perhaps were not fit for monarchies; except it be in the person of the monarch himself, or his sons; as it came to pass in the times of the Roman emperors, who did impropriate the actual triumphs to themselves and their sons, for such wars as they did achieve in person; and left only, for wars achieved by subjects, some triumphal garments and ensigns to the general.

To conclude: no man can *by care taking* (as the Scripture saith) *add a cubit to his stature,* in this little model of a man's body; but in the great frame of kingdoms and commonwealths, it is in the power of princes or estates to add amplitude and greatness to their kingdoms; for by introducing such ordinances, constitutions, and customs, as we have now touched, they may sow greatness to their posterity and succession. But these things are commonly not observed, but left to take their chance.

· 30 ·

OF REGIMENT OF HEALTH

THERE is a wisdom in this beyond the rules of physic: a man's own observation, what he finds good of, and what he finds hurt of, is the best physic to preserve health. But it is a safer conclusion to say, *This agreeth not well with me, therefore I will not continue it;* than this, *I find no offence of this, therefore I may use it.* For strength of nature in youth passeth over many excesses, which are owing a man till his age. Discern of the coming on of years, and think not to do the same things still; for age will not be defied. Beware of sudden change in any great point of diet, and if necessity inforce it, fit the rest to it. For it is a secret both in nature and state, that it is safer to change many things than one. Examine thy customs of diet, sleep, exercise, apparel, and the like; and try, in any thing thou shalt judge hurtful, to discontinue it by little and little but so, as if thou dost find any inconvenience by the change, thou come back to it again: for it is hard to distinguish that which is generally held good and wholesome, from that which is good particularly, and fit for thine own body. To be free-minded and cheerfully disposed at hours of meat and of sleep and of exercise, is one of the best precepts of long lasting. As for the passions and studies of the mind; avoid envy; anxious fears; anger fretting inwards; subtle and knotty inquisitions; joys and exhilarations in excess; sadness not communicated. Entertain hopes; mirth rather than joy; variety of delights, rather than surfeit of them; wonder and admiration, and therefore novelties; studies that fill the mind with splendid and illustrious objects, as histories, fables, and contemplations of nature. If you fly physic in health altogether, it will be too strange for your body when you shall need it. If you make it too familiar, it will work no extraordinary effect when sickness cometh. I commend rather some diet for certain seasons, than frequent use of physic, except it be grown into a custom. For those diets alter the body more, and trouble it less. Despise no new accident in your body, but ask opinion of it. In sickness, respect health principally; and in health, action. For those that put their bodies to endure in health, may in most sicknesses, which are not very sharp, be cured only with diet and tendering. Celsus could never have spoken it as a physician, had he not been a wise man withal, when he giveth it for one of the great precepts of health and lasting, that a man do vary and interchange contraries, but with an inclination to the more benign extreme: use fasting and full eating, but rather full eating; watching and sleep, but rather sleep; sitting and exercise, but rather exercise; and the like. So shall nature be cherished, and yet taught masteries. Physicians are some of them so pleasing and conformable to the humour of the patient, as they press not the true cure of the disease; and some other are so regular in proceeding according to art for the disease, as they respect not sufficiently the condition of the patient. Take one of a middle temper; or if it may not be found in one man, combine two of either sort; and forget not to call as well the best acquainted with your body, as the best reputed of for his faculty.

• 31 •

OF SUSPICION

SUSPICIONS amongst thoughts are like bats amongst birds, they ever fly by twilight. Certainly they are to be repressed, or at the least well guarded: for they cloud the mind; they leese friends; and they check with business, whereby business cannot go on currently and constantly. They dispose kings to tyranny, husbands to jealousy, wise men to irresolution and melancholy. They are defects, not in the heart, but in the brain; for they take place in the stoutest natures; as in the example of Henry the Seventh of England. There was not a more suspicious man, nor a more stout. And in such a composition they do small hurt. For commonly they are not admitted, but with examination, whether they be likely or no? But in fearful natures they gain ground too fast. There is nothing makes a man suspect much, more than to know little; and therefore men should remedy suspicion by procuring to know more, and not to keep their suspicions in smother. What would men have? Do they think those they employ and deal with are saints? Do they not think they will have their own ends, and be truer to themselves than to them? Therefore there is no better way to moderate suspicions, than to account upon such suspicions as true and yet to bridle them as false. For so far as a man ought to make use of suspicions, as to provide, as if that should be true that he suspects, yet it may do him no hurt. Suspicions that the mind of itself gathers are but buzzes; but suspicions that are artificially nourished, and put into men's heads by the tales and whisperings of others, have stings. Certainly, the best mean to clear the way in this same

wood of suspicions, is frankly to communicate them with
the party that he suspects; for thereby he shall be sure to
know more of the truth of them than he did before; and
withal shall make that party more circumspect not to give
further cause of suspicion. But this would not be done to
men of base natures; for they, if they find themselves once
suspected, will never be true. The Italian says, *Sospetto
licentia fede;* as if suspicion did give a passport to faith;
but it ought rather to kindle it to discharge itself.

· 32 ·

OF DISCOURSE

SOME in their discourse desire rather commendation of
wit, in being able to hold all arguments, than of judgment, in discerning what is true; as if it were a praise to
know what might be said, and not what should be
thought. Some have certain common places and themes
wherein they are good, and want variety; which kind of
poverty is for the most part tedious, and when it is once
perceived, ridiculous. The honourablest part of talk is to
give the occasion; and again to moderate and pass to
somewhat else; for then a man leads the dance. It is good,
in discourse and speech of conversation, to vary and in-
termingle speech of the present occasion with arguments,
tales with reasons, asking of questions with telling of
opinions, and jest with earnest: for it is a dull thing to
tire, and, as we say now, to jade, any thing too far. As for
jest, there be certain things which ought to be privileged
from it; namely, religion, matters of state, great persons,
any man's present business of importance, and any case
that deserveth pity. Yet there be some that think their
wits have been asleep, except they dart out somewhat
that is piquant, and to the quick. That is a vein which
would be bridled;

Parce, puer, stimulis, et fortius utere loris.
[Spare the whip, boy, and use the reins more strongly.]

And generally, men ought to find the difference between saltness and bitterness. Certainly, he that hath a satirical vein, as he maketh others afraid of his wit, so he had need be afraid of others' memory. He that questioneth much, shall learn much, and content much; but especially if he apply his questions to the skill of the persons whom he asketh; for he shall give them occasion to please themselves in speaking, and himself shall continually gather knowledge. But let his questions not be troublesome; for that is fit for a poser. And let him be sure to leave other men their turns to speak. Nay, if there be any that would reign and take up all the time, let him find means to take them off, and to bring others on; as musicians use to do with those that dance too long galliards. If you dissemble sometimes your knowledge of that you are thought to know, you shall be thought another time to know that you know not. Speech of a man's self ought to be seldom, and well chosen. I knew one was wont to say in scorn, *He must needs be a wise man, he speaks so much of himself:* and there is but one case wherein a man may commend himself with good grace; and that is in commending virtue in another; especially if it be such a virtue whereunto himself pretendeth. Speech of touch towards others should be sparingly used; for discourse ought to be as a field, without coming home to any man. I knew two noblemen, of the west part of England, whereof the one was given to scoff, but kept ever royal cheer in his house; the other would ask of those that had been at the other's table, *Tell truly, was there never a flout or dry blow given?* To which the guest would answer, *Such and such a thing passed.* The lord would say, *I thought he would mar a good dinner.* Discretion of speech is more than eloquence; and to speak agreeably to him with whom we deal, is more than to speak in good words or in good order. A good continued speech, without a good speech of interlocution, shews slowness; and a good reply or second speech, without a good settled speech, sheweth shallowness and weakness. As we see in beasts, that those that are weakest in the course, are yet nimblest in the turn; as it is betwixt the greyhound and the hare. To use too many circumstances ere one come to the matter, is wearisome; to use none at all, is blunt.

· 33 ·

OF PLANTATIONS

PLANTATIONS are amongst ancient, primitive and heroical works. When the world was young it begat more children; but now it is old it begets fewer: for I may justly account new plantations to be the children of former kingdoms. I like a plantation in a pure soil; that is, where people are not displanted to the end to plant in others. For else it is rather an extirpation than a plantation. Planting of countries is like planting of woods; for you must make account to leese almost twenty years profit, and expect your recompense in the end. For the principal thing that hath been the destruction of most plantations, hath been the base and hasty drawing of profit in the first years. It is true, speedy profit is not to be neglected, as far as may stand with the good of the plantation, but no further. It is a shameful and unblessed thing to take the scum of people, and wicked condemned men, to be the people with whom you plant; and not only so, but it spoileth the plantation; for they will ever live like rogues, and not fall to work, but be lazy, and do mischief, and spend victuals, and be quickly weary, and then certify over to their country to the discredit of the plantation. The people wherewith you plant ought to be gardeners, ploughmen, labourers, smiths, carpenters, joiners, fishermen, fowlers, with some few apothecaries, surgeons, cooks and bakers. In a country of plantation, first look about what kind of victual the country yields of itself to hand; as chestnuts, wallnuts, pine-apples, olives, dates, plums, cherries, wild honey, and the like; and make use of them. Then consider what victual or esculent things there are, which grow speedily, and within the year; as parsnips, carrots, turnips, onions, radish, artichokes of Hierusalem, maize, and the like. For wheat, barley, and oats, they ask too much labour; but with pease and beans you may begin, both because they ask less labour, and because they serve for meat as well as for bread. And of rice likewise cometh a great increase, and it is a kind of meat. Above all, there ought to be brought store of biscuit, oat-meal, flour, meal, and the like, in the beginning, till bread may be had. For beasts, or birds, take chiefly such as are least subject to diseases, and multiply fastest; as swine, goats, cocks, hens, turkeys, geese, house-doves, and the like. The victual in plantations ought to be expended almost as in a besieged town; that is, with certain allowance. And let the main part of the ground employed to gardens or corn, be to a common stock; and to be laid in, and stored up, and then delivered out in proportion; besides some spots of ground that any particular person will manure for his own private. Consider likewise what commodities the soil where the plantation is doth naturally yield, that they may some way help to defray the charge of the plantation, (so it be not, as was said, to the untimely prejudice of the main business,) as it hath fared with tobacco in Virginia. Wood commonly aboundeth but too much; and therefore timber is fit to be one. If there be iron ore, and streams whereupon to set the mills, iron is a brave commodity where wood aboundeth. Making of bay-salt, if the climate be proper for it, would be put in experience. Growing silk likewise, if any be, is a likely commodity. Pitch and tar, where store of firs and pines are, will not fail. So drugs and sweet woods, where they are, cannot but yield great profit. Soap-ashes likewise, and other things that may be thought of. But moil not too much under ground; for the hope of mines is very uncertain, and useth to make the planters lazy in other things. For government, let it be in the hands of one, assisted with some counsel; and let them have commission to exercise martial laws, with some limitation. And above all, let men make that profit of being in the wilderness, as they have God always, and his service, before their eyes. Let not the government of the plantation depend upon too many counsellors and undertakers in the country that planteth, but upon a temperate number; and let those be rather noblemen and gentlemen, than merchants; for they look ever to the present gain. Let there be freedoms from custom, till the plantation be of strength; and not only freedom from custom, but freedom to carry their commodities where they may make their best of them, except there be some special cause of caution. Cram not in people, by sending too fast company after company; but rather harken how they waste, and send supplies proportionably; but so as the number may live well in the plantation, and not by surcharge be in penury. It hath been a great endangering to the health of some plantations, that they have built along the sea and rivers, in marish and unwholesome grounds. Therefore, though you begin there, to avoid carriage and other like discommodities, yet build still rather upwards from the streams, than along. It concerneth likewise the health of the plantation that they have good store of salt with them, that they may use it in their victuals when it shall be necessary. If you plant where savages are, do not only entertain them with trifles and gingles; but use them justly and graciously, with sufficient guard nevertheless; and do not win their favour by helping them to invade their enemies, but for their defence it is not amiss; and send oft of them over to the country that plants, that they may see a better condition than their own, and commend it when they return. When the plantation grows to strength, then it is time to plant with women as well as with men; that the plantation may spread into generations, and not be ever pieced from without. It is the sinfullest thing in the world to forsake or destitute a plantation once in forwardness; for besides the dishonour, it is the guiltiness of blood of many commiserable persons.

OF RICHES

I CANNOT call Riches better than the baggage of virtue.
The Roman word is better, *impedimenta*. For as the baggage is to an army, so is riches to virtue. It cannot be
spared nor left behind, but it hindereth the march; yea
and the care of it sometimes loseth or disturbeth the
victory. Of great riches there is no real use, except it be
in the distribution; the rest is but conceit. So saith Salomon, *Where much is, there are many to consume it; and
what hath the owner but the sight of it with his eyes?*
The personal fruition in any man cannot reach to feel
great riches: there is a custody of them; or a power of
dole and donative of them; or a fame of them; but no
solid use to the owner. Do you not see what feigned
prices are set upon little stones and rarities? and what
works of ostentation are undertaken, because there might
seem to be some use of great riches? But then you will
say, they may be of use to buy men out of dangers or
troubles. As Salomon saith, *Riches are as a strong hold, in
the imagination of the rich man.* But this is excellently
expressed, that it is in imagination, and not always in
fact. For certainly great riches have sold more men than
they have bought out. Seek not proud riches, but such as
thou mayest get justly, use soberly, distribute cheerfully,
and leave contentedly. Yet have no abstract nor friarly
contempt of them. But distinguish, as Cicero saith well of
Rabirius Posthumus, *In studio rei amplificandæ appare-
bat, non avaritiæ prædam, sed instrumentum bonitati
quæri;* [In seeking to increase his estate it was apparent
that he sought not a prey for avarice to feed on, but an
instrument for goodness to work with.] Hearken also to
Salomon, and beware of hasty gathering of riches; *Qui
festinat ad divitias, non erit insons* [He that maketh haste
to be rich shall not be innocent]. The poets feign, that
when Plutus (which is Riches) is sent from Jupiter, he

limps and goes slowly; but when he is sent from Pluto, he runs and is swift of foot. Meaning that riches gotten by good means and just labour pace slowly; but when they come by the death of others (as by the course of inheritance, testaments, and the like), they come tumbling upon a man. But it mought be applied likewise to Pluto, taking him for the devil. For when riches come from the devil (as by fraud and oppression and unjust means), they come upon speed. The ways to enrich are many, and most of them foul. Parsimony is one of the best, and yet is not innocent; for it withholdeth men from works of liberality and charity. The improvement of the ground is the most natural obtaining of riches; for it is our great mother's blessing, the earth's; but it is slow. And yet where men of great wealth do stoop to husbandry, it multiplieth riches exceedingly. I knew a nobleman in England, that had the greatest audits of any man in my time; a great grazier, a great sheep-master, a great timber man, a great collier, a great corn-master, a great lead-man, and so of iron, and a number of the like points of husbandry. So as the earth seemed a sea to him, in respect of the perpetual importation. It was truly observed by one, that himself came very hardly to a little riches, and very easily to great riches. For when a man's stock is come to that, that he can expect the prime of markets, and overcome those bargains which for their greatness are few men's money, and be partner in the industries of younger men, he cannot but increase mainly. The gains of ordinary trades and vocations are honest; and furthered by two things chiefly; by diligence, and by a good name for good and fair dealing. But the gains of bargains are of a more doubtful nature; when men shall wait upon others' necessity, broke by servants and instruments to draw them on, put off others cunningly that would be better chapmen, and the like practices, which are crafty and naught. As for the chopping of bargains, when a man buys not to hold but to sell over again, that commonly grindeth double, both upon the seller and upon the buyer. Sharings do greatly enrich, if the hands be well chosen that are trusted. Usury is the certainest means of gain, though one of the worst;

as that whereby a man doth eat his bread *in sudore vultûs alieni;* [in the sweat of another man's face;] and besides, doth plough upon Sundays. But yet certain though it be, it hath flaws; for that the scriveners and brokers do value unsound men to serve their own turn. The fortune in being the first in an invention or in a privilege, doth cause sometimes a wonderful overgrowth in riches; as it was with the first sugar man in the Canaries. Therefore if a man can play the true logician, to have as well judgment as invention, he may do great matters; especially if the times be fit. He that resteth upon gains certain, shall hardly grow to great riches; and he that puts all upon adventures, doth oftentimes break and come to poverty: it is good therefore to guard adventures with certainties, that may uphold losses. Monopolies, and coemption of wares for re-sale, where they are not restrained, are great means to enrich; especially if the party have intelligence what things are like to come into request, and so store himself beforehand. Riches gotten by service, though it be of the best rise, yet when they are gotten by flattery, feeding humours, and other servile conditions, they may be placed amongst the worst. As for fishing for testaments and executorships (as Tacitus saith of Seneca, *testamenta et orbos tamquam indagine capi,* [wills and childless couples are caught with a net]) it is yet worse; by how much men submit themselves to meaner persons than in service. Believe not much them that seem to despise riches; for they despise them that despair of them; and none worse when they come to them. Be not penny-wise; riches have wings, and sometimes they fly away of themselves, sometimes they must be set flying to bring in more. Men leave their riches either to their kindred, or to the public; and moderate portions prosper best in both. A great state left to an heir, is as a lure to all the birds of prey round about to seize on him, if he be not the better stablished in years and judgment. Likewise glorious gifts and foundations are like *sacrifices without salt;* and but the painted sepulchres of alms, which soon will putrefy and corrupt inwardly. Therefore measure not thine advancements by quantity, but frame them by measure:

and defer not charities till death; for, certainly, if a man weigh it rightly, he that doth so is rather liberal of another man's than of his own.

· 35 ·

OF PROPHECIES

I MEAN not to speak of divine prophecies; nor of heathen oracles; nor of natural predictions; but only of prophecies that have been of certain memory, and from hidden causes. Saith the Pythonissa to Saul, *To-morrow thou and thy son shall be with me.* Homer hath these verses:

> At domus Æneæ cunctis dominabitur oris,
> Et nati natorum, et qui nascentur ab illis.

[The house of Æneas shall reign in all lands, and his children's children, and their generations.] A prophecy, as it seems, of the Roman empire. Seneca the tragedian hath these verses:

> —— Venient annis
> Sæcula seris, quibus Oceanus
> Vincula rerum laxet, et ingens
> Pateat Tellus, Tiphysque novos
> Detegat orbes; nec sit terris
> Ultima Thule:

[There shall come a time when the bands of ocean shall be loosened, and the vast earth shall be laid open; another Tiphys shall disclose new worlds, and lands shall be seen beyond Thule:] a prophecy of the discovery of America. The daughter of Polycrates dreamed that Jupiter bathed her father, and Apollo anointed him; and it came to pass that he was crucified in an open place, where the sun made his body run with sweat, and the rain washed it. Philip of Macedon dreamed he sealed up his wife's belly; whereby he did expound it, that his wife should be barren; but Aristander the soothsayer told him his wife was with child, because men do not use to seal vessels that are empty. A phantasm that appeared to M. Brutus in his tent, said to him, *Philippis iterum me videbis* [Thou shalt see me again at Philippi]. Tiberius said to Galba, *Tu quoque, Galba, degustabis imperium* [Thou likewise shall taste of empire]. In Vespasian's time, there went a prophecy in the East, that those that should come forth of Judea should reign over the world: which though it may be was meant of our Saviour, yet Tacitus expounds it of Vespasian. Domitian dreamed, the night before he was slain, that a golden head was growing out of the nape of his neck: and indeed the succession that followed him, for many years, made golden times. Henry the Sixth of England said of Henry the Seventh, when he was a lad, and gave him water, *This is the lad that shall enjoy the crown for which we strive.* When I was in France, I heard from one Dr. Pena, that the Queen Mother, who was given to curious arts, caused the King her husband's nativity to be calculated, under a false name; and the astrologer gave a judgment, that he should be killed in a duel; at which the Queen laughed, thinking her husband to be above challenges and duels: but he was slain upon a course at tilt, the splinters of the staff of Montgomery going in at his beaver. The trivial prophecy, which I heard when I was a child, and queen Elizabeth was in the flower of her years, was,

> When hempe is sponne
> England's done:

whereby it was generally conceived, that after the princes had reigned which had the principial letters of that word *hempe* (which were Henry, Edward, Mary, Philip, and Elizabeth), England should come to utter confusion; which, thanks be to God, is verified only in the change of the name; for that the King's style is now no more of England, but of Britain. There was also another prophecy, before the year of eighty-eight, which I do not well understand.

> There shall be seen upon a day,
> Between the Baugh and the May,
> The black fleet of Norway.
> When that that is come and gone,
> England build houses of lime and stone,
> For after wars shall you have none.

It was generally conceived to be meant of the Spanish fleet that came in eighty-eight: for that the king of Spain's surname, as they say, is Norway. The prediction of Regio-montanus,

> Octogesimus octavus mirabilis annus,

was thought likewise accomplished in the sending of that great fleet, being the greatest in strength, though not in number, of all that ever swam upon the sea. As for Cleon's dream, I think it was a jest. It was, that he was devoured of a long dragon; and it was expounded of a maker of sausages, that troubled him exceedingly. There are numbers of the like kind; especially if you include dreams, and predictions of astrology. But I have set down these few only of certain credit, for example. My judgment is, that they ought all to be despised; and ought to serve but for winter talk by the fireside. Though when I say *despised,* I mean it as for belief; for otherwise, the spreading or publishing of them is in no sort to be despised. For they have done much mischief; and I see many severe laws made to suppress them. That that hath given them grace, and some credit, consisteth in three things. First, that men mark when they hit, and never mark when they miss; as they do generally also of dreams. The second is, that probable conjectures, or obscure traditions, many times turn themselves into prophecies; while the nature of man, which coveteth divination, thinks it no peril to foretell that which indeed they do but collect. As that of Seneca's verse. For so much was then subject to demonstration, that the globe of the earth had great parts beyond the Atlantic, which mought be probably conceived not to be all sea: and adding thereto the tradition in Plato's Timæus, and his Atlanticus, it mought encourage one to turn it to a prediction. The third and last (which is the great one) is, that almost all of them, being infinite in number, have been impostures, and by idle and crafty brains merely contrived and feigned after the event past.

• 36 •

OF AMBITION

AMBITION is like choler; which is an humour that maketh men active, earnest, full of alacrity, and stirring, if it be not stopped. But if it be stopped, and cannot have his way, it becometh adust, and thereby malign and venomous. So ambitious men, if they find the way open for their rising, and still get forward, they are rather busy than dangerous; but if they be checked in their desires, they become secretly discontent, and look upon men and matters with an evil eye, and are best pleased when things go backward; which is the worst property in a servant of a prince or state. Therefore it is good for princes, if they use ambitious men, to handle it so as they be still progressive and not retrograde; which because it cannot be without inconvenience, it is good not to use such natures at all. For if they rise not with their service, they will take order to make their service fall with them. But since we have said it were good not to use men of ambitious natures, except it be upon necessity, it is fit we speak in what cases they are of necessity. Good commanders in the wars must be taken, be they never so ambitious; for the use of their service dispenseth with the rest; and to take a soldier without ambition is to pull off his spurs. There is also great use of ambitious men in being screens to princes in matters of danger and envy; for no man will take that part, except he be like a seeled dove, that mounts and mounts because he cannot see about him. There is use also of ambitious men in pulling down the greatness of any subject that overtops; as Tiberius used Macro in the pulling down of Sejanus.

Since therefore they must be used in such cases, there resteth to speak how they are to be bridled, that they may be less dangerous. There is less danger of them if they be of mean birth, than if they be noble; and if they be rather harsh of nature, than gracious and popular: and if they be rather new raised, than grown cunning and fortified in their greatness. It is counted by some a weakness in princes to have favourites; but it is of all others the best remedy against ambitious great-ones. For when the way of pleasuring and displeasuring lieth by the favourite, it is impossible any other should be over-great. Another means to curb them, is to balance them by others as proud as they. But then there must be some middle counsellors, to keep things steady; for without that ballast the ship will roll too much. At the least, a prince may animate and inure some meaner persons, to be as it were scourges to ambitious men. As for the having of them obnoxious to ruin; if they be of fearful natures, it may do well; but if they be stout and daring, it may precipitate their designs, and prove dangerous. As for the pulling of them down, if the affairs require it, and that it may not be done with safety suddenly, the only way is, the interchange continually of favours and disgraces; whereby they may not know what to expect, and be as it were in a wood. Of ambitions, it is less harmful, the ambition to prevail in great things, than that other to appear in every thing; for that breeds confusion, and mars business. But yet it is less danger to have an ambitious man stirring in business, than great in dependances. He that seeketh to be eminent amongst able men hath a great task; but that is ever good for the public. But he that plots to be the only figure amongst ciphers is the decay of a whole age. Honour hath three things in it; the vantage ground to do good; the approach to kings and principal persons; and the raising of a man's own fortunes. He that hath the best of these intentions, when he aspireth, is an honest man; and that prince that can discern of these intentions in another that aspireth, is a wise prince. Generally, let princes and states choose such ministers as are more sensible of duty than of rising; and

such as love business rather upon conscience than upon
bravery; and let them discern a busy nature from a willing
mind.

• 37 •

OF MASQUES AND TRIUMPHS

THESE things are but toys, to come amongst such serious
observations. But yet, since princes will have such things,
it is better they should be graced with elegancy than
daubed with cost. Dancing to song, is a thing of great
state and pleasure. I understand it, that the song be in
quire, placed aloft, and accompanied with some broken
music; and the ditty fitted to the device. Acting in song,
especially in dialogues, hath an extreme good grace; I
say acting, not dancing (for that is a mean and vulgar
thing); and the voices of the dialogue would be strong
and manly, (a base and a tenor; no treble;) and the ditty
high and tragical; not nice or dainty. Several quires,
placed one over against another, and taking the voice by
catches, anthem-wise, give great pleasure. Turning dances
into figure is a childish curiosity. And generally let it be
noted, that those things which I here set down are such
as do naturally take the sense, and not respect petty won-
derments. It is true, the alterations of scenes, so it be
quietly and without noise, are things of great beauty and
pleasure; for they feed and relieve the eye, before it be
full of the same object. Let the scenes abound with light,
specially coloured and varied; and let the masquers, or
any other, that are to come down from the scene, have
some motions upon the scene itself before their coming
down; for it draws the eye strangely, and makes it with
great pleasure to desire to see that it cannot perfectly
discern. Let the songs be loud and cheerful, and not
chirpings or pulings. Let the music likewise be sharp and
loud, and well placed. The colours that shew best by
candle-light, are white, carnation, and a kind of sea-water-
green; and oes, or spangs, as they are of no great cost, so

they are of most glory. As for rich embroidery, it is lost and not discerned. Let the suits of the masquers be graceful, and such as become the person when the vizards are off; not after examples of known attires; Turks, soldiers, mariners, and the like. Let anti-masques not be long; they have been commonly of fools, satyrs, baboons, wild-men, antics, beasts, sprites, witches, Ethiops, pigmies, turquets, nymphs, rustics, Cupids, statua's moving, and the like. As for angels, it is not comical enough to put them in anti-masques; and any thing that is hideous, as devils, giants, is on the other side as unfit. But chiefly, let the music of them be recreative, and with some strange changes. Some sweet odours suddenly coming forth, without any drops falling, are, in such a company as there is steam and heat, things of great pleasure and refreshment. Double masques, one of men, another of ladies, addeth state and variety. But all is nothing except the room be kept clear and neat.

For justs, and tourneys, and barriers; the glories of them are chiefly in the chariots, wherein the challengers make their entry; especially if they be drawn with strange beasts: as lions, bears, camels, and the like; or in the devices of their entrance; or in the bravery of their liveries; or in the goodly furniture of their horses and armour. But enough of these toys.

· 38 ·

OF NATURE IN MAN

NATURE is often hidden; sometimes overcome; seldom extinguished. Force maketh nature more violent in the return; doctrine and discourse maketh nature less importune; but custom only doth alter and subdue nature. He that seeketh victory over his nature, let him not set himself too great nor too small tasks; for the first will make him dejected by often failings; and the second will make him a small proceeder, though by often prevailings. And at the first let him practise with helps, as swimmers

do with bladders or rushes; but after a time let him practise with disadvantages, as dancers do with thick shoes.
For it breeds great perfection, if the practice be harder
than the use. Where nature is mighty, and therefore the
victory hard, the degrees had need be, first to stay and
arrest nature in time; like to him that would say over
the four and twenty letters when he was angry; then to
go less in quantity; as if one should, in forbearing wine,
come from drinking healths to a draught at a meal; and
lastly, to discontinue altogether. But if a man have the
fortitude and resolution to enfranchise himself at once,
that is the best:

Optimus ille animi vindex lædentia pectus
Vincula qui rupit, dedoluitque semel.

[Wouldst thou be free? The chains that gall thy breast
With one strong effort burst, and be at rest.]

Neither is the ancient rule amiss, to bend nature as a
wand to a contrary extreme, whereby to set it right; understanding it, where the contrary extreme is no vice. Let
not a man force a habit upon himself with a perpetual
continuance, but with some intermission. For both the
pause reinforceth the new onset; and if a man that is not
perfect be ever in practice, he shall as well practise his
errors as his abilities, and induce one habit of both; and
there is no means to help this but by seasonable inter-
missions. But let not a man trust his victory over his nature too far; for nature will lay buried a great time, and
yet revive upon the occasion or temptation. Like as it
was with Æsop's damsel, turned from a cat to a woman,
who sat very demurely at the board's end, till a mouse
ran before her. Therefore let a man either avoid the occasion altogether; or put himself often to it, that he may
be little moved with it. A man's nature is best perceived
in privateness, for there is no affectation; in passion, for
that putteth a man out of his precepts; and in a new case
or experiment, for there custom leaveth him. They are
happy men whose natures sort with their vocations; other-

wise they may say, *multum incola fuit anima mea,* [my soul hath been a stranger and a sojourner;] when they converse in those things they do not affect. In studies, whatsoever a man commandeth upon himself, let him set hours for it; but whatsoever is agreeable to his nature, let him take no care for any set times; for his thoughts will fly to it of themselves; so as the spaces of other business or studies will suffice. A man's nature runs either to herbs or weeds; therefore let him seasonably water the one, and destroy the other.

· 39 ·

OF CUSTOM AND EDUCATION

MEN's thoughts are much according to their inclination; their discourse and speeches according to their learning and infused opinions; but their deeds are after as they have been accustomed. And therefore as Machiavel well noteth (though in an evil-favoured instance,) there is no trusting to the force of nature nor to the bravery of words, except it be corroborate by custom. His instance is, that for the achieving of a desperate conspiracy, a man should not rest upon the fierceness of any man's nature, or his resolute undertakings; but take such an one as hath had his hands formerly in blood. But Machiavel knew not of a friar Clement, nor a Ravillac, nor a Jaureguy, nor a Baltazar Gerard; yet his rule holdeth still, that nature, nor the engagement of words, are not so forcible as custom. Only superstition is now so well advanced, that men of the first blood are as firm as butchers by occupation; and votary resolution is made equipollent to custom even in matter of blood. In other things the predominancy of custom is every where visible; insomuch as a man would wonder to hear men profess, protest, engage, give great words, and then do just as they have done before; as if they were dead images, and engines moved only by the wheels of custom. We see also the reign or tyranny of custom, what it is. The Indians (I mean the sect of their wise men) lay themselves quietly upon a stack of wood, and so sacrifice themselves by fire. Nay the wives strive to be burned with the corpses of their husbands. The lads of Sparta, of ancient time, were wont to be scourged upon the altar of Diana, without so much as queching. I remember, in the beginning of Queen Elizabeth's time of England, an Irish rebel condemned, put up a petition to the Deputy that he might be hanged in a with, and not in an halter; because it had been so used with former rebels. There be monks in Russia, for penance, that will sit a whole night in a vessel of water, till they be engaged with hard ice. Many examples may be put of the force of custom, both upon mind and body. Therefore, since custom is the principal magistrate of man's life, let men by all means endeavour to obtain good customs. Certainly custom is most perfect when it beginneth in young years: this we call education; which is, in effect, but an early custom. So we see, in languages the tongue is more pliant to all expressions and sounds, the joints are more supple to all feats of activity and motions, in youth than afterwards. For it is true that late learners cannot so well take the ply; except it be in some minds that have not suffered themselves to fix, but have kept themselves open and prepared to receive continual amendment, which is exceeding rare. But if the force of custom simple and separate be great, the force of custom copulate and conjoined and collegiate is far greater. For there example teacheth, company comforteth, emulation quickeneth, glory raiseth: so as in such places the force of custom is in his exaltation. Certainly the great multiplication of virtues upon human nature resteth upon societies well ordained and disciplined. For commonwealths and good governments do nourish virtue grown, but do not much mend the seeds. But the misery is, that the most effectual means are now applied to the ends least to be desired.

OF FORTUNE

IT cannot be denied, but outward accidents conduce much to fortune; favour, opportunity, death of others, occasion fitting virtue. But chiefly, the mould of a man's fortune is in his own hands. *Faber quisque fortunæ suæ* [every man is the architect of his own fortune], saith the poet. And the most frequent of external causes is, that the folly of one man is the fortune of another. For no man prospers so suddenly as by others' errors. *Serpens nisi serpentem comederit non fit draco.* [A serpent must have eaten another serpent, before he can become a dragon.] Overt and apparent virtues bring forth praise; but there be secret and hidden virtues that bring forth fortune; certain deliveries of a man's self, which have no name. The Spanish name, *desemboltura,* partly expresseth them; when there be not stonds nor restiveness in a man's nature; but that the wheels of his mind keep way with the wheels of his fortune. For so Livy (after he had described Cato Major in these words, *In illo viro tantum robur corporis et animi fuit, ut quocunque loco natus esset, fortunam sibi facturus videretur*) [Such was his strength of body and mind, that wherever he had been born he could have made himself a fortune;] falleth upon that, that he had *versatile ingenium* [a wit that could turn well]. Therefore if a man look sharply and attentively, he shall see Fortune: for though she be blind, yet she is not invisible. The way of fortune is like the milken way in the sky; which is a meeting or knot of a number of small stars; not seen asunder, but giving light together. So are there a number of little and scarce discerned virtues, or rather faculties and customs, that make men fortunate. The Italians note some of them, such as a man would little think. When they speak of one that cannot do amiss, they will throw in into his other conditions, that he hath *Poco di matto* [a little of the fool]. And certainly there be not two more fortunate properties, than to have a little of the fool, and not too much of the honest. Therefore extreme lovers of their country or masters were never fortunate, neither can they be. For when a man placeth his thoughts without himself, he goeth not his own way. An hasty fortune maketh an enterpriser and remover; (the French hath it better, *enterprenant,* or *remuant;*) but the exercised fortune maketh the able man. Fortune is to be honoured and respected, and it be but for her daughters, Confidence and Reputation. For those two felicity breedeth; the first within a man's self, the latter in others towards him. All wise men, to decline the envy of their own virtues, use to ascribe them to Providence and Fortune; for so they may the better assume them: and, besides, it is greatness in a man to be the care of the higher powers. So Cæsar said to the pilot in the tempest, *Cæsarem portas, et fortunam ejus* [You carry Cæsar and his fortune]. So Sylla chose the name of *Felix* [Fortunate], and not of *Magnus* [Great]. And it hath been noted, that those who ascribe openly too much to their own wisdom and policy, end infortunate. It is written that Timotheus the Athenian, after he had, in the account he gave to the state of his government, often interlaced this speech, *and in this Fortune had no part,* never prospered in any thing he undertook afterwards. Certainly there be, whose fortunes are like Homer's verses, that have a slide and easiness more than the verses of other poets; as Plutarch saith of Timoleon's fortune, in respect of that of Agesilaus or Epaminondas. And that this should be, no doubt it is much in a man's self.

· 41 ·

OF USURY

MANY have made witty invectives against Usury. They say that it is a pity the devil should have God's part, which is the tithe. That the usurer is the greatest sabbath-

breaker, because his plough goeth every Sunday. That
the usurer is the drone that Virgil speaketh of;

Ignavum fucos pecus a præsepibus arcent.
[They drive the lazy swarm of drones from the hive].

That the usurer breaketh the first law that was made for
mankind after the fall, which was, *in sudore vultûs tui
comedes panem tuum;* not, *in sudore vultûs alieni;* [in the
sweat of thy face shalt thou eat bread—not in the sweat
of another's face]. That usurers should have orange-tawny
bonnets, because they do judaize. That it is against nature
for money to beget money; and the like. I say this only,
that usury is a *concessum propter duritiem cordis:* [a
thing allowed by reason of the hardness of men's hearts:]
for since there must be borrowing and lending, and men
are so hard of heart as they will not lend freely, usury
must be permitted. Some others have made suspicious
and cunning propositions of banks, discovery of men's
estates, and other inventions. But few have spoken of
usury usefully. It is good to set before us the incom-
modities and commodities of usury, that the good may be
either weighed out or culled out; and warily to provide,
that while we make forth to that which is better, we meet
not with that which is worse.

The discommodities of usury are, First, that it makes
fewer merchants. For were it not for this lazy trade of
usury, money would not lie still, but would in great part
be employed upon merchandizing; which is the *vena
porta* of wealth in a state. The second, that it makes poor
merchants. For as a farmer cannot husband his ground so
well if he sit at a great rent; so the merchant cannot drive
his trade so well, if he sit at great usury. The third is incident to the other two; and that is the decay of customs
of kings or states, which ebb or flow with merchandizing.
The fourth, that it bringeth the treasure of a realm or
state into a few hands. For the usurer being at certainties,
and others at uncertainties, at the end of the game most
of the money will be in the box; and ever a state flour-
isheth when wealth is more equally spread. The fifth, that

it beats down the price of land; for the employment of money is chiefly either merchandizing or purchasing; and usury waylays both. The sixth, that it doth dull and damp all industries, improvements, and new inventions, wherein money would be stirring, if it were not for this slug. The last, that it is the canker and ruin of many men's estates; which in process of time breeds a public poverty.

On the other side, the commodities of usury are, first, that howsoever usury in some respect hindereth merchandizing, yet in some other it advanceth it; for it is certain that the greatest part of trade is driven by young merchants, upon borrowing at interest; so as if the usurer either call in or keep back his money, there will ensue presently a great stand of trade. The second is, that were it not for this easy borrowing upon interest, men's necessities would draw upon them a most sudden undoing; in that they would be forced to sell their means (be it lands or goods) far under foot; and so, whereas usury doth but gnaw upon them, bad markets would swallow them quite up. As for mortgaging or pawning, it will little mend the matter: for either men will not take pawns without use; or if they do, they will look precisely for the forfeiture. I remember a cruel monied man in the country, that would say, The devil take this usury, it keeps us from forfeitures of mortgages and bonds. The third and last is, that it is a vanity to conceive that there would be ordinary borrowing without profit; and it is impossible to conceive the number of inconveniences that will ensue, if borrowing be cramped. Therefore to speak of the abolishing of usury is idle. All states have ever had it, in one kind or rate, or other. So as that opinion must be sent to Utopia.

To speak now of the reformation and reiglement of usury; how the discommodities of it may be best avoided, and the commodities retained. It appears by the balance of commodities and discommodities of usury, two things are to be reconciled. The one, that the tooth of usury be grinded, that it bite not too much; the other, that there be left open a means to invite monied men to lend to the merchants, for the continuing and quickening of trade. This cannot be done, except you introduce two several sorts of usury, a less and a greater. For if you reduce usury to one low rate, it will ease the common borrower, but the merchant will be to seek for money. And it is to be noted, that the trade of merchandize, being the most lucrative, may bear usury at a good rate: other contracts not so.

To serve both intentions, the way would be briefly thus. That there be two rates of usury; the one free, and general for all; the other under licence only, to certain persons and in certain places of merchandizing. First therefore, let usury in general be reduced to five in the hundred; and let that rate be proclaimed to be free and current; and let the state shut itself out to take any penalty for the same. This will preserve borrowing from any general stop or dryness. This will ease infinite borrowers in the country. This will, in good part, raise the price of land, because land purchased at sixteen years' purchase will yield six in the hundred, and somewhat more; whereas this rate of interest yields but five. This by like reason will encourage and edge industrious and profitable improvements; because many will rather venture in that kind than take five in the hundred, especially having been used to greater profit. Secondly, let there be certain persons licenced to lend to known merchants upon usury at a higher rate; and let it be with the cautions following. Let the rate be, even with the merchant himself, somewhat more easy than that he used formerly to pay; for by that means all borrowers shall have some ease by this reformation, be he merchant, or whosoever. Let it be no bank or common stock, but every man be master of his own money. Not that I altogether mislike banks, but they will hardly be brooked, in regard of certain suspicions. Let the state be answered some small matter for the licence, and the rest left to the lender; for if the abatement be but small, it will no whit discourage the lender. For he, for example, that took before ten or nine in the hundred, will sooner descend to eight in the hundred, than give over his trade of usury, and go from certain gains to gains of hazard. Let these licensed lenders be in number indefinite, but restrained to certain principal cities and towns of merchandizing; for then they will be hardly able to colour other men's monies in the country: so as the licence of nine will not suck away the current rate of five; for no man will lend his monies far off, nor put them into unknown hands.

If it be objected that this doth in a sort authorize usury, which before was in some places but permissive; the answer is, that it is better to mitigate usury by declaration, than to suffer it to rage by connivance.

• 42 •

OF YOUTH AND AGE

A MAN that is young in years may be old in hours, if he have lost no time. But that happeneth rarely. Generally, youth is like the first cogitations, not so wise as the second. For there is a youth in thoughts, as well as in ages. And yet the invention of young men is more lively than that of old; and imaginations stream into their minds better, and as it were more divinely. Natures that have much heat and great and violent desires and perturbations, are not ripe for action till they have passed the meridian of their years; as it was with Julius Cæsar, and Septimius Severus. Of the latter of whom it is said, *Juventutem egit erroribus, imo furoribus, plenam;* [He passed a youth full of errors, yea of madnesses.] And yet he was the ablest emperor, almost, of all the list. But reposed natures may do well in youth. As it is seen in Augustus Cæsar, Cosmus Duke of Florence, Gaston de Fois, and others. On the other side, heat and vivacity in age is an excellent composition for business. Young men are fitter to invent than to judge; fitter for execution than for counsel; and fitter for new projects than for settled business. For the experience of age, in things that fall within the compass of it, directeth them; but in new things, abuseth them. The errors of young men are the ruin of business; but the errors of aged men amount but to this, that more might have been done, or sooner. Young men, in the conduct and manage of actions, embrace more than they can hold; stir more than they can quiet; fly to the end, without consideration of the means and degrees; pursue some few principles which they have chanced upon absurdly; care not to innovate, which draws unknown inconveniences; use extreme remedies at first; and that which doubleth all errors, will not acknowledge or retract them; like an unready horse, that will neither stop nor turn. Men of age object too much, consult too long, adventure too little, repent too soon, and seldom drive business home to the full period, but content themselves with a mediocrity of success. Certainly it is good to compound employments of both; for that will be good for the present, because the virtues of either age may correct the defects of both; and good for succession, that young men may be learners, while men in age are actors; and, lastly, good for extern accidents, because authority followeth old men, and favour and popularity youth. But for the moral part, perhaps youth will have the pre-eminence, as age hath for the politic. A certain rabbin, upon the text, *Your young men shall see visions, and your old men shall dream dreams,* inferreth that young men are admitted nearer to God than old, because vision is a clearer revelation than a dream. And certainly, the more a man drinketh of the world, the more it intoxicateth: and age doth profit rather in the powers of understanding, than in the virtues of the will and affections. There be some have an over-early ripeness in their years, which fadeth betimes. These are, first, such as have brittle wits, the edge whereof is soon turned; such as was Hermogenes the rhetorician, whose books are exceeding subtle; who afterwards waxed stupid. A second sort is of those that have some natural dispositions which have better grace in youth than in age; such as is a fluent and luxuriant speech; which becomes youth well, but not age: so Tully saith of Hortensius, *Idem manebat, neque idem decebat* [He continued the same, when the same was not becoming]. The third is of such as take too high a strain at the first, and are magnanimous

more than tract of years can uphold. As was Scipio Africanus, of whom Livy saith in effect, *Ultima primis cede-
bant* [His last actions were not equal to his first].

• 43 •

OF BEAUTY

VIRTUE is like a rich stone, best plain set; and surely virtue
is best in a body that is comely, though not of delicate
features; and that hath rather dignity of presence, than
beauty of aspect. Neither is it almost seen, that very beautiful persons are otherwise of great virtue; as if nature
were rather busy not to err, than in labour to produce
excellency. And therefore they prove accomplished, but
not of great spirit; and study rather behaviour than virtue. But this holds not always: for Augustus Cæsar, Titus
Vespasianus, Philip le Bel of France, Edward the Fourth
of England, Alcibiades of Athens, Ismael the Sophy of
Persia, were all high and great spirits; and yet the most
beautiful men of their times. In beauty, that of favour is
more than that of colour; and that of decent and gracious
motion more than that of favour. That is the best part of
beauty, which a picture cannot express; no nor the first
sight of life. There is no excellent beauty that hath not
some strangeness in the proportion. A man cannot tell
whether Apelles or Albert Durer were the more trifler;
whereof the one would make a personage by geometrical
proportions; the other, by taking the best parts out of
divers faces, to make one excellent. Such personages, I
think, would please nobody but the painter that made
them. Not but I think a painter may make a better face
than ever was; but he must do it by a kind of felicity, (as
a musician that maketh an excellent air in music,) and
not by rule. A man shall see faces, that if you examine
them part by part, you shall find never a good; and yet
altogether do well. If it be true that the principal part
of beauty is in decent motion, certainly it is no marvel
though persons in years seem many times more amiable;

pulchrorum autumnus pulcher; [beautiful persons have a beautiful Autumn;] for no youth can be comely but by pardon, and considering the youth as to make up the comeliness. Beauty is as summer fruits, which are easy to corrupt, and cannot last; and for the most part it makes a dissolute youth, and an age a little out of countenance; but yet certainly again, if it light well, it maketh virtue shine, and vices blush.

· 44 ·

OF DEFORMITY

DEFORMED persons are commonly even with nature; for as nature hath done ill by them, so do they by nature; being for the most part (as the Scripture saith) *void of natural affection;* and so they have their revenge of nature. Certainly there is a consent between the body and the mind; and where nature erreth in the one, she ventureth in the other. *Ubi peccat in uno, periclitatur in altero.* But because there is in man an election touching the frame of his mind, and a necessity in the frame of his body, the stars of natural inclination are sometimes obscured by the sun of discipline and virtue. Therefore it is good to consider of deformity, not as a sign, which is more deceivable; but as a cause, which seldom faileth of the effect. Whosoever hath any thing fixed in his person that doth induce contempt, hath also a perpetual spur in himself to rescue and deliver himself from scorn. Therefore all deformed persons are extreme bold. First, as in their own defence, as being exposed to scorn; but in process of time by a general habit. Also it stirreth in them industry, and especially of this kind, to watch and observe the weakness of others, that they may have somewhat to repay. Again, in their superiors, it quencheth jealousy towards them, as persons that they think they may at pleasure despise: and it layeth their competitors and emulators asleep; as never believing they should be in possibility of advancement, till they see them in possession. So that upon the matter, in a great wit, deformity is an advantage to rising. Kings in ancient times (and at this present in some countries) were wont to put great trust in eunuchs; because they that are envious towards all are more obnoxious and officious towards one. But yet their trust towards them hath rather been as to good spials and good whisperers, than good magistrates and officers. And much like is the reason of deformed persons. Still the ground is, they will, if they be of spirit, seek to free themselves from scorn; which must be either by virtue or malice; and therefore let it not be marvelled if sometimes they prove excellent persons; as was Agesilaus, Zanger the son of Solyman, Æsop, Gasca President of Peru; and Socrates may go likewise amongst them; with others.

· 45 ·

OF BUILDING

HOUSES are built to live in, and not to look on; therefore let use be preferred before uniformity, except where both may be had. Leave the goodly fabrics of houses, for beauty only, to the enchanted palaces of the poets; who build them with small cost. He that builds a fair house upon an ill seat, committeth himself to prison. Neither do I reckon it an ill seat only where the air is unwholesome; but likewise where the air is unequal; as you shall see many fine seats set upon a knap of ground, environed with higher hills round about it; whereby the heat of the sun is pent in, and the wind gathereth as in troughs; so as you shall have, and that suddenly, as great diversity of heat and cold as if you dwelt in several places. Neither is it ill air only that maketh an ill seat, but ill ways, ill markets: and, if you will consult with Momus, ill neighbours. I speak not of many more; want of water; want of wood, shade, and shelter; want of fruitfulness, and mixture of grounds of several natures; want of prospect; want of level grounds; want of places at some near distance for sports of hunting, hawking, and races; too near the sea, too remote; [not] having the commodity of navigable rivers, or the discommodity of their overflowing; too far off from great cities, which may hinder business, or too near them, which lurcheth all provisions, and maketh every thing dear; where a man hath a great living laid together, and where he is scanted: all which, as it is impossible perhaps to find together, so it is good to know them, and think of them, that a man may take as many as he can; and if he have several dwellings, that he sort them so, that what he wanteth in the one he may find in the other. Lucullus answered Pompey well; who, when he saw his stately galleries, and rooms so large and lightsome, in one of his houses, said, *Surely an excellent place for summer, but how do you in winter?* Lucullus answered, *Why, do you not think me as wise as some fowl are, that ever change their abode towards the winter?*

To pass from the seat to the house itself; we will do as Cicero doth in the orator's art; who writes books *De Oratore,* and a book he entitles *Orator;* whereof the former delivers the precepts of the art, and the latter the perfection. We will therefore describe a princely palace, making a brief model thereof. For it is strange to see, now in Europe, such huge buildings as the Vatican and Escurial and some others be, and yet scarce a very fair room in them.

First therefore, I say you cannot have a perfect palace, except you have two several sides; a side for the banquet, as is spoken of in the book of Hester, and a side for the household; the one for feasts and triumphs, and the other for dwelling. I understand both these sides to be not only returns, but parts of the front; and to be uniform without, though severally partitioned within; and to be on both sides of a great and stately tower in the midst of the front, that, as it were, joineth them together on either hand. I would have on the side of the banquet, in front, one only goodly room above stairs, of some forty foot high; and under it a room for a dressing or preparing place at times of triumphs. On the other side, which is the household side, I wish it divided at the first into a hall and a chapel, (with a partition between;) both of good state and bigness; and those not to go all the length, but to have at the further end a winter and a summer parlour, both fair. And under these rooms, a fair and large cellar sunk under ground; and likewise some privy kitch-ens, with butteries and pantries, and the like. As for the tower, I would have it two stories, of eighteen foot high a piece, above the two wings; and a goodly leads upon the top, railed with statua's interposed; and the same tower to be divided into rooms, as shall be thought fit. The stairs likewise to the upper rooms, let them be upon a fair open newel, and finely railed in with images of wood, cast into a brass colour; and a very fair landing-place at the top. But this to be, if you do not point any of the lower rooms for a dining place of servants. For otherwise you shall have the servants' dinner after your own: for the steam of it will come up as in a tunnel. And so much for the front. Only I understand the height of the first stairs to be sixteen foot, which is the height of the lower room.

Beyond this front is there to be a fair court, but three sides of it, of a far lower building than the front. And in all the four corners of that court fair stair-cases, cast into turrets, on the outside, and not within the row of build-ings themselves. But those towers are not to be of the height of the front, but rather proportionable to the lower building. Let the court not be paved, for that striketh up a great heat in summer, and much cold in winter. But only some side alleys, with a cross, and the quarters to graze, being kept shorn, but not too near shorn. The row of return on the banquet side, let it be all stately galleries: in which galleries let there be three, or five, fine cupolas in the length of it, placed at equal distance; and fine coloured windows of several works. On the household side, chambers of presence and ordinary entertainments, with some bed-chambers; and let all three sides be a double house, without thorough lights on the sides, that you may have rooms from the sun, both for forenoon and afternoon. Cast it also, that you may have rooms both for summer and winter; shady for summer, and warm for winter. You shall have sometimes fair houses so full of glass, that one cannot tell where to become to be out of the sun or cold. For inbowed windows, I hold them of good use; (in cities, indeed, upright do better, in respect of the uniformity towards the street;) for they be pretty retiring places for conference; and besides, they keep both the wind and sun off; for that which would strike almost thorough the room doth scarce pass the window. But let them be but few, four in the court, on the sides only.

Beyond this court, let there be an inward court, of the same square and height; which is to be environed with the garden on all sides; and in the inside, cloistered on all sides, upon decent and beautiful arches, as high as the first story. On the under story, towards the garden, let it be turned to a grotta, or place of shade, or estivation. And only have opening and windows towards the garden; and be level upon the floor, no whit sunken under ground, to avoid all dampishness. And let there be a fountain, or some fair work of statua's in the midst of this court; and to be paved as the other court was. These buildings to be for privy lodgings on both sides; and the end for privy galleries. Whereof you must foresee that one of them be for an infirmary, if the prince or any special person should be sick, with chambers, bed-chamber, antecamera, and recamera, joining to it. This upon the second story. Upon the ground story, a fair gallery, open, upon pillars; and upon the third story likewise, an open gallery, upon pillars, to take the prospect and freshness of the garden. At both corners of the further side, by way of return, let there be two delicate or rich cabinets, daintily paved, richly hanged, glazed with crystalline glass, and a rich cupola in the midst; and all other elegancy that may be thought upon. In the upper gallery too, I wish that there may be, if the place will yield it, some fountains running in divers places from the wall, with some fine avoidances. And thus much for the model of the palace; save that you must have, before you come to the front, three courts. A green court plain, with a wall about it; a second court of the same, but more garnished, with little turrets, or rather embellishments, upon the wall; and a third court, to make a square with the front, but not to be built, nor yet enclosed with a naked wall, but enclosed with tarrasses, leaded aloft, and fairly garnished, on the three sides; and cloistered on the inside, with pillars, and not with arches below. As for offices, let them stand at distance, with some low galleries, to pass from them to the palace itself.

• 46 •

OF GARDENS

GOD ALMIGHTY first planted a Garden. And indeed it is the purest of human pleasures. It is the greatest refreshment to the spirits of man; without which buildings and palaces are but gross handyworks: and a man shall ever see that when ages grow to civility and elegancy, men come to build stately sooner than to garden finely; as if gardening were the greater perfection. I do hold it, in the royal ordering of gardens, there ought to be gardens for all the months in the year; in which severally things of beauty may be then in season. For December, and January, and the latter part of November, you must take such things as are green all winter: holly; ivy; bays; juniper; cypress-trees; yew; pine-apple-trees; fir-trres; rosemary; lavender; periwinkle, the white, the purple, and the blue; germander; flags; orange-trees; lemon-trees; and myrtles, if they be stoved; and sweet marjoram, warm set. There followeth, for the latter part of January and February, the mezereon-tree, which then blossoms; crocus vernus, both the yellow and the grey; primroses; anemones; the early tulippa; hyacinthus orientalis; chamaïris; fritellaria. For March, there come violets, specially the single blue, which are the earliest; the yellow daffodil; the daisy; the almond-tree in blossom; the peach-tree in blossom; the cornelian-tree in blossom; sweet-briar. In April follow, the double white violet; the wall-flower; the stock-gilliflower; the cowslip; flower-de-lices, and lilies of all natures; rosemary-flowers; the tulippa; the double piony; the pale daffodil; the French honeysuckle; the cherry-tree in blossom; the dammasin and plum-trees in blossom; the white thorn in leaf; the lilac-tree. In May and June come pinks of all sorts, specially the blush-pink; roses of all kinds, except the musk, which comes later; honey-suckles; strawberries; bugloss; columbine; the French marigold; flos Africanus; cherry-tree in fruit; ribes; figs in fruit; rasps; vine-flowers; lavender in flowers; the sweet satyrian, with the white flower; herba muscaria; lilium convallium; the apple-tree in blossom. In July come gilliflowers of all varieties; musk-roses; the lime-tree in blossom; early pears and plums in fruit; genitings, quadlins. In August come plums of all sorts in fruit; pears; apricocks; berberries; filberds; musk-melons; monks-hoods, of all colours. In September come grapes; apples; poppies of all colours; peaches; melocotones; nectarines; cornelians; wardens; quinces. In October and the beginning of November come services; medlars; bullaces; roses cut or removed to come late; holly-oaks; and such like. These particulars are for the climate of London; but my meaning is perceived, that you may have *ver perpetuum* [eternal spring], as the place affords.

And because the breath of flowers is far sweeter in the air (where it comes and goes like the warbling of music) than in the hand, therefore nothing is more fit for that delight, than to know what be the flowers and plants that do best perfume the air. Roses, damask and red, are fast flowers of their smells; so that you may walk by a whole row of them, and find nothing of their sweetness; yea though it be in a morning's dew. Bays likewise yield no smell as they grow. Rosemary little; nor sweet marjoram. That which above all others yields the sweetest smell in the air, is the violet, specially the white double violet, which comes twice a year; about the middle of April, and about Bartholomew-tide. Next to that is the musk-rose. Then the strawberry-leaves dying, with a most excellent cordial smell. Then the flower of the vines; it is a little dust, like the dust of a bent, which grows upon the cluster in the first coming forth. Then sweet-briar. Then wallflowers, which are very delightful to be set under a parlour or lower chamber window. Then pinks and gilliflowers, specially the matted pink and clove gilliflower.

Then the flowers of the lime-tree. Then the honeysuckles,
so they be somewhat afar off. Of bean-flowers I speak not,
because they are field flowers. But those which perfume
the air most delightfully, not passed by as the rest, but
being trodden upon and crushed, are three; that is,
burnet, wild-thyme, and watermints. Therefore you are to
set whole alleys of them, to have the pleasure when you
walk or tread.

For gardens (speaking of those which are indeed
princelike, as we have done of buildings), the contents
ought not well to be under thirty acres of ground; and
to be divided into three parts; a green in the entrance; a
heath or desert in the going forth; and the main garden in
the midst; besides alleys on both sides. And I like well
that four acres of ground be assigned to the green; six
to the heath; four and four to either side; and twelve to
the main garden. The green hath two pleasures: the one,
because nothing is more pleasant to the eye than green
grass kept finely shorn; the other, because it will give you
a fair alley in the midst, by which you may go in front
upon a stately hedge, which is to enclose the garden. But
because the alley will be long, and, in great heat of the
year or day, you ought not to buy the shade in the garden
by going in the sun thorough the green, therefore you are,
of either side the green, to plant a covert alley, upon carpenter's work, about twelve foot in height, by which you
may go in shade into the garden. As for the making of
knots or figures with divers coloured earths, that they may
lie under the windows of the house on that side which the
garden stands, they be but toys: you may see as good
sights many times in tarts. The garden is best to be square,
encompassed on all the four sides with a stately arched
hedge. The arches to be upon pillars of carpenter's work,
of some ten foot high, and six foot broad; and the spaces
between of the same dimension with the breadth of the
arch. Over the arches let there be an entire hedge of some
four foot high, framed also upon carpenter's work; and
upon the upper hedge, over every arch, a little turret,
with a belly, enough to receive a cage of birds: and over
every space between the arches some other little figure,

with broad plates of round coloured glass gilt, for the sun to play upon. But this hedge I intend to be raised upon a bank, not steep, but gently slope, of some six foot, set all with flowers. Also I understand, that this square of the garden should not be the whole breadth of the ground, but to leave on either side ground enough for diversity of side alleys; unto which the two covert alleys of the green may deliver you. But there must be no alleys with hedges at either end of this great enclosure; not at the hither end, for letting your prospect upon this fair hedge from the green; nor at the further end, for letting your prospect from the hedge through the arches upon the heath.

For the ordering of the ground within the great hedge, I leave it to variety of device; advising nevertheless that whatsoever form you cast it into, first, it be not too busy, or full of work. Wherein I, for my part, do not like images cut out in juniper or other garden stuff; they be for children. Little low hedges, round, like welts, with some pretty pyramides, I like well; and in some places, fair columns upon frames of carpenter's work. I would also have the alleys spacious and fair. You may have closer alleys upon the side grounds, but none in the main garden. I wish also, in the very middle, a fair mount, with three ascents, and alleys, enough for four to walk abreast; which I would have to be perfect circles, without any bulwarks or embossments; and the whole mount to be thirty foot high; and some fine banqueting-house, with some chimneys neatly cast, and without too much glass.

For fountains, they are a great beauty and refreshment; but pools mar all, and make the garden unwholesome, and full of flies and frogs. Fountains I intend to be of two natures: the one that sprinkleth or spouteth water; the other a fair receipt of water, of some thirty or forty foot square, but without fish, or slime, or mud. For the first, the ornaments of images gilt, or of marble, which are in use, do well: but the main matter is so to convey the water, as it never stay, either in the bowls or in the cistern; that the water be never by rest discoloured, green

or red or the like; or gather any mossiness or putrefaction.
Besides that, it is to be cleansed every day by the hand.
Also some steps up to it, and some fine pavement about
it, doth well. As for the other kind of fountain, which we
may call a bathing pool, it may admit much curiosity and
beauty; wherewith we will not trouble ourselves: as, that
the bottom be finely paved, and with images; the sides
likewise; and withal embellished with coloured glass, and
such things of lustre; encompassed also with fine rails of
low statua's. But the main point is the same which we
mentioned in the former kind of fountain; which is, that
the water be in perpetual motion, fed by a water higher
than the pool, and delivered into it by fair spouts, and
then discharged away under ground, by some equality of
bores, that it stay little. And for fine devices, of arching
water without spilling, and making it rise in several forms
(of feathers, drinking glasses, canopies, and the like),
they be pretty things to look on, but nothing to health
and sweetness.

For the heath, which was the third part of our plot, I
wish it to be framed, as much as may be, to a natural
wildness. Trees I would have none in it, but some thick-
ets made only of sweet-briar and honeysuckle, and some
wild vine amongst; and the ground set with violets, strawberries, and primroses. For these are sweet, and prosper
in the shade. And these to be in the heath, here and there,
not in any order. I like also little heaps, in the nature of
mole-hills (such as are in wild heaths), to be set, some
with wild thyme; some with pinks; some with germander,
that gives a good flower to the eye; some with periwinkle; some with violets; some with strawberries; some
with cowslips; some with daisies; some with red roses;
some with lilium convallium; some with sweet-williams
red; some with bear's-foot: and the like low flowers, being withal sweet and sightly. Part of which heaps are to
be with standards of little bushes pricked upon their top,
and part without. The standards to be roses; juniper;
holly; berberries; (but here and there, because of the
smell of their blossom;) red currants; gooseberry; rose-

mary; bays; sweet-briar; and such like. But these standards to be kept with cutting, that they grow not out of course.

For the side grounds, you are to fill them with variety of alleys, private, to give a full shade, some of them, wheresoever the sun be. You are to frame some of them likewise for shelter, that when the wind blows sharp, you may walk as in a gallery. And those alleys must be likewise hedged at both ends, to keep out the wind; and these closer alleys must be ever finely gravelled, and no grass, because of going wet. In many of these alleys likewise, you are to set fruit-trees of all sorts; as well upon the walls as in ranges. And this would be generally observed, that the borders wherein you plant your fruit-trees be fair and large, and low, and not steep; and set with fine flowers, but thin and sparingly, lest they deceive the trees. At the end of both the side grounds, I would have a mount of some pretty height, leaving the wall of the enclosure breast high, to look abroad into the fields.

For the main garden, I do not deny but there should be some fair alleys ranged on both sides, with fruit trees; and some pretty tufts of fruit trees, and arbours with seats, set in some decent order; but these to be by no means set too thick; but to leave the main garden so as it be not close, but the air open and free. For as for shade, I would have you rest upon the alleys of the side grounds, there to walk, if you be disposed, in the heat of the year or day; but to make account that the main garden is for the more temperate parts of the year; and in the heat of summer, for the morning and the evening, or overcast days.

For aviaries, I like them not, except they be of that largeness as they may be turfed, and have living plants and bushes set in them; that the birds may have more scope, and natural nestling, and that no foulness appear in the floor of the aviary. So I have made a platform of a princely garden, partly by precept, partly by drawing, not a model, but some general lines of it; and in this I have spared for no cost. But it is nothing for great princes, that for the most part taking advice with workmen, with no less cost set their things together; and sometimes add statua's, and such things, for state and magnificence, but nothing to the true pleasure of a garden.

· 47 ·

OF NEGOCIATING

IT is generally better to deal by speech than by letter; and by the mediation of a third than by a man's self. Letters are good, when a man would draw an answer by letter back again; or when it may serve for a man's justification afterwards to produce his own letter; or where it may be danger to be interrupted, or heard by pieces. To deal in person is good, when a man's face breedeth regard, as commonly with inferiors; or in tender cases, where a man's eye upon the countenance of him with whom he speaketh may give him a direction how far to go; and generally, where a man will reserve to himself liberty either to disavow or to expound. In choice of instruments, it is better to choose men of a plainer sort, that are like to do that that is committed to them, and to report back again faithfully the success, than those that are cunning to contrive out of other men's business somewhat to grace themselves, and will help the matter in report for satisfaction sake. Use also such persons as affect the business wherein they are employed; for that quickeneth much; and such as are fit for the matter; as bold men for expostulation, fair-spoken men for persuasion, crafty men for inquiry and observation, froward and absurd men for business that doth not well bear out itself. Use also such as have been lucky, and prevailed before in things wherein you have employed them; for that breeds confidence, and they will strive to maintain their prescription. It is better to sound a person with whom one deals afar off, than to fall upon the point at first; except you mean to surprise him by some short question. It is better dealing with men in appetite, than with those that are where they would be. If a man deal with another upon conditions, the start or first performance is all; which a man cannot reasonably demand, except either the nature of the thing be such, which must go before; or else a man can persuade the other party that he shall still need him in some other thing; or else that he be counted the honester man. All practice is to discover, or to work. Men discover themselves in trust, in passion, at unawares, and of necessity, when they would have somewhat done and cannot find an apt pretext. If you would work any man, you must either know his nature and fashions, and so lead him; or his ends, and so persuade him; or his weakness and disadvantages, and so awe him; or those that have interest in him, and so govern him. In dealing with cunning persons, we must ever consider their ends, to interpret their speeches; and it is good to say little to them, and that which they least look for. In all negociations of difficulty, a man may not look to sow and reap at once; but must prepare business, and so ripen it by degrees.

· 48 ·

OF FOLLOWERS AND FRIENDS

COSTLY followers are not to be liked; lest while a man maketh his train longer, he make his wings shorter. I reckon to be costly, not them alone which charge the purse, but which are wearisome and importune in suits. Ordinary followers ought to challenge no higher conditions than countenance, recommendation, and protection from wrongs. Factious followers are worse to be liked, which follow not upon affection to him with whom they range themselves, but upon discontentment conceived against some other; whereupon commonly ensueth that ill intelligence that we many times see between great personages. Likewise glorious followers, who make themselves as trumpets of the commendation of those they follow, are full of inconvenience; for they taint business through want of secrecy; and they export honour from a man, and make him a return in envy. There is a kind of followers likewise which are dangerous, being indeed espials; which inquire the secrets of the house, and bear tales of them to others. Yet such men, many times, are in great favour; for they are officious, and commonly exchange tales. The following by certain estates of men, answerable to that which a great person himself professeth, (as of soldiers to him that hath been employed in the wars, and the like,) hath ever been a thing civil, and well taken even in monarchies; so it be without too much pomp or popularity. But the most honourable kind of following is to be followed as one that apprehendeth to advance virtue and desert in all sorts of persons. And yet, where there is no eminent odds in sufficiency, it is better to take with the more passable, than with the more able. And besides, to speak truth, in base times active men are of more use than virtuous. It is true that in government it is good to use men of one rank equally: for to countenance some extraordinarily, is to make them insolent, and the rest discontent; because they may claim a due. But contrariwise, in favour, to use men with much difference and election is good; for it maketh the persons preferred more thankful, and the rest more officious: because all is of favour. It is good discretion not to make too much of any man at the first; because one cannot hold out that proportion. To be governed (as we call it) by one, is not safe; for it shews softness, and gives a freedom to scandal and disreputation; for those that would not censure or speak ill of a man immediately, will talk more boldly of those that are so great with them, and thereby wound their honour. Yet to be distracted with many is worse; for it makes men to be of the last impression, and full of change. To take advice of some few friends is ever honourable; *for lookers-on many times see more than gamesters; and the vale best discovereth the hill.* There is little friendship in the world, and least of all between equals, which was wont to be magnified. That that is, is between superior and inferior, whose fortunes may comprehend the one the other.

OF SUITORS

MANY ill matters and projects are undertaken; and private suits do putrefy the public good. Many good matters are undertaken with bad minds; I mean not only corrupt minds, but crafty minds, that intend not performance. Some embrace suits, which never mean to deal effectually in them; but if they see there may be life in the matter by some other mean, they will be content to win a thank, or take a second reward, or at least to make use in the mean time of the suitor's hopes. Some take hold of suits only for an occasion to cross some other; or to make an information whereof they could not otherwise have apt pretext; without care what become of the suit when that turn is served; or, generally, to make other men's business a kind of entertainment to bring in their own. Nay some undertake suits, with a full purpose to let them fall; to the end to gratify the adverse party or competitor. Surely there is in some sort a right in every suit; either a right in equity, if it be a suit of controversy; or a right of desert, if it be a suit of petition. If affection lead a man to favour the wrong side in justice, let him rather use his countenance to compound the matter than to carry it. If affection lead a man to favour the less worthy in desert, let him do it without depraving or disabling the better deserver. In suits which a man doth not well understand, it is good to refer them to some friend of trust and judgment, that may report whether he may deal in them with honour: but let him choose well his referendaries, for else he may be led by the nose. Suitors are so distasted with delays and abuses, that plain dealing in denying to deal in suits at first, and reporting the success barely, and in challenging no more thanks than one hath deserved, is grown not only honourable but also gracious. In suits of favour, the first coming ought to take little place: so far forth consideration may be had of his trust, that if intelligence of the matter could not otherwise have been had but by him, advantage be not taken of the note, but the party left to his other means; and in some sort recompensed for his discovery. To be ignorant of the value of a suit is simplicity; as well as to be ignorant of the right thereof is want of conscience. Secrecy in suits is a great mean of obtaining; for voicing them to be in forwardness may discourage some kind of suitors, but doth quicken and awake others. But timing of the suit is the principal. Timing, I say, not only in respect of the person that should grant it, but in respect of those which are like to cross it. Let a man, in the choice of his mean, rather choose the fittest mean than the greatest mean; and rather them that deal in certain things, than those that are general. The reparation of a denial is sometimes equal to the first grant; if a man shew himself neither dejected nor discontented. *Iniquum petas ut æquum feras,* [Ask more than is reasonable, that you may get no less,] is a good rule, where a man hath strength of favour: but otherwise a man were better rise in his suit; for he that would have ventured at first to have lost the suitor, will not in the conclusion lose both the suitor and his own former favour. Nothing is thought so easy a request to a great person, as his letter; and yet, if it be not in a good cause, it is so much out of his reputation. There are no worse instruments than these general contrivers of suits; for they are but a kind of poison and infection to public proceedings.

· 50 ·

OF STUDIES

STUDIES serve for delight, for ornament, and for ability. Their chief use for delight, is in privateness and retiring; for ornament, is in discourse; and for ability, is in the judgment and disposition of business. For expert men can execute, and perhaps judge of particulars, one by one; but the general counsels, and the plots and marshalling of affairs, come best from those that are learned. To spend too much time in studies is sloth; to use them too much for ornament, is affectation; to make judgment wholly by their rules, is the humour of a scholar. They perfect nature, and are perfected by experience: for natural abilities are like natural plants, that need proyning by study; and studies themselves do give forth directions too much at large, except they be bounded in by experience. Crafty men contemn studies, simple men admire them, and wise men use them; for they teach not their own use; but that is a wisdom without them, and above them, won by observation. Read not to contradict and confute; nor to believe and take for granted; nor to find talk and discourse; but to weigh and consider. Some books are to be tasted, others to be swallowed, and some few to be chewed and digested; that is, some books are to be read only in parts; others to be read, but not curiously; and some few to be read wholly, and with diligence and attention. Some books also may be read by deputy, and extracts made of them by others; but that would be only in the less important arguments, and the meaner sort of books; else distilled books are like common distilled waters, flashy things. Reading maketh a full man; conference a ready man; and writing an exact man. And therefore, if a man write little, he had need have a great memory; if he confer little, he had need have a present wit: and if he read little, he had need have much cunning, to seem to know that he doth not. Histories make men wise; poets witty; the mathematics subtile; natural philosophy deep; moral grave; logic and rhetoric able to contend. *Abeunt studia in mores.* [The studies pass into the manners.] Nay there is no stond or impediment in the wit, but may be wrought out by fit studies: like as diseases of the body may have appropriate exercises. Bowling is good for the stone and reins; shooting for the lungs and breast; gentle walking for the stomach; riding for the head; and the like. So if a man's wit be wandering, let him study the mathematics; for in demonstrations, if his wit be called away never so little, he must begin again. If his wit be not apt to distinguish or find differences, let him study the schoolmen; for they are *cymini sectores,* [splitters of hairs.] If he be not apt to beat over matters, and to call up one thing to prove and illustrate another, let him study the lawyers' cases. So every defect of the mind may have a special receipt.

· 51 ·

OF FACTION

MANY have an opinion not wise, that for a prince to govern his estate, or for a great person to govern his proceedings, according to the respect of factions, is a principal part of policy; whereas contrariwise, the chiefest wisdom is either in ordering those things which are general, and wherein men of several factions do nevertheless agree; or in dealing with correspondence to particular persons, one by one. But I say not that the consideration of factions is to be neglected. Mean men, in their rising, must adhere; but great men, that have strength in themselves, were better to maintain themselves indifferent and neutral. Yet even in beginners, to adhere so moderately, as he be a man of the one faction which is most passable with the other, commonly giveth best way. The lower and weaker faction is the firmer in conjunction; and it is often seen that a few that are stiff do tire out a greater number that are more moderate. When one of the factions is extinguished, the remaining subdivideth; as the faction between Lucullus and the rest of the nobles of the senate (which they called *Optimates*) held out awhile against the faction of Pompey and Cæsar; but when the senate's authority was pulled down, Cæsar and Pompey soon after brake. The faction or party of Antonius and Octavianus Cæsar against Brutus and Cassius, held out likewise for a time; but when Brutus and Cassius were overthrown, then soon after Antonius and Octavianus brake and subdivided. These examples are of wars, but the same holdeth in private factions. And therefore those that are seconds in factions do many times, when the faction subdivideth, prove principals; but many times also they prove cyphers and cashiered; for many a man's strength is in opposition; and when that faileth he groweth out of use. It is commonly seen that men once placed take in with the contrary faction to that by which they enter: thinking belike that they have the first sure, and now are ready for a new purchase. The traitor in faction lightly goeth away with it; for when matters have stuck long in balancing, the winning of some one man casteth them, and he getteth all the thanks. The even carriage between two factions proceedeth not always of moderation, but of a trueness to a man's self, with end to make use of both. Certainly in Italy they hold it a little suspect in popes, when they have often in their mouth *Padre commune* [the Common Father]: and take it to be a sign of one that meaneth to refer all to the greatness of his own house. Kings had need beware how they side themselves, and make themselves as of a faction or party; for leagues within the state are ever pernicious to monarchies: for they raise an obligation paramount to obligation of sovereignty, and make the king *tanquam unus ex nobis* [like one of themselves]; as was to be seen in the League of France. When factions are carried too high and too violently, it is a sign of weakness in princes; and much to the prejudice both of their authority and business. The motions of factions under kings ought to be like the motions (as the astronomers speak) of the inferior orbs, which may have their proper motions, but yet still are quietly carried by the higher motion of *primum mobile*.

· 52 ·

OF CEREMONIES AND RESPECTS

HE that is only real, had need have exceeding great parts of virtue; as the stone had need to be rich that is set without foil. But if a man mark it well, it is in praise and commendation of men as it is in gettings and gains: for the proverb is true, *That light gains make heavy purses;* for light gains come thick, whereas great come but now and then. So it is true that small matters win great commendation, because they are continually in use and in note: whereas the occasion of any great virtue cometh but on festivals. Therefore it doth much add to a man's reputation, and is (as queen Isabella said) *like perpetual letters commendatory*, to have good forms. To attain them it almost sufficeth not to despise them; for so shall a man observe them in others; and let him trust himself with the rest. For if he labour too much to express them, he shall lose their grace; which is to be natural and unaffected. Some men's behaviour is like a verse, wherein every syllable is measured; how can a man comprehend great matters, that breaketh his mind too much to small observations? Not to use ceremonies at all, is to teach others not to use them again; and so diminisheth respect to himself; especially they be not to be omitted to strangers and formal natures; but the dwelling upon them, and exalting them above the moon, is not only tedious, but doth diminish the faith and credit of him that speaks. And certainly there is a kind of conveying of effectual and imprinting passages amongst compliments, which is of singular use, if a man can hit upon it. Amongst a man's peers a man shall be sure of familiarity; and therefore it is good a little to keep state. Amongst a man's inferiors one shall be sure of reverence; and therefore it is good a little to be familiar. He that is too much in anything, so that he giveth another occasion of satiety, maketh himself cheap. To apply one's self to others is good; so it be with demonstration that a man doth it upon regard, and not upon facility. It is a good precept generally in seconding another, yet to add somewhat of one's own: as if you will grant his opinion, let it be with some distinction; if you will follow his motion, let it be with condition; if you allow his counsel, let it be with alleging further reason. Men had need beware how they be too perfect in compliments; for be they never so sufficient otherwise, their enviers will be sure to give them that attribute, to the disadvantage of their greater virtues. It is loss also in business to be too full of respects, or to be curious in observing times and opportunities.

Salomon saith, *He that considereth the wind shall not sow, and he that looketh to the clouds shall not reap.* A wise man will make more opportunities than he finds. Men's behaviour should be like their apparel, not too strait or point device, but free for exercise or motion.

• 53 •

OF PRAISE

PRAISE is the reflexion of virtue. But it is as the glass or body which giveth the reflexion. If it be from the common people, it is commonly false and naught; and rather followeth vain persons than virtuous. For the common people understand not many excellent virtues. The lowest virtues draw praise from them; the middle virtues work in them astonishment or admiration; but of the highest virtues they have no sense of perceiving at all. But shews, and *species virtutibus similes* [appearances resembling virtues], serve best with them. Certainly fame is like a river, that beareth up things light and swoln, and drowns things weighty and solid. But if persons of quality and judgment concur, then it is (as the Scripture saith), *Nomen bonum instar unguenti fragrantis;* [a good name like unto a sweet ointment]. It filleth all round about, and will not easily away. For the odours of ointments are more durable than those of flowers. There be so many false points of praise, that a man may justly hold it a suspect. Some praises proceed merely of flattery; and if he be an ordinary flatterer, he will have certain common attributes, which may serve every man; if he be a cunning flatterer, he will follow the arch-flatterer, which is a man's self; and wherein a man thinketh best of himself, therein the flatterer will uphold him most: but if he be an impudent flatterer, look wherein a man is conscious to himself that he is most defective, and is most out of countenance in himself, that will the flatterer entitle him to perforce, *spretâ conscientiâ* [in spite of his conscience]. Some praises come of good wishes and respects, which is a form due in civility to kings and great persons, *laudando præcipere* [to teach by praising]; when by telling men what they are, they represent to them what they should be. Some men are praised maliciously to their hurt, thereby to stir envy and jealousy towards them; *pessimum genus inimicorum laudantium;* [the worst kind of enemies are they that praise;] insomuch as it was a proverb amongst the Grecians, that *he that was praised to his hurt, should have a push rise upon his nose;* as we say, *that a blister will rise upon one's tongue that tells a lie.* Certainly moderate praise, used with opportunity, and not vulgar, is that which doth the good. Salomon saith, *He that praiseth his friend aloud, rising early, it shall be to him no better than a curse.* Too much magnifying of man or matter doth irritate contradiction, and procure envy and scorn. To praise a man's self cannot be decent, except it be in rare cases; but to praise a man's office or profession, he may do it with good grace, and with a kind of magnanimity. The Cardinals of Rome, which are theologues, and friars, and schoolmen, have a phrase of notable contempt and scorn towards civil business: for they call all temporal business of wars, embassages, judicature, and other employments, *sbirrerie*, which is *under-sheriffries;* as if they were but matters for under-sheriffs and catch-poles: though many times those under-sheriffries do more good than their high speculations. St. Paul, when he boasts of himself, he doth oft interlace, *I speak like a fool;* but speaking of his calling, he saith, *magnificabo apostolatum meum* [I will magnify my mission].

• 54 •

OF VAIN-GLORY

IT was prettily devised of Æsop; *the fly sat upon the axle-tree of the chariot wheel, and said, What a dust do I raise!* So are there some vain persons, that whatsoever goeth alone or moveth upon greater means, if they have never so little hand in it, they think it is they that carry it. They that are glorious must needs be factious; for all bravery stands upon comparisons. They must needs be violent, to make good their own vaunts. Neither can they be secret, and therefore not effectual; but according to the French proverb, *Beaucoup de bruit, peu de fruit; Much bruit, little fruit.* Yet certainly there is use of this quality in civil affairs. Where there is an opinion and fame to be created either of virtue or greatness, these men are good trumpeters. Again, as Titus Livius noteth in the case of Antiochus and the Ætolians, *There are sometimes great effects of cross lies,* as if a man that negociates between two princes, to draw them to join in a war against the third, doth extol the forces of either of them above meassure, the one to the other: and sometimes he that deals between man and man, raiseth his own credit with both, by pretending greater interest than he hath in either. And in these and the like kinds, it often falls out that somewhat is produced of nothing; for lies are sufficient to breed opinion, and opinion brings on substance. In militar commanders and soldiers, vain-glory is an essential point; for as iron sharpens iron, so by glory one courage sharpeneth another. In cases of great enterprise upon charge and adventure, a composition of glorious natures doth put life into business; and those that are of solid and sober natures have more of the ballast than of the sail. In fame of learning, the flight will be slow without some feathers of ostentation. *Qui de contemnendâ gloriâ libros scribunt, nomen suum inscribunt.* [They that write books on the worthlessness of glory, take care to put their names on the title page.] Socrates, Aristotle, Galen, were men full of ostentation. Certainly vain-glory helpeth to perpetuate a man's memory; and virtue was never so beholding to human nature, as it received his due at the second hand. Neither had the fame of Cicero, Seneca, Plinius Secundus, borne her age so well, if it had not been joined with some vanity in themselves; like unto varnish, that makes ceilings not only shine but last. But all this while, when I speak of vain-glory, I mean not of that property that Tacitus doth attribute to Mucianus; *Omnium, quæ dixerat feceratque, arte quâdam ostentator:* [A man that had a kind of art of setting forth to advantage all that he had said or done:] for that proceeds not of vanity, but of natural magnanimity and discretion; and in some persons is not only comely, but gracious. For excusations, cessions, modesty itself well governed, are but arts, of ostentation. And amongst those arts there is none better than that which Plinius Secundus speaketh of, which is to be liberal of praise and commendation to others, in that wherein a man's self hath any perfection. For saith Pliny very wittily, *In commending another you do yourself right; for he that you commend is either superior to you in that you commend, or inferior. If he be inferior, if he be to be commended, you much more; if he be superior, if he be not to be commended, you much less.* Glorious men are the scorn of wise men, the admiration of fools, the idols of parasites, and the slaves of their own vaunts.

· 55 ·

OF HONOUR AND REPUTATION

THE winning of Honour is but the revealing of a man's virtue and worth without disadvantage. For some in their actions do woo and affect honour and reputation; which sort of men are commonly much talked of, but inwardly little admired. And some, contrariwise, darken their virtue in the shew of it; so as they be undervalued in opinion. If a man perform that which hath not been attempted before; or attempted and given over; or hath been achieved, but not with so good circumstance; he shall purchase more honour, than by effecting a matter of greater difficulty or virtue, wherein he is but a follower. If a man so temper his actions, as in some one of them he doth content every faction or combination of people, the music will be the fuller. A man is an ill husband of his honour, that entereth into any action, the failing wherein may disgrace him more than the carrying of it through can honour him. Honour that is gained and broken upon another hath the quickest reflexion, like diamonds cut with fascets. And therefore let a man contend to excel any competitors of his in honour, in outshooting them, if he can, in their own bow. Discreet followers and servants help much to reputation. *Omnis fama a domesticis emanat* [All fame comes from servants]. Envy, which is the canker of honour, is best extinguished by declaring a man's self in his ends rather to seek merit than fame; and by attributing a man's successes rather to divine Providence and felicity, than to his own virtue or policy. The true marshalling of the degrees of sovereign honour are these. In the first place are *conditores imperiorum,* founders of states and commonwealths; such as were Romulus, Cyrus, Cæsar, Ottoman, Ismael. In the second place are *legislatores,* lawgivers; which are also called *second founders,* or *perpetui principes,* because they govern by their ordinances after they are gone; such were Lycurgus, Solon, Justinian, Eadgar, Alphonsus of Castile, the wise, that made the *Siete partidas.* In the third place are *liberatores,* or *salvatores,* such as compound the long miseries of civil wars, or deliver their countries from servitude of strangers or tyrants; as Augustus Cæsar, Vespasianus, Aurelianus, Theodoricus, King Henry the Seventh of England, King Henry the Fourth of France. In the fourth place are *propagatores* or *propugnatores imperii* [extenders or defenders of empire]; such as in honourable wars enlarge their territories, or make noble defence against invaders. And in the last place are *patres patriæ,* [fathers of their country;] which reign justly, and make the times good wherein they live. Both which last kinds need no examples, they are in such number. Degrees of honour in subjects are, first *participes curarum* [sharers of cares], those upon whom princes do discharge the greatest weight of their affairs; their *right hands,* as we call them. The next are *duces belli,* great leaders; such as are princes' lieutenants, and do them notable services in the wars. The third are *gratiosi,* favourites; such as exceed not this scantling, to be solace to the sovereign, and harmless to the people. And the fourth, *negotiis pares* [those equal to the business]; such as have great places under princes, and execute their places with sufficiency. There is an honour, likewise, which may be ranked amongst the greatest, which happeneth rarely; that is, of such as sacrifice themselves to death or danger for the good of their country; as was M. Regulus, and the two Decii.

· 56 ·

OF JUDICATURE

JUDGES ought to remember that their office is *jus dicere*, and not *jus dare*; to interpret law, and not to make law, or give law. Else will it be like the authority claimed by the church of Rome, which under pretext of exposition of Scripture doth not stick to add and alter; and to pronounce that which they do not find; and by shew of antiquity to introduce novelty. Judges ought to be more learned than witty, more reverend than plausible, and more advised than confident. Above all things, integrity is their portion and proper virtue. *Cursed* (saith the law) *is he that removeth the landmark.* The mislayer of a mere-stone is to blame. But it is the unjust judge that is the capital remover of landmarks, when he defineth amiss of lands and property. One foul sentence doth more hurt than many foul examples. For these do but corrupt the stream, the other corrupteth the fountain. So saith Salomon, *Fons turbatus, et vena corrupta, est justus cadens in causâ suâ coram adversario* [A righteous man falling down before the wicked is as a troubled fountain or a corrupt spring]. The office of judges may have reference unto the parties that sue, unto the advocates that plead, unto the clerks and ministers of justice underneath them, and to the sovereign or state above them.

First, for the causes or parties that sue. *There be* (saith the Scripture) *that turn judgment into wormwood;* and surely there be also that turn it into vinegar; for injustice maketh it bitter, and delays make it sour. The principal duty of a judge is to suppress force and fraud; whereof force is the more pernicious when it is open, and fraud

when it is close and disguised. Add thereto contentious
suits, which ought to be spewed out, as the surfeit of
courts. A judge ought to prepare his way to a just sentence, as God useth to prepare his way, by raising valleys
and taking down hills: so when there appeareth on either
side an high hand, violent prosecution, cunning advantages taken, combination, power, great counsel, then is the
virtue of a judge seen, to make inequality equal; that he
may plant his judgment as upon an even ground. *Qui
fortiter emungit, elicit sanguinem;* [Violent blowing makes
the nose bleed;] and where the wine-press is hard
wrought, it yields a harsh wine, that tastes of the grape-
stone. Judges must beware of hard constructions and
strained inferences; for there is no worse torture than the
torture of laws. Specially in case of laws penal, they
ought to have care that that which was meant for terror
be not turned into rigour; and that they bring not upon
the people that shower whereof the Scripture speaketh,
Pluet super eos laqueos [He shall rain snares upon
them]; for penal laws pressed are a *shower of snares* upon
the people. Therefore let penal laws, if they have been
sleepers of long, or if they be grown unfit for the present
time, be by wise judges confined in the execution: *Judicis
officium est, ut res, ita tempora rerum, &c.* [A judge must
have regard to the time as well as to the matter.] In
causes of life and death, judges ought (as far as the law
permitteth) in justice to remember mercy; and to cast a
severe eye upon the example, but a merciful eye upon
the person.

Secondly, for the advocates and counsel that plead. Patience and gravity of hearing is an essential part of
justice; and an overspeaking judge is no well-tuned
cymbal. It is no grace to a judge first to find that which he
might have heard in due time from the bar; or to show
quickness of conceit in cutting off evidence or counsel
too short; or to prevent information by questions, though
pertinent. The parts of a judge in hearing are four: to
direct the evidence; to moderate length, repetition, or im-
pertinency of speech; to recapitulate, select, and collate
the material points of that which hath been said; and

to give the rule or sentence. Whatsoever is above these is too much; and proceedeth either of glory and willingness to speak, or of impatience to hear, or of shortness of memory, or of want of a staid and equal attention. It is a strange thing to see that the boldness of advocates should prevail with judges; whereas they should imitate God, in whose seat they sit; who *represseth the presumptuous, and giveth grace to the modest*. But it is more strange, that judges should have noted favourites; which cannot but cause multiplication of fees, and suspicion of bye-ways. There is due from the judge to the advocate some commendation and gracing, where causes are well handled and fair pleaded; especially towards the side which obtaineth not; for that upholds in the client the reputation of his counsel, and beats down in him the conceit of his cause. There is likewise due to the public a civil reprehension of advocates, where there appeareth cunning counsel, gross neglect, slight information, indiscreet pressing, or an over-bold defence. And let not the counsel at the bar chop with the judge, nor wind himself into the handling of the cause anew after the judge hath declared his sentence; but on the other side, let not the judge meet the cause half way, nor give occasion for the party to say his counsel or proofs were not heard.

Thirdly, for that that concerns clerks and ministers. The place of justice is an hallowed place; and therefore not only the bench, but the foot-pace and precincts and purprise thereof, ought to be preserved without scandal and corruption. For certainly *Grapes* (as the Scripture saith) *will not be gathered of thorns or thistles;* neither can justice yield her fruit with sweetness amongst the briars and brambles of catching and polling clerks and ministers. The attendance of courts is subject to four bad instruments. First, certain persons that are sowers of suits; which make the court swell, and the country pine. The second sort is of those that engage courts in quarrels of jurisdiction, and are not truely *amici curiæ* [friends of the court] but *parasiti curiæ* [parasites of the court], in puffing a court up beyond her bounds, for their own scraps and advantage. The third sort is of those that may be accounted the left hands of courts; persons that are full of nimble and sinister tricks and shifts, whereby they pervert the plain and direct courses of courts, and bring justice into oblique lines and labyrinths. And the fourth is the poller and exacter of fees; which justifies the common resemblance of the courts of justice to the bush whereunto while the sheep flies for defence in weather, he is sure to lose part of his fleece. On the other side, an ancient clerk, skilful in precedents, wary in proceeding, and understanding in the business of the court, is an excellent finger of a court; and doth many times point the way to the judge himself.

Fourthly, for that which may concern the sovereign and estate. Judges ought above all to remember the conclusion of the Roman Twelve Tables; *Salus populi suprema lex;* [The supreme law of all is the weal of the people;] and to know that laws, except they be in order to that end, are but things captious, and oracles not well inspired. Therefore it is an happy thing in a state when kings and states do often consult with judges; and again when judges do often consult with the king and state: the one, when there is matter of law intervenient in business of state; the other, when there is some consideration of state intervenient in matter of law. For many times the things deduced to judgment may be *meum* and *tuum*, when the reason and consequence thereof may trench to point of estate: I call matter of estate, not only the parts of sovereignty, but whatsoever introduceth any great alteration or dangerous precedent; or concerneth manifestly any great portion of people. And let no man weakly conceive that just laws and true policy have any antipathy; for they are like the spirits and sinews, that one moves with the other. Let judges also remember, that Salomon's throne was supported by lions on both sides: let them be lions, but yet lions under the throne; being circumspect that they do not check or oppose any points of sovereignty. Let not judges also be so ignorant of their own right, as to think there is not left to them, as a principal part of their office, a wise use and application of laws. For they may remember what the apostle saith of a greater law than theirs; *Nos scimus quia lex bona est, modo quis eâ utatur legitime.* [We know that the law is good, if a man use it lawfully.]

· 57 ·

OF ANGER

To seek to extinguish Anger utterly is but a bravery of the Stoics. We have better oracles: *Be angry, but sin not. Let not the sun go down upon your anger.* Anger must be limited and confined both in race and in time. We will first speak how the natural inclination and habit to be angry may be attempered and calmed. Secondly, how the particular motions of anger may be repressed, or at least refrained from doing mischief. Thirdly, how to raise anger or appease anger in another.

For the first; there is no other way but to meditate and ruminate well upon the effects of anger, how it troubles man's life. And the best time to do this, is to look back upon anger when the fit is throughly over. Seneca saith well, *That anger is like ruin, which breaks itself upon that it falls.* The Scripture exhorteth us *To possess our souls in patience.* Whosoever is out of patience, is out of possession of his soul. Men must not turn bees;

...... animasque in vulnere ponunt:

[that put their lives in the sting.]

Anger is certainly a kind of baseness; as it appears well in the weakness of those subjects in whom it reigns; children, women, old folks, sick folks. Only men must beware that they carry their anger rather with scorn than with fear; so that they may seem rather to be above the injury than below it; which is a thing easily done, if a man will give law to himself in it.

For the second point; the causes and motives of anger are chiefly three. First, to be too sensible of hurt; for no man is angry that feels not himself hurt; and therefore tender and delicate persons must needs be oft angry; they have so many things to trouble them, which more robust natures have little sense of. The next is, the apprehension and construction of the injury offered to be, in the circumstances thereof, full of contempt: for contempt is that which putteth an edge upon anger, as much or more than the hurt itself. And therefore when men are ingenious in picking out circumstances of contempt, they do kindle their anger much. Lastly, opinion of the touch of a man's reputation doth multiply and sharpen anger. Wherein the remedy is, that a man should have, as Consalvo was wont to say, *telam honoris crassiorem*, [an honour of a stouter web.] But in all refrainings of anger, it is the best remedy to win time; and to make a man's self believe, that the opportunity of his revenge is not yet come, but that he foresees a time for it; and so to still himself in the mean time, and reserve it.

To contain anger from mischief, though it take hold of a man, there be two things whereof you must have special caution. The one, of extreme bitterness of words, especially if they be aculeate and proper; for *communia maledicta* are nothing so much; and again, that in anger a man reveal no secrets; for that makes him not fit for society. The other, that you do not peremptorily break off, in any business, in a fit of anger; but howsoever you shew bitterness, do not act anything that is not revocable.

For raising and appeasing anger in another; it is done chiefly by choosing of times, when men are frowardest and worst disposed, to incense them. Again, by gathering (as was touched before) all that you can find out to aggravate the contempt. And the two remedies are by the contraries. The former to take good times, when first to relate to a man an angry business; for the first impression is much; and the other is, to sever, as much as may be, the construction of the injury from the point of contempt; imputing it to misunderstanding, fear, passion, or what you will.

OF VICISSITUDE OF THINGS

SALOMON saith, *There is no new thing upon the earth.*
So that as Plato had an imagination, *That all knowledge
was but remembrance;* so Salomon giveth his sentence,
That all novelty is but oblivion. Whereby you may see
that the river of Lethe runneth as well above ground as
below. There is an abstruse astrologer that saith, *if it
were not for two things that are constant, (the one is, that
the fixed stars ever stand at like distance one from another, and never come nearer together, nor go further
asunder; the other, that the diurnal motion perpetually
keepeth time,) no individual would last one moment.*
Certain it is, that the matter is in a perpetual flux, and
never at a stay. The great winding-sheets, that bury all
things in oblivion, are two; deluges and earthquakes. As
for conflagrations and great droughts, they do not merely
dispeople and destroy. Phaëton's car went but a day.
And the three years' drought in the time of Elias was
but particular, and left people alive. As for the great
burnings by lightnings, which are often in the West
Indies, they are but narrow. But in the other two destruc-
tions, by deluge and earthquake, it is further to be noted,
that the remnant of people which hap to be reserved, are
commonly ignorant and mountainous people, that can
give no account of the time past; so that the oblivion is
all one as if none had been left. If you consider well of
the people of the West Indies, it is very probable that
they are a newer or a younger people than the people
of the old world. And it is much more likely that the
destruction that hath heretofore been there, was not by
earthquakes (as the Ægyptian priest told Solon concerning the island of Atlantis, *that it was swallowed by
an earthquake*), but rather that it was desolated by a
particular deluge. For earthquakes are seldom in those
parts. But on the other side, they have such pouring

rivers, as the rivers of Asia and Africk and Europe are but brooks to them. Their Andes likewise, or mountains, are far higher than those with us; whereby it seems that the remnants of generation of men were in such a particular deluge saved. As for the observation that Machiavel hath, that the jealousy of sects doth much extinguish the memory of things; traducing Gregory the Great, that he did what in him lay to extinguish all heathen antiquities; I do not find that those zeals do any great effects, nor last long; as it appeared in the succession of Sabinian, who did revive the former antiquities.

The vicissitude or mutations in the Superior Globe are no fit matter for this present argument. It may be, Plato's great year, if the world should last so long, would have some effect; not in renewing the state of like individuals, (for that is the fume of those that conceive the celestial bodies have more accurate influences upon these things below than indeed they have,) but in gross. Comets, out of question, have likewise power and effect over the gross and mass of things; but they are rather gazed upon, and waited upon in their journey, than wisely observed in their effects; specially in their respective effects; that is, what kind of comet, for magnitude, colour, version of the beams, placing in the region of heaven, or lasting, produceth what kind of effects.

There is a toy which I have heard, and I would not have it given over, but waited upon a little. They say it is observed in the Low Countries (I know not in what part) that every five and thirty years the same kind and suit of years and weathers comes about again; as great frosts, great wet, great droughts, warm winters, summers with little heat, and the like; and they call it the *Prime*. It is a thing I do the rather mention, because, computing backwards, I have found some concurrence.

But to leave these points of nature, and to come to men. The greatest vicissitude of things amongst men, is the vicissitude of sects and religions. For those orbs rule in men's minds most. The true religion is *built upon the rock*; the rest are tossed upon the waves of time. To speak therefore of the causes of new sects; and to give some counsel concerning them, as far as the weakness of human judgment can give stay to so great revolutions.

When the religion formerly received is rent by discords; and when the holiness of the professors of religion is decayed and full of scandal; and withal the times be stupid, ignorant, and barbarous; you may doubt the springing up of a new sect; if then also there should arise any extravagant and strange spirit to make himself author thereof. All which points held when Mahomet published his law. If a new sect have not two properties, fear it not; for it will not spread. The one is, the supplanting or the opposing of authority established; for nothing is more popular than that. The other is, the giving licence to pleasures and a voluptuous life. For as for speculative heresies, (such as were in ancient times the Arians, and now the Arminians,) though they work mightily upon men's wits, yet they do not produce any great alterations in states; except it be by the help of civil occasions. There be three manner of plantations of new sects. By the power of signs and miracles; by the eloquence and wisdom of speech and persuasion; and by the sword. For martyrdoms, I reckon them amongst miracles; because they seem to exceed the strength of human nature: and I may do the like of superlative and admirable holiness of life. Surely there is no better way to stop the rising of new sects and schisms, than to reform abuses; to compound the smaller differences; to proceed mildly, and not with sanguinary persecutions; and rather to take off the principal authors by winning and advancing them, than to enrage them by violence and bitterness.

The changes and vicissitude in wars are many; but chiefly in three things; in the seats or stages of the war; in the weapons; and in the manner of the conduct. Wars, in ancient time, seemed more to move from east to west; for the Persians, Assyrians, Arabians, Tartars, (which were the invaders,) were all eastern people. It is true, the Gauls were western; but we read but of two incursions of theirs: the one to Gallo-Græcia, the other to Rome. But East and West have no certain points of heaven; and no more have the wars, either from the east or west, any certainty of observation. But North and South are fixed; and it hath seldom or never been seen that the far southern people have invaded the northern, but contrariwise. Whereby it is manifest that the northern tract of the world is in nature the more martial region: be it in respect of the stars of that hemisphere; or of the great continents that are upon the north, whereas the south part, for aught that is known, is almost all sea; or (which is most apparent) of the cold of the northern parts, which is that which, without aid of discipline, doth make the bodies hardest, and the courages warmest.

Upon the breaking and shivering of a great state and empire, you may be sure to have wars. For great empires, while they stand, do enervate and destroy the forces of the natives which they have subdued, resting upon their own protecting forces; and then when they fail also, all goes to ruin, and they become a prey. So was it in the decay of the Roman empire; and likewise in the empire of Almaigne, after Charles the Great, every bird taking a feather; and were not unlike to befal to Spain, if it should break. The great accessions and unions of kingdoms do likewise stir up wars: for when a state grows to an overpower, it is like a great flood, that will be sure to overflow. As it hath been seen in the states of Rome, Turkey, Spain, and others. Look when the world hath fewest barbarous peoples, but such as commonly will not marry or generate, except they know means to live, (as it is almost every where at this day, except Tartary,) there is no danger of inundations of people: but when there be great shoals of people, which go on to populate, without foreseeing means of life and sustentation, it is of necessity that once in an age or two they discharge a portion of their people upon other nations; which the ancient northern people were wont to do by lot; casting lots what part should stay at home, and what should seek their fortunes. When a war-like state grows soft and effeminate, they may be sure of a war. For commonly such states are grown rich in the time of their degenerating; and so the prey inviteth, and their decay in valour encourageth a war.

As for the weapons, it hardly falleth under rule and observation: yet we see even they have returns and vicissitudes. For certain it is, that ordnance was known in the city of the Oxidrakes in India; and was that which the Macedonians called thunder and lightning, and magic. And it is well known that the use of ordnance hath been in China above two thousand years. The conditions of weapons, and their improvement, are, First, the fetching afar off; for that outruns the danger; as it is seen in ordnance and muskets. Secondly, the strength of the percussion; wherein likewise ordnance do exceed all arietations and ancient inventions. The third is, the commodious use of them; as that they may serve in all weathers; that the carriage may be light and manageable; and the like.

For the conduct of the war: at the first, men rested extremely upon number: they did put the wars likewise upon main force and valour; pointing days for pitched fields, and so trying it out upon an even match: and they were more ignorant in ranging and arraying their battles. After they grew to rest upon number rather competent than vast; they grew to advantages of place, cunning diversions, and the like: and they grew more skilful in the ordering of their battles.

In the youth of a state, arms do flourish; in the middle age of a state, learning; and then both of them together for a time; in the declining age of a state, mechanical arts and merchandise. Learning hath his infancy, when it is but beginning and almost childish: then his youth, when it is luxuriant and juvenile: then his strength of years, when it is solid and reduced: and lastly, his old age, when it waxeth dry and exhaust. But it is not good to look too long upon these turning wheels of vicissitude, lest we become giddy. As for the philology of them, that is but a circle of tales, and therefore not fit for this writing.

THE

GREAT INSTAURATION

INSTAURATIO MAGNA

[1620]

PROEMIUM

FRANCIS OF VERULAM

REASONED THUS WITH HIMSELF

AND JUDGED IT TO BE FOR THE INTEREST OF THE PRESENT AND FUTURE GENERATIONS THAT THEY SHOULD BE MADE ACQUAINTED WITH HIS THOUGHTS

BEING convinced that the human intellect makes its own difficulties, not using the true helps which are at man's disposal soberly and judiciously; whence follows manifold ignorance of things, and by reason of that ignorance mischiefs innumerable; he thought all trial should be made, whether that commerce between the mind of man and the nature of things, which is more precious than anything on earth, or at least than anything that is of the earth, might by any means be restored to its perfect and original condition, or if that may not be, yet reduced to a better condition than that in which it now is. Now that the errors which have hitherto prevailed, and which will prevail for ever, should (if the mind be left to go its own way), either by the natural force of the understanding or by help of the aids and instruments of Logic, one by one correct themselves, was a thing not to be hoped for: because the primary notions of things which the mind readily and passively imbibes, stores up, and accumulates (and it is from them that all the rest flow) are false, confused, and overhastily abstracted from the facts; nor are the secondary and subsequent notions less arbitrary and inconstant; whence it follows that the entire fabric of human reason which we employ in the inquisition of nature, is badly put together and built up, and like some magnificent structure without any foundation. For while men are occupied in admiring and applauding the false powers of the mind, they pass by and throw away those true powers, which, if it be supplied with the proper aids and can itself be content to wait upon nature instead of vainly affecting to overrule her, are within its reach. There was but one course left, therefore,—to try the whole thing anew upon a better plan, and to commence a total reconstruction of sciences, arts, and all human knowledge, raised upon the proper foundations. And this, though in the project and undertaking it may seem a thing infinite and beyond the powers of man, yet when it comes to be dealt with it will be found sound and sober, more so than what has been done hitherto. For of this there is some issue; whereas in what is now done in the matter of science there is only a whirling round about, and perpetual agitation, ending where it began. And although he was well aware how solitary an enterprise it is, and how hard a thing to win faith and credit for, nevertheless he was resolved not to abandon either it or himself; nor to be deterred from trying and entering upon that one path, which is alone open to the human mind. For better it is to make a beginning of that which may lead to something, than to engage in a perpetual struggle and pursuit in courses which have no exit. And certainly the two ways of contemplation are much like those two ways of action, so much celebrated, in this— that the one, arduous and difficult in the beginning, leads out at last into the open country; while the other, seeming at first sight easy and free from obstruction, leads to pathless and precipitous places.

Moreover, because he knew not how long it might be before these things would occur to any one else, judging especially from this, that he has found no man hitherto who has applied his mind to the like, he resolved to publish at once so much as he has been able to complete. The cause of which haste was not ambition for himself, but solicitude for the work; that in case of his death there might remain some outline and project of that which he had conceived, and some evidence likewise of his honest mind and inclination towards the benefit of the human race. Certain it is that all other ambition whatsoever seemed poor in his eyes compared with the work which he had in hand; seeing that the matter at issue is either nothing, or a thing so great that it may well be content with its own merit, without seeking other recompence.

EPISTLE DEDICATORY

TO OUR MOST GRACIOUS AND MIGHTY PRINCE AND LORD

JAMES

BY THE GRACE OF GOD
OF GREAT BRITAIN, FRANCE, AND IRELAND KING
DEFENDER OF THE FAITH, ETC.

MOST GRACIOUS AND MIGHTY KING

Your Majesty may perhaps accuse me of larceny, having stolen from your affairs so much time as was required for this work. I know not what to say for myself. For of time there can be no restitution, unless it be that what has been abstracted from your business may perhaps go to the memory of your name and the honour of your age; if these things are indeed worth anything. Certainly they are quite new; totally new in their very kind: and yet they are copied from a very ancient model; even the world itself and the nature of things and of the mind. And to say truth, I am wont for my own part to regard this work as a child of time rather than of wit; the only wonder being that the first notion of the thing, and such great suspicions concerning matters long established, should have come into any man's mind. All the rest follows readily enough. And no doubt there is something of accident (as we call it) and luck as well in what men think as in what they do or say. But for this accident which I speak of, I wish that if there be any good in what I have to offer, it may be ascribed to the infinite mercy and goodness of God, and to the felicity of your Majesty's

153

times; to which as I have been an honest and affectionate servant in my life, so after my death I may yet perhaps, through the kindling of this new light in the darkness of philosophy, be the means of making this age famous to posterity; and surely to the times of the wisest and most learned of kings belongs of right the regeneration and restoration of the sciences. Lastly, I have a request to make—a request no way unworthy of your Majesty, and which especially concerns the work in hand; namely, that you who resemble Solomon in so many things—in the gravity of your judgments, in the peacefulness of your reign, in the largeness of your heart, in the noble variety of the books which you have composed—would further follow his example in taking order for the collecting and perfecting of a Natural and Experimental History, true and severe (unincumbered with literature and book-learning), such as philosophy may be built upon,—such, in fact, as I shall in its proper place describe: that so at length, after the lapse of so many ages, philosophy and the sciences may no longer float in air, but rest on the solid foundation of experience of every kind, and the same well examined and weighed. I have provided the machine, but the stuff must be gathered from the facts of nature. May God Almighty long preserve your Majesty!

Your Majesty's

Most bounden and devoted

Servant,

FRANCIS VERULAM,

CHANCELLOR

PREFACE

That the state of knowledge is not prosperous
nor greatly advancing; and that a way must
be opened for the human understanding
entirely different from any hitherto known,
and other helps provided, in order that the
mind may exercise over the nature of things
the authority which properly belongs to it.

IT seems to me that men do not rightly understand either their store or their strength, but overrate the one and underrate the other. Hence it follows, that either from an extravagant estimate of the value of the arts which they possess, they seek no further; or else from too mean an estimate of their own powers, they spend their strength in small matters and never put it fairly to the trial in those which go to the main. These are as the pillars of fate set in the path of knowledge; for men have neither desire nor hope to encourage them to penetrate further. And since opinion of store is one of the chief causes of want, and satisfaction with the present induces neglect of provision for the future, it becomes a thing not only useful, but absolutely necessary, that the excess of honour and admiration with which our existing stock of inventions is regarded be in the very entrance and threshold of the work, and that frankly and without circumlocution, stripped off, and men be duly warned not to exaggerate or make too much of them. For let a man look carefully into all that variety of books with which the arts and sciences abound, he will find everywhere endless repetitions of the same thing, varying in the method of treatment, but not new in substance, insomuch that the whole stock, numerous as it appears at first view, proves on examination to be but scanty. And for its value and utility it must be plainly avowed that that wisdom which we have derived principally from the Greeks is but like the boyhood of knowledge, and has the characteristic property of boys: it can talk, but it cannot generate; for it is fruitful of controversies but barren of works. So that the state of learning as it now is appears to be represented to the life in the old fable of Scylla, who had the head and face of a virgin, but her womb was hung round with barking monsters, from which she could not be delivered. For in like manner the sciences to which we are accustomed have certain general positions which are specious and flattering; but as soon as they come to particulars, which are as the parts of generation, when they should produce fruit and works, then arise contentions and barking disputations, which are the end of the matter and all the issue they can yield. Observe also, that if sciences of this kind had any life in them, that could never have come to pass which has been the case now for many ages—that they stand almost at a stay, without receiving any augmentations worthy of the human race; insomuch that many times not only what was asserted once is asserted still, but what was a question once is a question still, and instead of being resolved by discussion is only fixed and fed; and all the tradition and succession of schools is still a succession of masters and scholars, not of inventors and those who bring to further perfection the things invented. In the mechanical arts we do not find it so; they, on the contrary, as having in them some breath of life, are continually growing and becoming more perfect. As originally invented they are commonly rude, clumsy, and shapeless; afterwards they acquire new powers and more commodious arrangements and constructions; in so far that men shall sooner leave the study and pursuit of them and turn to something else, than they arrive at the ultimate perfection of which they are capable. Philosophy and the intellectual sciences, on the contrary, stand like statues, worshipped and celebrated, but not moved or advanced. Nay, they sometimes flourish most in the hands of the first author, and afterwards degenerate. For when men have once made over their judgments to others' keeping, and (like those senators whom they called *Pedarii*) have agreed to support some one person's opinion, from that time they make no enlargement of the sciences themselves, but fall to the servile office of embellishing certain individual authors and increasing their retinue. And let it not be said that the sciences have been growing gradually till they have at last reached their full stature, and so (their course being completed) have settled in the works of a few writers; and that there being now no room for the invention of better, all that remains is to embellish and cultivate those things which have been invented already. Would it were so! But the truth is that this appropriating of the sciences has its origin in nothing better than the confidence of a few persons and the sloth and indolence of the rest. For after the sciences had been in several parts perhaps cultivated and handled diligently, there has risen up some man of bold disposition, and famous for methods and short ways which people like, who has in appearance reduced them to an art, while he has in fact only spoiled all that the others had done. And yet this is what posterity like, because it makes the work short and easy, and saves further inquiry, of which they are weary and impatient. And if any one take this general acquiescence and consent for an argument of weight, as being the judgment of Time, let me tell him that the reasoning on which he relies is most fallacious and weak. For, first, we are far from knowing all that in the matter of sciences and arts has in various ages and places been brought to light and published; much less, all that has been by private persons secretly attempted and stirred; so neither the births nor the miscarriages of Time are entered in our records. Nor, secondly, is the consent itself and the time it has continued a consideration of much worth. For however various are the forms of civil polities, there is but one form of polity in the sciences; and that always has been and always will be popular. Now the doctrines which find most favour with the populace are those which are either contentious and pugnacious, or specious and empty; such, I say, as either entangle assent or tickle it.

And therefore no doubt the greatest wits in each successive age have been forced out of their own course; men of capacity and intellect above the vulgar having been fain, for reputation's sake, to bow to the judgment of the time and the multitude; and thus if any contemplations of a higher order took light anywhere, they were presently blown out by the winds of vulgar opinions. So that Time is like a river, which has brought down to us things light and puffed up, while those which are weighty and solid have sunk. Nay, those very authors who have usurped a kind of dictatorship in the sciences and taken upon them to lay down the law with such confidence, yet when from time to time they come to themselves again, they fall to complaints of the subtlety of nature, the hiding-places of truth, the obscurity of things, the entanglement of causes, the weakness of the human mind; wherein nevertheless they show themselves never the more modest, seeing that they will rather lay the blame upon the common condition of men and nature than upon themselves. And then whatever any art fails to attain, they ever set it down upon the authority of that art itself as impossible of attainment; and how can art be found guilty when it is judge in its own cause? So it is but a device for exempting ignorance from ignominy. Now for those things which are delivered and received, this is their condition: barren of works, full of questions; in point of enlargement slow and languid; carrying a show of perfection in the whole, but in the parts ill filled up; in selection popular, and unsatisfactory even to those who propound them; and therefore fenced round and set forth with sundry artifices. And if there be any who have determined to make trial for themselves, and put their own strength to the work of advancing the boundaries of the sciences, yet have they not ventured to cast themselves completely loose from received opinions or to seek their knowledge at the fountain; but they think they have done some great thing if they do but add and introduce into the existing sum of science something of their own; prudently considering with themselves that by making the addition they can assert their liberty, while they retain the credit of modesty by assenting to the rest. But these mediocrities and middle ways so much praised, in deferring to opinions and customs, turn to the great detriment of the sciences. For it is hardly possible at once to admire an author and to go beyond him; knowledge being as water, which will not rise above the level from which it fell. Men of this kind, therefore, amend some things, but advance little; and improve the condition of knowledge, but do not extend its range. Some, indeed, there have been who have gone more boldly to work, and taking it all for an open matter and giving their genius full play, have made a passage for themselves and their own opinions by pulling down and demolishing former ones; and yet all their stir has but little advanced the matter; since their aim has been not to extend philosophy and the arts in substance and value, but only to change doctrines and transfer the kingdom of opinions to themselves; whereby little has indeed been gained, for though the error be the opposite of the other, the causes of erring are the same in both. And if there have been any who, not binding themselves either to other men's opinions or to their own, but loving liberty, have desired to engage others along with themselves in search, these, though honest in intention, have been weak in endeavour. For they have been content to follow probable reasons, and are carried round in a whirl of arguments, and in the promiscuous liberty of search have relaxed the severity of inquiry. There is none who has dwelt upon experience and the facts of nature as long as is necessary. Some there are indeed who have committed themselves to the waves of experience, and almost turned mechanics; yet these again have in their very experiments pursued a kind of wandering inquiry, without any regular system of operations. And besides they have mostly proposed to themselves certain petty tasks, taking it for a great matter to work out some single discovery;—a course of proceeding at once poor in aim and unskilful in design. For no man can rightly and successfully investigate the nature of anything in the thing itself; let him vary his experiments as laboriously as he will, he never comes to a resting-place, but still finds something to seek beyond. And there is another thing to be remembered; namely, that all industry in experimenting has begun with proposing to itself certain definite works to be accomplished, and has pursued them with premature and unseasonable eagerness; it has sought, I say, experiments of Fruit, not experiments of Light; not imitating the divine procedure, which in its first day's work created light only and assigned to it one entire day; on which day it produced no material work, but proceeded to that on the days following. As for those who have given the first place to Logic, supposing that the surest helps to the sciences were to be found in that, they have indeed most truly and excellently perceived that the human intellect left to its own course is not to be trusted; but then the remedy is altogether too weak for the disease; nor is it without evil in itself. For the Logic which is received, though it be very properly applied to civil business and to those arts which rest in discourse and opinion, is not nearly subtle enough to deal with nature; and in offering at what it cannot master, has done more to establish and perpetuate error than to open the way to truth.

Upon the whole therefore, it seems that men have not been happy hitherto either in the trust which they have placed in others or in their own industry with regard to the sciences; especially as neither the demonstrations nor the experiments as yet known are much to be relied upon. But the universe to the eye of the human understanding is framed like a labyrinth; presenting as it does on every side so many ambiguities of way, such deceitful resemblances of objects and signs, natures so irregular in their lines, and so knotted and entangled. And then the way is still to be made by the uncertain light of the sense, sometimes shining out, sometimes clouded over, through the woods of experience and particulars; while those who offer themselves for guides are (as was said) themselves also puzzled, and increase the number of errors and wanderers. In circumstances so difficult neither the natural force of man's judgment nor even any accidental felicity offers any chance of success. No excellence of wit, no repetition of chance experiments, can overcome such difficulties as these. Our steps must be guided by a clue, and the whole way from the very first perception of the senses must be laid out upon a sure plan. Not that I would be understood to mean that nothing whatever has been done in so many ages by so great labours. We have no reason to be ashamed of the discoveries which have been made, and no doubt the ancients proved themselves in everything that turns on wit and abstract meditation, wonderful men. But as in former ages when men sailed only by observation of the stars, they could indeed coast along the shores of the old continent or cross a few small and mediterranean seas; but before the ocean could be traversed and the new world discovered, the use of the mariner's needle, as a more faithful and certain guide, had to be found out; in like manner the discoveries which have been hitherto made in the arts and sciences are such as might be made by practice, meditation, observation, argumentation,—for they lay near to the senses, and immediately beneath common notions; but before we can reach the remoter and more hidden parts of nature, it is necessary that a more perfect use and application of the human mind and intellect be introduced.

For my own part at least, in obedience to the everlasting love of truth, I have committed myself to the uncertainties and difficulties and solitudes of the ways, and relying on the divine assistance have upheld my mind both against the shocks and embattled ranks of opinion, and against my own private and inward hesitations and scruples, and against the fogs and clouds of nature, and the phantoms flitting about on every side; in the hope of providing at last for the present and future generations guidance more faithful and secure. Wherein if I have made any progress, the way has been opened to me by no other means than the true and legitimate humiliation of the human spirit. For all those who before me have applied themselves to the invention of arts have but cast a glance or two upon facts and examples and experience, and straightway proceeded, as if invention were nothing more than an exercise of thought, to invoke their own spirits to give them oracles. I, on the contrary, dwelling purely and constantly among the facts of nature, withdraw my intellect from them no further than may suffice to let the images and rays of natural objects meet in a point, as they do in the sense of vision; whence it follows that the strength and excellency of the wit has but little to do in the matter. And the same humility which I use in inventing I employ likewise in teaching. For I do not endeavour either by triumphs of confutation, or pleadings of antiquity, or assumption of authority, or even by the veil of obscurity, to invest these inventions of mine with any majesty; which might easily be done by one who sought to give lustre to his own name rather than light to other men's minds. I have not sought (I say) nor do I seek either to force or ensnare men's judgments, but I lead them to things themselves and the concordances of things, that they may see for themselves what they have, what they can dispute, what they can add and contribute to the common stock. And for myself, if in anything I have been either too credulous or too little awake and attentive, or if I have fallen off by the way and left the inquiry incomplete, nevertheless I so present these things naked and open, that my errors can be marked and set aside before the mass of knowledge be further infected by them; and it will be easy also for others to continue and carry on my labours. And by these means I suppose that I have established for ever a true and lawful marriage between the empirical and the rational faculty, the unkind and ill-starred divorce and separation of which has thrown into confusion all the affairs of the human family.

Wherefore, seeing that these things do not depend upon myself, at the outset of the work I most humbly and fervently pray to God the Father, God the Son, and God the Holy Ghost, that remembering the sorrows of mankind and the pilgrimage of this our life wherein we wear out days few and evil, they will vouchsafe through my hands to endow the human family with new mercies. This likewise I humbly pray, that things human may not interfere with things divine, and that from the opening

of the ways of sense and the increase of natural light
there may arise in our minds no incredulity or darkness
with regard to the divine mysteries; but rather that the
understanding being thereby purified and purged of
fancies and vanity, and yet not the less subject and entirely submissive to the divine oracles, may give to
faith that which is faith's. Lastly, that knowledge being
now discharged of that venom which the serpent infused
into it, and which makes the mind of man to swell, we
may not be wise above measure and sobriety, but cultivate truth in charity.

And now having said my prayers I turn to men; to
whom I have certain salutary admonitions to offer and
certain fair requests to make. My first admonition (which
was also my prayer) is that men confine the sense within
the limits of duty in respect of things divine: for the
sense is like the sun, which reveals the face of earth, but
seals and shuts up the face of heaven. My next, that in
flying from this evil they fall not into the opposite error,
which they will surely do if they think that the inquisition
of nature is in any part interdicted or forbidden. For it
was not that pure and uncorrupted natural knowledge
whereby Adam gave names to the creatures according
to their propriety, which gave occasion to the fall. It was
the ambitious and proud desire of moral knowledge to
judge of good and evil, to the end that man may revolt
from God and give laws to himself, which was the form
and manner of the temptation. Whereas of the sciences
which regard nature, the divine philosopher declares
that "it is the glory of God to conceal a thing, but it is
the glory of the King to find a thing out." Even as
though the divine nature took pleasure in the innocent
and kindly sport of children playing at hide and seek,
and vouchsafed of his kindness and goodness to admit
the human spirit for his playfellow at that game. Lastly,
I would address one general admonition to all; that they
consider what are the true ends of knowledge, and that
they seek it not either for pleasure of the mind, or for
contention, or for superiority to others, or for profit, or

fame, or power, or any of these inferior things; but for the benefit and use of life; and that they perfect and govern it in charity. For it was from lust of power that the angels fell, from lust of knowledge that man fell; but of charity there can be no excess, neither did angel or man ever come in danger by it.

The requests I have to make are these. Of myself I say nothing; but in behalf of the business which is in hand I entreat men to believe that it is not an opinion to be held, but a work to be done; and to be well assured that I am labouring to lay the foundation, not of any sect or doctrine, but of human utility and power. Next, I ask them to deal fairly by their own interests, and laying aside all emulations and prejudices in favour of this or that opinion, to join in consultation for the common good; and being now freed and guarded by the securities and helps which I offer from the errors and impediments of the way, to come forward themselves and take part in that which remains to be done. Moreover, to be of good hope, nor to imagine that this Instauration of mine is a thing infinite and beyond the power of man, when it is in fact the true end and termination of infinite error; and seeing also that it is by no means forgetful of the conditions of mortality and humanity, (for it does not suppose that the work can be altogether completed within one generation, but provides for its being taken up by another); and finally that it seeks for the sciences not arrogantly in the little cells of human wit, but with reverence in the greater world. But it is the empty things that are vast: things solid are most contracted and lie in little room. And now I have only one favour more to ask (else injustice to me may perhaps imperil the business itself)— that men will consider well how far, upon that which I must needs assert (if I am to be consistent with myself), they are entitled to judge and decide upon these doctrines of mine; inasmuch as all that premature human reasoning which anticipates inquiry, and is abstracted from the facts rashly and sooner than is fit, is by me rejected (so far as the inquisition of nature is concerned), as a thing uncertain, confused, and ill built up; and I cannot be fairly asked to abide by the decision of a tribunal which is itself on its trial.

THE PLAN OF THE WORK

THE WORK IS IN SIX PARTS:

1. *The Divisions of the Sciences*
2. *The New Organon; or Directions concerning the Interpretation of Nature*
3. *The Phenomena of the Universe; or a Natural and Experimental History for the foundation of Philosophy*
4. *The Ladder of the Intellect*
5. *The Forerunners; or Anticipations of the New Philosophy*
6. *The New Philosophy; or Active Science*

THE ARGUMENTS OF THE SEVERAL PARTS

IT being part of my design to set everything forth, as far as may be, plainly and perspicuously (for nakedness of the mind is still, as nakedness of the body once was, the companion of innocence and simplicity), let me first explain the order and plan of the work. I distribute it into six parts.

The first part exhibits a summary or general description of the knowledge which the human race at present possesses. For I thought it good to make some pause upon that which is received; that thereby the old may be more easily made perfect and the new more easily approached. And I hold the improvement of that which we have to be as much an object as the acquisition of more. Besides which it will make me the better listened to; for "He that is ignorant (says the proverb) receives not the words of knowledge, unless thou first tell him that which is in his own heart." We will therefore make a coasting voyage along the shores of the arts and sciences received; not without importing into them some useful things by the way.

In laying out the divisions of the sciences however, I take into account not only things already invented and known, but likewise things omitted which ought to be there. For there are found in the intellectual as in the terrestial globe waste regions as well as cultivated ones. It is no wonder therefore if I am sometimes obliged to depart from the ordinary divisions. For in adding to the total you necessarily alter the parts and sections; and the received divisions of the sciences are fitted only to the received sum of them as it stands now.

With regard to those things which I shall mark as omitted, I intend not merely to set down a simple title or a concise argument of that which is wanted. For as often as I have occasion to report anything as deficient, the nature of which is at all obscure, so that men may not perhaps easily understand what I mean or what the work is which I have in my head, I shall always (provided it be a matter of any worth) take care to subjoin either directions for the execution of such work, or else a portion of the work itself executed by myself as a sample of the whole: thus giving assistance in every case either by work or by counsel. For if it were for the sake of my own reputation only and other men's interests were not concerned in it, I would not have any man think that in such cases merely some light and vague notion has crossed my mind, and that the things which I desire and offer at are no better than wishes; when they are in fact things which men may certainly command if they will, and of which I have formed in my own mind a clear and detailed conception. For I do not propose merely to survey these regions in my mind, like an augur taking auspices, but to enter them like a general who means to take possession.—So much for the first part of the work.

Having thus coasted past the ancient arts, the next point

is to equip the intellect for passing beyond. To the second part therefore belongs the doctrine concerning the better and more perfect use of human reason in the inquisition of things, and the true helps of the understanding: that thereby (as far as the condition of mortality and humanity allows) the intellect may be raised and exalted, and made capable of overcoming the difficulties and obscurities of nature. The art which I introduce with this view (which I call *Interpretation of Nature*) is a kind of logic; though the difference between it and the ordinary logic is great; indeed immense. For the ordinary logic professes to contrive and prepare helps and guards for the understanding, as mine does; and in this one point they agree. But mine differs from it in three points especially; viz. in the end aimed at; in the order of demonstration; and in the starting point of the inquiry.

For the end which this science of mine proposes is the invention not of arguments but of arts; not of things in accordance with principles, but of principles themselves; not of probable reasons, but of designations and directions for works. And as the intention is different, so accordingly is the effect; the effect of the one being to overcome an opponent in argument, of the other to command nature in action.

In accordance with this end is also the nature and order of the demonstrations. For in the ordinary logic almost all the work is spent about the syllogism. Of induction the logicians seem hardly to have taken any serious thought, but they pass it by with a slight notice, and hasten on to the formulæ of disputation. I on the contrary reject demonstration by syllogism, as acting too confusedly, and letting nature slip out of its hands. For although no one can doubt that things which agree in a middle term agree with one another (which is a proposition of mathematical certainty), yet it leaves an opening for deception; which is this. The syllogism consists of propositions; propositions of words; and words are the tokens and signs of notions. Now if the very notions of the mind (which are as the soul of words and the basis of the whole structure) be improperly and overhastily abstracted from facts, vague, not sufficiently definite, faulty in short in many ways, the whole edifice tumbles. I therefore reject the syllogism; and that not only as regards principles (for to principles the logicians themselves do not apply it) but also as regards middle propositions; which, though obtainable no doubt by the syllogism, are, when so obtained, barren of works, remote from practice, and altogether unavailable for the active department of the sciences. Although therefore I leave to the syllogism and these famous and boasted modes of demonstration their jurisdiction over popular arts and such as are matter of opinion (in which department I leave all as it is), yet in dealing with the nature of things I use induction throughout, and that in the minor propositions as well as the major. For I consider induction to be that form of demonstration which upholds the sense, and closes with nature, and comes to the very brink of operation, if it does not actually deal with it.

Hence it follows that the order of demonstration is likewise inverted. For hitherto the proceeding has been to fly at once from the sense and particulars up to the most general propositions, as certain fixed poles for the argument to turn upon, and from these to derive the rest by middle terms: a short way, no doubt, but precipitate; and one which will never lead to nature, though it offers an easy and ready way to disputation. Now my plan is to proceed regularly and gradually from one axiom to another, so that the most general are not reached till the last: but then when you do come to them you find them to be not empty notions, but well defined, and such as nature would really recognise as her first principles, and such as lie at the heart and marrow of things.

But the greatest change I introduce is in the form itself of induction and the judgment made thereby. For the induction of which the logicians speak, which proceeds by simple enumeration, is a puerile thing; concludes at hazard; is always liable to be upset by a contradictory instance; takes into account only what is known and ordinary; and leads to no result.

Now what the sciences stand in need of is a form of induction which shall analyse experience and take it to pieces, and by a due process of exclusion and rejection lead to an inevitable conclusion. And if that ordinary mode of judgment practised by the logicians was so laborious, and found exercise for such great wits, how much more labour must we be prepared to bestow upon this other, which is extracted not merely out of the depths of the mind, but out of the very bowels of nature.

Nor is this all. For I also sink the foundations of the sciences deeper and firmer; and I begin the inquiry nearer the source than men have done heretofore; submitting to examination those things which the common logic takes on trust. For first, the logicians borrow the principles of each science from the science itself; secondly, they hold in reverence the first notions of the mind; and lastly, they receive as conclusive the immediate informations of the sense, when well disposed. Now upon the first point, I hold that true logic ought to enter the several provinces of science armed with a higher authority than belongs to the principles of those sciences themselves, and ought to call those putative principles to account until they are fully established. Then with regard to the first notions of the intellect; there is not one of the impressions taken by the intellect when left to go its own way, but I hold it for suspected, and no way established, until it has submitted to a new trial and a fresh judgment has been thereupon pronounced. And lastly, the information of the sense itself I sift and examine in many ways. For certain it is that the senses deceive; but then at the same time they supply the means of discovering their own errors; only the errors are here, the means of discovery are to seek.

The sense fails in two ways. Sometimes it gives no information, sometimes it gives false information. For first, there are very many things which escape the sense, even when best disposed and no way obstructed; by reason either of the subtlety of the whole body, or the minuteness of the parts, or distance of place, or slowness or else swiftness of motion, or familiarity of the object, or other causes. And again when the sense does apprehend a thing its apprehension is not much to be relied upon. For the testimony and information of the sense has reference always to man, not to the universe; and it is a great error to assert that the sense is the measure of things.

To meet these difficulties, I have sought on all sides diligently and faithfully to provide helps for the sense—substitutes to supply its failures, rectifications to correct its errors; and this I endeavour to accomplish not so much by instruments as by experiments. For the subtlety of experiments is far greater than that of the sense itself, even when assisted by exquisite instruments; such experiments, I mean, as are skilfully and artificially devised for the express purpose of determining the point in question. To the immediate and proper perception of the sense therefore I do not give much weight; but I contrive that the office of the sense shall be only to judge of the experiment, and that the experiment itself shall judge of the thing. And thus I conceive that I perform the office of a true priest of the sense (from which all knowledge in nature must be sought, unless men mean to go mad) and a not unskilful interpreter of its oracles; and that while others only profess to uphold and cultivate the sense, I do so in fact. Such then are the provisions I make for finding the genuine light of nature and kindling and bringing it to bear. And they would be sufficient of themselves, if the human intellect were even, and like a fair sheet of paper with no writing on it. But since the minds of men are strangely possessed and beset, so that there is no true and even surface left to reflect the genuine rays of things, it is necessary to seek a remedy for this also.

Now the idols, or phantoms, by which the mind is occupied are either adventitious or innate. The adventitious come into the mind from without; namely, either from the doctrines and sects of philosophers, or from perverse rules of demonstration. But the innate are inherent in the very nature of the intellect, which is far more prone to error than the sense is. For let men please themselves as they will in admiring and almost adoring the human mind, this is certain: that as an uneven mirror distorts the rays of objects according to its own figure and section, so the mind, when it receives impressions of objects through the sense, cannot be trusted to report them truly, but in forming its notions mixes up its own nature with the nature of things.

And as the first two kinds of idols are hard to eradicate, so idols of this last kind cannot be eradicated at all. All that can be done is to point them out, so that this insidious action of the mind may be marked and reproved (else as fast as old errors are destroyed new ones will spring up out of the ill complexion of the mind itself, and so we shall have but a change of errors, and not a clearance); and to lay it down once for all as a fixed and established maxim, that the intellect is not qualified to judge except by means of induction, and induction in its legitimate form. This doctrine then of the expurgation of the intellect to qualify it for dealing with truth, is comprised in three refutations: the refutation of the Philosophies; the refutation of the Demonstrations; and the refutation of the Natural Human Reason. The explanation of which things, and of the true relation between the nature of things and the nature of the mind, is as the strewing and decoration of the bridal chamber of the Mind and the Universe, the Divine Goodness assisting; out of which marriage let us hope (and be this the prayer of the bridal song) there may spring helps to man, and a line and race of inventions that may in some degree subdue and overcome the necessities and miseries of humanity. This is the second part of the work.

But I design not only to indicate and mark out the ways, but also to enter them. And therefore the third part of the work embraces the Phenomena of the Universe; that is to say, experience of every kind, and such a natural history as may serve for a foundation to build philosophy upon. For a good method of demonstration or form of interpreting nature may keep the mind from going astray or stumbling, but it is not any excellence of method that can supply it with the material of knowledge. Those however who aspire not to guess and divine, but to discover and know; who propose not to devise mimic and fabulous worlds of their own, but to examine and dissect the nature of this very world itself; must go to facts themselves for everything. Nor can the place of this labour and search and worldwide perambulation be supplied by any genius or meditation or argumentation; no, not if all men's wits could meet in one. This therefore we must have, or the business must be for ever abandoned. But up to this day such has been the condition of men in this matter, that it is no wonder if nature will not give herself into their hands.

For first, the information of the sense itself, sometimes failing, sometimes false; observation, careless, irregular, and led by chance; tradition, vain and fed on rumour; practice, slavishly bent upon its work; experiment, blind, stupid, vague, and prematurely broken off; lastly, natural history trivial and poor;—all these have contributed to supply the understanding with very bad materials for philosophy and the sciences.

Then an attempt is made to mend the matter by a preposterous subtlety and winnowing of argument. But this comes too late, the case being already past remedy; and is far from setting the business right or sifting away the errors. The only hope therefore of any greater increase or progress lies in a reconstruction of the sciences.

Of this reconstruction the foundation must be laid in natural history, and that of a new kind and gathered on a new principle. For it is in vain that you polish the mirror if there are no images to be reflected; and it is as necessary that the intellect should be supplied with fit matter to work upon, as with safeguards to guide its working. But my history differs from that in use (as my logic does) in many things,—in end and office, in mass and composition, in subtlety, in selection also and setting forth, with a view to the operations which are to follow.

For first, the object of the natural history which I propose is not so much to delight with variety of matter or to help with present use of experiments, as to give light to the discovery of causes and supply a suckling philosophy with its first food. For though it be true that I am principally in pursuit of works and the active department of the sciences, yet I wait for harvest-time, and do not attempt to mow the moss or to reap the green corn. For I well know that axioms once rightly discovered will carry whole troops of works along with them, and produce them, not here and there one, but in clusters. And that unseasonable and puerile hurry to snatch by way of earnest at the first works which come within reach, I utterly condemn and reject, as an Atalanta's apple that hinders the race. Such then is the office of this natural history of mine.

Next, with regard to the mass and composition of it: I mean it to be a history not only of nature free and at large (when she is left to her own course and does her work her own way),—such as that of the heavenly bodies, meteors, earth and sea, minerals, plants, animals,—but much more of nature under constraint and vexed; that is to say, when by art and the hand of man she is forced out of her natural state, and squeezed and moulded. Therefore I set down at length all experiments of the mechanical arts, of the operative part of the liberal arts, of the many crafts which have not yet grown into arts properly so called, so far as I have been able to examine them and as they conduce to the end in view. Nay (to say the plain truth) I do in fact (low and vulgar as men may think it) count more upon this part both for helps and safeguards than upon the other; seeing that the nature of things betrays itself more readily under the vexations of art than in its natural freedom.

Nor do I confine the history to Bodies; but I have thought it my duty besides to make a separate history of such Virtues as may be considered cardinal in nature. I mean those original passions or desires of matter which constitute the primary elements of nature; such as Dense and Rare, Hot and Cold, Solid and Fluid, Heavy and Light, and several others.

Then again, to speak of subtlety: I seek out and get together a kind of experiments much subtler and simpler than those which occur accidentally. For I drag into light many things which no one who was not proceeding by a regular and certain way to the discovery of causes would have thought of inquiring after; being indeed in themselves of no great use; which shows that they were not sought for on their own account; but having just the same relation to things and works which the letters of the alphabet have to speech and words—which, though in themselves useless, are the elements of which all discourse is made up.

Further, in the selection of the relations and experiments I conceive I have been a more cautious purveyor than those who have hitherto dealt with natural history. For I admit nothing but on the faith of eyes, or at least of careful and severe examination; so that nothing is exaggerated for wonder's sake, but what I state is sound and without mixture of fables or vanity. All received or current falsehoods also (which by strange negligence have been allowed for many ages to prevail and become established) I proscribe and brand by name; that the sciences may be no more troubled with them. For it has been well observed that the fables and superstitions and follies which nurses instil into children do serious injury to their minds; and the same consideration makes me anxious, having the management of the childhood as it were of philosophy in its course of natural history, not to let it accustom itself in the beginning to any vanity. Moreover, whenever I come to a new experiment of any subtlety (though it be in my own opinion certain and approved), I nevertheless subjoin a clear account of the manner in which I made it; that men knowing exactly how each point was made out, may see whether there be any error connected with it, and may arouse themselves to devise proofs more trustworthy and exquisite, if such can be found; and finally, I interpose everywhere admonitions and scruples and cautions, with a religious care to eject, repress, and as it were exorcise every kind of phantasm.

Lastly, knowing how much the sight of man's mind is distracted by experience and history, and how hard it is at the first (especially for minds either tender or preoccupied) to become familiar with nature, I not unfrequently subjoin observations of my own, being as the first offers, inclinations, and as it were glances of history towards philosophy; both by way of an assurance to men that they will not be kept for ever tossing on the waves of experience, and also that when the time comes for the intellect to begin its work, it may find everything the more ready. By such a natural history then as I have described, I conceive that a safe and convenient approach may be made to nature, and matter supplied of good quality and well prepared for the understanding to work upon.

And now that we have surrounded the intellect with faithful helps and guards, and got together with most careful selection a regular army of divine works, it may seem that we have no more to do but to proceed to philosophy itself. And yet in a matter so difficult and doubtful there are still some things which it seems necessary to premise, partly for convenience of explanation, partly for present use.

Of these the first is to set forth examples of inquiry and invention according to my method, exhibited by anticipation in some particular subjects; choosing such subjects as are at once the most noble in themselves among those under inquiry, and most different one from another; that there may be an example in every kind. I do not speak of those examples which are joined to the several precepts and rules by way of illustration (for of these I have given plenty in the second part of the work); but I mean actual types and models, by which the entire process of the mind and the whole fabric and order of invention from the beginning to the end, in certain subjects, and those various and remarkable, should be set as it were before the eyes. For I remember that in the mathematics it is easy to follow the demonstration when you have a machine beside you; whereas without that help all appears involved and more subtle than it really is. To examples of this kind,—being in fact nothing more than an application of the second part in detail and at large,—the fourth part of the work is devoted.

The fifth part is for temporary use only, pending the completion of the rest; like interest payable from time to time until the principal be forthcoming. For I do not make so blindly for the end of my journey, as to neglect anything useful that may turn up by the way. And therefore I include in this fifth part such things as I have myself discovered, proved, or added,—not however according to the true rules and methods of interpretation, but by the ordinary use of the understanding in inquiring and discovering. For besides that I hope my speculations may in virtue of my continual conversancy with nature have a value beyond the pretensions of my wit, they will serve in the meantime for wayside inns, in which the mind may rest and refresh itself on its journey to more certain conclusions. Nevertheless I wish it to be understood in the meantime that they are conclusions by which (as not being discovered and proved by the true form of interpretation) I do not at all mean to bind myself. Nor need any one be alarmed at such suspension of judgment, in one who maintains not simply that nothing can be known, but only that nothing can be known except in a certain course and way; and yet establishes provisionally certain degrees of assurance, for use and relief until the mind shall arrive at a knowledge of causes in which it can rest. For even those schools of philosophy which held the absolute impossibility of knowing anything were not inferior to those which took upon them to pronounce. But then they did not provide helps for the sense and understanding, as I have done, but simply took away all their authority: which is quite a different thing—almost the reverse.

The sixth part of my work (to which the rest is subservient and ministrant) discloses and sets forth that philosophy which by the legitimate, chaste, and severe course of inquiry which I have explained and provided is at length developed and established. The completion however of this last part is a thing both above my strength and beyond my hopes. I have made a beginning of the work— a beginning, as I hope, not unimportant:—the fortune of the human race will give the issue;—such an issue, it may be, as in the present condition of things and men's minds cannot easily be conceived or imagined. For the matter in hand is no mere felicity of speculation, but the real business and fortunes of the human race, and all power of operation. For man is but the servant and interpreter of nature: what he does and what he knows is only what he has observed of nature's order in fact or in thought; beyond this he knows nothing and can do nothing. For the chain of causes cannot by any force be loosed or broken, nor can nature be commanded except by being obeyed. And so those twin objects, human Knowledge and human Power, do really meet in one; and it is from ignorance of causes that operation fails.

And all depends on keeping the eye steadily fixed upon the facts of nature and so receiving their images simply as they are. For God forbid that we should give out a dream of our own imagination for a pattern of the world; rather may he graciously grant to us to write an apocalypse or true vision of the footsteps of the Creator imprinted on his creatures.

Therefore do thou, O Father, who gavest the visible light as the first fruits of creation, and didst breathe into the face of man the intellectual light as the crown and consummation thereof, guard and protect this work, which coming from thy goodness returneth to thy glory. Thou when thou turnedst to look upon the works which thy hands had made, sawest that all was very good, and didst rest from thy labours. But man, when he turned to look upon the work which his hands had made, saw that all was vanity and vexation of spirit, and could find no rest therein. Wherefore if we labour in thy works with the sweat of our brows thou wilt make us partakers of thy vision and thy sabbath. Humbly we pray that this mind may be steadfast in us, and that through these our hands, and the hands of others to whom thou shalt give the same spirit, thou wilt vouchsafe to endow the human family with new mercies.

THE

FIRST PART OF THE INSTAURATION

WHICH COMPRISES THE

DIVISIONS OF THE SCIENCES

IS WANTING

But some account of them will be found in
the Second Book of the

"PROFICIENCE AND ADVANCEMENT OF

LEARNING

DIVINE AND HUMAN"

NEXT COMES

THE

SECOND PART OF THE INSTAURATION

WHICH EXHIBITS

THE ART ITSELF OF INTERPRETING

NATURE

AND OF THE TRUER EXERCISE

OF THE INTELLECT

Not however in the form of a regular Treatise,
but only a Summary digested
into Aphorisms

THE

SECOND PART OF THE WORK

WHICH IS CALLED

THE NEW ORGANON

OR

TRUE DIRECTIONS

CONCERNING

THE INTERPRETATION

OF NATURE

[NOVUM ORGANUM]

[1620]

PREFACE

THOSE who have taken upon them to lay down the law of
nature as a thing already searched out and understood,
whether they have spoken in simple assurance or professional affectation, have therein done philosophy and the
sciences great injury. For as they have been successful in
inducing belief, so they have been effective in quenching

and stopping inquiry; and have done more harm by spoiling and putting an end to other men's efforts than good by their own. Those on the other hand who have taken a contrary course, and asserted that absolutely nothing can be known,—whether it were from hatred of the ancient sophists, or from uncertainty and fluctuation of mind, or even from a kind of fulness of learning, that they fell upon this opinion,—have certainly advanced reasons for it that are not to be despised; but yet they have neither started from true principles nor rested in the just conclusion, zeal and affectation having carried them much too far. The more ancient of the Greeks (whose writings are lost) took up with better judgment a position between these two extremes,—between the presumption of pronouncing on everything, and the despair of comprehending anything; and though frequently and bitterly complaining of the difficulty of inquiry and the obscurity of things, and like impatient horses champing the bit, they did not the less follow up their object and engage with Nature; thinking (it seems) that this very question,—viz. whether or no anything can be known,—was to be settled not by arguing, but by trying. And yet they too, trusting entirely to the force of their understanding, applied no rule, but made everything turn upon hard thinking and perpetual working and exercise of the mind.

Now my method, though hard to practise, is easy to explain; and it is this. I propose to establish progressive stages of certainty. The evidence of the sense, helped and guarded by a certain process of correction, I retain. But the mental operation which follows the act of sense I for the most part reject; and instead of it I open and lay out a new and certain path for the mind to proceed in, starting directly from the simple sensuous perception. The necessity of this was felt no doubt by those who attributed so much importance to Logic; showing thereby that they were in search of helps for the understanding, and had no confidence in the native and spontaneous process of the mind. But this remedy comes too late to do any good, when the mind is already, through the daily intercourse and conversation of life, occupied with unsound doctrines and beset on all sides by vain imaginations. And therefore that art of Logic, coming (as I said) too late to the rescue, and no way able to set matters right again, has had the effect of fixing errors rather than disclosing truth. There remains but one course for the recovery of a sound and healthy condition,—namely, that the entire work of the understanding be commenced afresh, and the mind itself be from the very outset not left to take its own course, but guided at every step; and the business be done as if by machinery. Certainly if in things mechanical men had set to work with their naked hands, without help or force of instruments, just as in things intellectual they have set to work with little else than the naked forces of the understanding, very small would the matters have been which, even with their best efforts applied in conjunction, they could have attempted or accomplished. Now (to pause awhile upon this example and look in it as in a glass) let us suppose that some vast obelisk were (for the decoration of a triumph or some such magnificence) to be removed from its place, and that men should set to work upon it with their naked hands; would not any sober spectator think them mad? And if they should then send for more people, thinking that in that way they might manage it, would he not think them all the madder? And if they then proceeded to make a selection, putting away the weaker hands, and using only the strong and vigorous, would he not think them madder than ever? And if lastly, not content with this, they resolved to call in aid the art of athletics, and required all their men to come with hands, arms, and sinews well anointed and medicated according to the rules of art, would he not cry out that they were only taking pains to show a kind of method and discretion in their madness? Yet just so it is that men proceed in matters intellectual,—with just the same kind of mad effort and useless combination of forces,—when they hope great things either from the number and co-operation or from the excellency and acuteness of individual wits; yea, and when they endeavour by Logic (which may be considered as a kind of athletic art) to strengthen the sinews of the understanding; and yet with all this study and endeavour it is apparent to any true judgment that they are but applying the naked intellect all the time; whereas in every great work to be done by the hand of man it is manifestly impossible, without instruments and machinery, either for the strength of each to be exerted or the strength of all to be united.

Upon these premises two things occur to me of which, that they may not be overlooked, I would have men reminded. First it falls out fortunately as I think for the allaying of contradictions and heart-burnings, that the honour and reverence due to the ancients remains untouched and undiminished; while I may carry out my designs and at the same time reap the fruit of my modesty. For if I profess that I, going the same road as the ancients, have something better to produce, there must needs have been some comparison or rivalry between us (not to be avoided by any art of words) in respect of excellency or ability of wit; and though in this there would be nothing unlawful or new (for if there be anything misapprehended by them, or falsely laid down, why may not I, using a liberty common to all, take exception to it?) yet the contest, however just and allowable, would have been an unequal one perhaps, in respect of the measure of my own powers. As it is however,—my object being to open a new way for the understanding, a way by them untried and unknown,—the case is altered; party zeal and emulation are at an end; and I appear merely as a guide to point out the road; an office of small authority, and depending more upon a kind of luck than upon any ability or excellency. And thus much relates to the persons only. The other point of which I would have men reminded relates to the matter itself.

Be it remembered then that I am far from wishing to interfere with the philosophy which now flourishes, or with any other philosophy more correct and complete than this which has been or may hereafter be propounded. For I do not object to the use of this received philosophy, or others like it, for supplying matter for disputations or ornaments for discourse,—for the professor's lecture and for the business of life. Nay more, I declare openly that for these uses the philosophy which I bring forward will not be much available. It does not lie in the way. It cannot be caught up in passage. It does not flatter the understanding by conformity with preconceived notions. Nor will it come down to the apprehension of the vulgar except by its utility and effects.

Let there be therefore (and may it be for the benefit of both) two streams and two dispensations of knowledge; and in like manner two tribes or kindreds of students in philosophy—tribes not hostile or alien to each other, but bound together by mutual services;—let there in short be one method for the cultivation, another for the invention, of knowledge.

And for those who prefer the former, either from hurry or from considerations of business or for want of mental power to take in and embrace the other (which must needs be most men's case), I wish that they may succeed to their desire in what they are about, and obtain what they are pursuing. But if any man there be who, not content to rest in and use the knowledge which has already been discovered, aspires to penetrate further; to overcome, not an adversary in argument, but nature in action; to seek, not pretty and probable conjectures but certain and demonstrable knowledge;—I invite all such to join themselves, as true sons of knowledge, with me, that passing by the outer courts of nature, which numbers have trodden, we may find a way at length into her inner chambers. And to make my meaning clearer and to familiarise the thing by giving it a name, I have chosen to call one of these methods or ways *Anticipation of the Mind,* the other *Interpretation of Nature.*

Moreover I have one request to make. I have on my own part made it my care and study that the things which I shall propound should not only be true, but should also be presented to men's minds, how strangely soever preoccupied and obstructed, in a manner not harsh or unpleasant. It is but reasonable however (especially in so great a restoration of learning and knowledge) that I should claim of men one favour in return; which is this; If any one would form an opinion or judgment either out of his own observation, or out of the crowd of authorities, or out of the forms of demonstration (which have now acquired a sanction like that of judicial laws), concerning these speculations of mine, let him not hope that he can do it in passage or by the by; but let him examine the thing thoroughly; let him make some little trial for himself of the way which I describe and lay out; let him familiarise his thoughts with that subtlety of nature to which experience bears witness; let him correct by seasonable patience and due delay the depraved and deeprooted habits of his mind; and when all this is done and he has begun to be his own master, let him (if he will) use his own judgment.

[BOOK I]

APHORISMS
CONCERNING
THE INTERPRETATION OF NATURE
AND
THE KINGDOM OF MAN

APHORISM

I

Man, being the servant and interpreter of Nature, can do and understand so much and so much only as he has observed in fact or in thought of the course of nature: beyond this he neither knows anything nor can do anything.

II

Neither the naked hand nor the understanding left to itself can effect much. It is by instruments and helps that the work is done, which are as much wanted for the understanding as for the hand. And as the instruments of the hand either give motion or guide it, so the instruments of the mind supply either suggestions for the understanding or cautions.

III

Human knowledge and human power meet in one; for where the cause is not known the effect cannot be produced. Nature to be commanded must be obeyed; and that which in contemplation is as the cause is in operation as the rule.

IV

Towards the effecting of works, all that man can do is

to put together or put asunder natural bodies. The rest
is done by nature working within.

V

The study of nature with a view to works is engaged in
by the mechanic, the mathematician, the physician, the
alchemist, and the magician; but by all (as things now
are) with slight endeavour and scanty success.

VI

It would be an unsound fancy and self-contradictory to
expect that things which have never yet been done can be
done except by means which have never yet been tried.

VII

The productions of the mind and hand seem very numerous in books and manufactures. But all this variety lies
in an exquisite subtlety and derivations from a few things
already known; not in the number of axioms.

VIII

Moreover the works already known are due to chance
and experiment rather than to sciences; for the sciences
we now possess are merely systems for the nice ordering
and setting forth of things already invented; not methods
of invention or directions for new works.

IX

The cause and root of nearly all evils in the sciences is
this—that while we falsely admire and extol the powers of
the human mind we neglect to seek for its true helps.

X

The subtlety of nature is greater many times over than
the subtlety of the senses and understanding; so that all
those specious meditations, speculations, and glosses in

which men indulge are quite from the purpose, only there is no one by to observe it.

XI

As the sciences which we now have do not help us in finding out new works, so neither does the logic which we now have help us in finding out new sciences.

XII

The logic now in use serves rather to fix and give stability to the errors which have their foundation in commonly received notions than to help the search after truth. So it does more harm than good.

XIII

The syllogism is not applied to the first principles of sciences, and is applied in vain to intermediate axioms; being no match for the subtlety of nature. It commands assent therefore to the proposition, but does not take hold of the thing.

XIV

The syllogism consists of propositions, propositions consist of words, words are symbols of notions. Therefore if the notions themselves (which is the root of the matter) are confused and over-hastily abstracted from the facts, there can be no firmness in the superstructure. Our only hope therefore lies in a true induction.

XV

There is no soundness in our notions whether logical or physical. Substance, Quality, Action, Passion, Essence itself, are not sound notions: much less are Heavy, Light, Dense, Rare, Moist, Dry, Generation, Corruption, Attraction, Repulsion, Element, Matter, Form, and the like; but all are fantastical and ill defined.

XVI

Our notions of less general species, as Man, Dog, Dove, and of the immediate perceptions of the sense, as Hot, Cold, Black, White, do not materially mislead us; yet even these are sometimes confused by the flux and alteration of matter and the mixing of one thing with another. All the others which men have hitherto adopted are but wanderings, not being abstracted and formed from things by proper methods.

XVII

Nor is there less of wilfulness and wandering in the construction of axioms than in the formations of notions; not excepting even those very principles which are obtained by common induction; but much more in the axioms and lower propositions educed by the syllogism.

XVIII

The discoveries which have hitherto been made in the sciences are such as lie close to vulgar notions, scarcely beneath the surface. In order to penetrate into the inner and further recesses of nature, it is necessary that both notions and axioms be derived from things by a more sure and guarded way; and that a method of intellectual operation be introduced altogether better and more certain.

XIX

There are and can be only two ways of searching into and discovering truth. The one flies from the senses and particulars to the most general axioms, and from these principles, the truth of which it takes for settled and immoveable, proceeds to judgment and to the discovery of middle axioms. And this way is now in fashion. The other derives axioms from the senses and particulars, rising by a gradual and unbroken ascent, so that it arrives at the most general axioms last of all. This is the true way, but as yet untried.

XX

The understanding left to itself takes the same course (namely, the former) which it takes in accordance with logical order. For the mind longs to spring up to positions of higher generality, that it may find rest there; and so after a little while wearies of experiment. But this evil is increased by logic, because of the order and solemnity of its disputations.

XXI

The understanding left to itself, in a sober, patient, and grave mind, especially if it be not hindered by received doctrines, tries a little that other way, which is the right one, but with little progress; since the understanding, unless directed and assisted, is a thing unequal, and quite unfit to contend with the obscurity of things.

XXII

Both ways set out from the senses and particulars, and rest in the highest generalities; but the difference between them is infinite. For the one just glances at experiment and particulars in passing, the other dwells duly and orderly among them. The one, again, begins at once by establishing certain abstract and useless generalities, the other rises by gradual steps to that which is prior and better known in the order of nature.

XXIII

There is a great difference between the Idols of the human mind and the Ideas of the divine. That is to say, between certain empty dogmas, and the true signatures and marks set upon the works of creation as they are found in nature.

XXIV

It cannot be that axioms established by argumentation should avail for the discovery of new works; since the subtlety of nature is greater many times over than the subtlety of argument. But axioms duly and orderly formed from particulars easily discover the way to new particulars, and thus render sciences active.

XXV

The axioms now in use, having been suggested by a scanty and manipular experience and a few particulars of most general occurrence, are made for the most part just large enough to fit and take these in: and therefore it is no wonder if they do not lead to new particulars. And if some opposite instance, not observed or not known before, chance to come in the way, the axiom is rescued and preserved by some frivolous distinction; whereas the truer course would be to correct the axiom itself.

XXVI

The conclusions of human reason as ordinarily applied in matter of nature, I call for the sake of distinction *Anticipations of Nature* (as a thing rash or premature). That reason which is elicited from facts by a just and methodical process, I call *Interpretation of Nature*.

XXVII

Anticipations are a ground sufficiently firm for consent; for even if men went mad all after the same fashion, they might agree one with another well enough.

XXVIII

For the winning of assent, indeed, anticipations are far more powerful than interpretations; because being collected from a few instances, and those for the most part of familiar occurrence, they straightway touch the understanding and fill the imagination; whereas interpretations on the other hand, being gathered here and there from very various and widely dispersed facts, cannot suddenly strike the understanding; and therefore they must needs, in respect of the opinions of the time, seem harsh and out of tune; much as the mysteries of faith do.

XXIX

In sciences founded on opinions and dogmas, the use of anticipations and logic is good; for in them the object is to command assent to the proposition, not to master the thing.

XXX

Though all the wits of all the ages should meet together and combine and transmit their labours, yet will no great progress ever be made in science by means of anticipations; because radical errors in the first concoction of the mind are not to be cured by the excellence of functions and remedies subsequent.

XXXI

It is idle to expect any great advancement in science from the superinducing and engrafting of new things upon old. We must begin anew from the very foundations, unless we would revolve for ever in a circle with mean and contemptible progress.

XXXII

The honour of the ancient authors, and indeed of all, remains untouched; since the comparison I challenge is not of wits or faculties, but of ways and methods, and the part I take upon myself is not that of a judge, but of a guide.

XXXIII

This must be plainly avowed: no judgment can be rightly formed either of my method or of the discoveries to which it leads, by means of anticipations (that is to say, of the reasoning which is now in use); since I cannot be called on to abide by the sentence of a tribunal which is itself on its trial.

XXXIV

Even to deliver and explain what I bring forward is no easy matter; for things in themselves new will yet be apprehended with reference to what is old.

XXXV

It was said by Borgia of the expedition of the French into Italy, that they came with chalk in their hands to mark out their lodgings, not with arms to force their way in. I in like manner would have my doctrine enter quietly into the minds that are fit and capable of receiving it; for confutations cannot be employed, when the difference is upon first principles and very notions and even upon forms of demonstration.

XXXVI

One method of delivery alone remains to us; which is simply this: we must lead men to the particulars themselves, and their series and order; while men on their side must force themselves for awhile to lay their notions by and begin to familiarise themselves with facts.

XXXVII

The doctrine of those who have denied that certainty could be attained at all, has some agreement with my way of proceeding at the first setting out; but they end in being infinitely separated and opposed. For the holders of that doctrine assert simply that nothing can be known; I also assert that not much can be known in nature by the way which is now in use. But then they go on to destroy the authority of the senses and understanding; whereas I proceed to devise and supply helps for the same.

XXXVIII

The idols and false notions which are now in possession of the human understanding, and have taken deep root therein, not only so beset men's minds that truth can hardly find entrance, but even after entrance obtained, they will again in the very instauration of the sciences meet and trouble us, unless men being forewarned of the danger fortify themselves as far as may be against their assaults.

XXXIX

There are four classes of Idols which beset men's minds. To these for distinction's sake I have assigned names,— calling the first class *Idols of the Tribe;* the second, *Idols of the Cave;* the third, *Idols of the Market-place;* the fourth, *Idols of the Theatre.*

XL

The formation of ideas and axioms by true induction is no doubt the proper remedy to be applied for the keeping off and clearing away of idols. To point them out, however, is of great use; for the doctrine of Idols is to the Interpretation of Nature what the doctrine of the refutation of Sophisms is to common Logic.

XLI

The Idols of the Tribe have their foundation in human nature itself, and in the tribe or race of men. For it is a false assertion that the sense of man is the measure of things. On the contrary, all perceptions as well of the sense as of the mind are according to the measure of the individual and not according to the measure of the universe. And the human understanding is like a false mirror, which, receiving rays irregularly, distorts and discolours the nature of things by mingling its own nature with it.

XLII

The Idols of the Cave are the idols of the individual man. For every one (besides the errors common to human nature in general) has a cave or den of his own, which refracts and discolours the light of nature; owing either to his own proper and peculiar nature; or to his education and conversation with others; or to the reading of books, and the authority of those whom he esteems and admires; or to the differences of impressions, accordingly as they take place in a mind preoccupied and predisposed or in a mind indifferent and settled; or the like. So that the spirit of man (according as it is meted out to different individuals) is in fact a thing variable and full of perturbation, and governed as it were by chance. Whence it was well observed by Heraclitus that men look for sciences in their own lesser worlds, and not in the greater or common world.

XLIII

There are also Idols formed by the intercourse and association of men with each other, which I call Idols of the Market-place, on account of the commerce and consort of men there. For it is by discourse that men associate; and words are imposed according to the apprehension of the vulgar. And therefore the ill and unfit choice of words wonderfully obstructs the understanding. Nor do the definitions or explanations wherewith in some things learned men are wont to guard and defend themselves, by any means set the matter right. But words plainly force and overrule the understanding, and throw all into confusion, and lead men away into numberless empty controversies and idle fancies.

XLIV

Lastly, there are Idols which have immigrated into men's minds from the various dogmas of philosophies, and also from wrong laws of demonstration. These I call Idols of the Theatre; because in my judgment all the re-

ceived systems are but so many stage-plays, representing
worlds of their own creation after an unreal and scenic
fashion. Nor is it only of the systems now in vogue, or
only of the ancient sects and philosophies, that I speak;
for many more plays of the same kind may yet be composed and in like artificial manner set forth; seeing that
errors the most widely different have nevertheless causes
for the most part alike. Neither again do I mean this only
of entire systems, but also of many principles and axioms
in science, which by tradition, credulity, and negligence
have come to be received.

But of these several kinds of Idols I must speak more
largely and exactly, that the understanding may be duly
cautioned.

XLV

The human understanding is of its own nature prone to
suppose the existence of more order and regularity in the
world than it finds. And though there be many things in
nature which are singular and unmatched, yet it devises
for them parallels and conjugates and relatives which do
not exist. Hence the fiction that all celestial bodies move
in perfect circles; spirals and dragons being (except in
name) utterly rejected. Hence too the element of Fire
with its orb is brought in, to make up the square with the
other three which the sense perceives. Hence also the
ratio of density of the so-called elements is arbitrarily
fixed at ten to one. And so on of other dreams. And these
fancies affect not dogmas only, but simple notions also.

XLVI

The human understanding when it has once adopted
an opinion (either as being the received opinion or as
being agreeable to itself) draws all things else to support and agree with it. And though there be a greater
number and weight of instances to be found on the
other side, yet these it either neglects and despises, or
else by some distinction sets aside and rejects; in order
that by this great and pernicious predetermination the

authority of its former conclusions may remain inviolate. And therefore it was a good answer that was made by one who when they showed him hanging in a temple a picture of those who had paid their vows as having escaped shipwreck, and would have him say whether he did not now acknowledge the power of the gods,—"Aye," asked he again, "but where are they painted that were drowned after their vows?" And such is the way of all superstition, whether in astrology, dreams, omens, divine judgments, or the like; wherein men, having a delight in such vanities, mark the events where they are fulfilled, but where they fail, though this happen much oftener, neglect and pass them by. But with far more subtlety does this mischief insinuate itself into philosophy and the sciences; in which the first conclusion colours and brings into conformity with itself all that come after, though far sounder and better. Besides, independently of that delight and vanity which I have described, it is the peculiar and perpetual error of the human intellect to be more moved and excited by affirmatives than by negatives; whereas it ought properly to hold itself indifferently disposed towards both alike. Indeed in the establishment of any true axiom, the negative instance is the more forcible of the two.

XLVII

The human understanding is moved by those things which strike and enter the mind simultaneously and suddenly, and so fill the imagination; and then it feigns and supposes all other things to be somehow, though it cannot see how, similar to those few things by which it is surrounded. But for that going to and fro to remote and heterogeneous instances, by which axioms are tried as in the fire, the intellect is altogether slow and unfit, unless it be forced thereto by severe laws and overruling authority.

XLVIII

The human understanding is unquiet; it cannot stop or

rest, and still presses onward, but in vain. Therefore it is that we cannot conceive of any end or limit to the world; but always as of necessity it occurs to us that there is something beyond. Neither again can it be conceived how eternity has flowed down to the present day; for that distinction which is commonly received of infinity in time past and in time to come can by no means hold; for it would thence follow that one infinity is greater than another, and that infinity is wasting away and tending to become finite. The like subtlety arises touching the infinite divisibility of lines, from the same inability of thought to stop. But this inability interferes more mischievously in the discovery of causes: for although the most general principles in nature ought to be held merely positive, as they are discovered, and cannot with truth be referred to a cause; nevertheless the human understanding being unable to rest still seeks something prior in the order of nature. And then it is that in struggling towards that which is further off it falls back upon that which is more nigh at hand; namely, on final causes: which have relation clearly to the nature of man rather than to the nature of the universe; and from this source have strangely defiled philosophy. But he is no less an unskilled and shallow philosopher who seeks causes of that which is most general, than he who in things subordinate and subaltern omits to do so.

XLIX

The human understanding is no dry light, but receives an infusion from the will and affections; whence proceed sciences which may be called "sciences as one would." For what a man had rather were true he more readily believes. Therefore he rejects difficult things from impatience of research; sober things, because they narrow hope; the deeper things of nature, from superstition; the light of experience, from arrogance and pride, lest his mind should seem to be occupied with things mean and transitory; things not commonly believed, out of deference to the opinion of the vulgar. Numberless in short are the ways, and sometimes imperceptible, in which the affections colour and infect the understanding.

L

But by far the greatest hindrance and aberration of the human understanding proceeds from the dulness, incompetency, and deceptions of the senses; in that things which strike the sense outweigh things which do not immediately strike it, though they be more important. Hence it is that speculation commonly ceases where sight ceases; insomuch that of things invisible there is little or no observation. Hence all the working of the spirits inclosed in tangible bodies lies hid and unobserved of men. So also all the more subtle changes of form in the parts of coarser substances (which they commonly call alteration, though it is in truth local motion through exceedingly small spaces) is in like manner unobserved. And yet unless these two things just mentioned be searched out and brought to light, nothing great can be achieved in nature, as far as the production of works is concerned. So again the essential nature of our common air, and of all bodies less dense than air (which are very many), is almost unknown. For the sense by itself is a thing infirm and erring; neither can instruments for enlarging or sharpening the senses do much; but all the truer kind of interpretation of nature is effected by instances and experiments fit and apposite; wherein the sense decides touching the experiment only, and the experiment touching the point in nature and the thing itself.

LI

The human understanding is of its own nature prone to abstractions and gives a substance and reality to things which are fleeting. But to resolve nature into abstractions is less to our purpose than to dissect her into parts; as did the school of Democritus, which went further into nature than the rest. Matter rather than forms should be the object of our attention, its configurations and changes of configuration, and simple action, and law of action or

motion; for forms are figments of the human mind, unless
you will call those laws of action forms.

LII

Such then are the idols which I call *Idols of the Tribe;*
and which take their rise either from the homogeneity of
the substance of the human spirit, or from its preoccupation, or from its narrowness, or from its restless motion, or
from an infusion of the affections, or from the incompetency of the senses, or from the mode of impression.

LIII

The *Idols of the Cave* take their rise in the peculiar
constitution, mental or bodily, of each individual; and
also in education, habit, and accident. Of this kind there
is a great number and variety; but I will instance those
the pointing out of which contains the most important
caution, and which have most effect in disturbing the
clearness of the understanding.

LIV

Men become attached to certain particular sciences and
speculations, either because they fancy themselves the
authors and inventors thereof, or because they have bestowed the greatest pains upon them and become most
habituated to them. But men of this kind, if they betake
themselves to philosophy and contemplations of a general
character, distort and colour them in obedience to their
former fancies; a thing especially to be noticed in Aristotle, who made his natural philosophy a mere bond-
servant to his logic, thereby rendering it contentious and
well nigh useless. The race of chemists again out of a few
experiments of the furnace have built up a fantastic
philosophy, framed with reference to a few things; and
Gilbert also, after he had employed himself most laboriously in the study and observation of the loadstone, proceeded at once to construct an entire system in accordance with his favourite subject.

LV

There is one principal and as it were radical distinction between different minds, in respect of philosophy and the sciences; which is this: that some minds are stronger and apter to mark the differences of things, others to mark their resemblances. The steady and acute mind can fix its contemplations and dwell and fasten on the subtlest distinctions: the lofty and discursive mind recognises and puts together the finest and most general resemblances. Both kinds however easily err in excess, by catching the one at gradations the other at shadows.

LVI

There are found some minds given to an extreme admiration of antiquity, others to an extreme love and appetite for novelty; but few so duly tempered that they can hold the mean, neither carping at what has been well laid down by the ancients, nor despising what is well introduced by the moderns. This however turns to the great injury of the sciences and philosophy; since these affectations of antiquity and novelty are the humours of partisans rather than judgments; and truth is to be sought for not in the felicity of any age, which is an unstable thing, but in the light of nature and experience, which is eternal. These factions therefore must be abjured, and care must be taken that the intellect be not hurried by them into assent.

LVII

Contemplations of nature and of bodies in their simple form break up and distract the understanding, while contemplations of nature and bodies in their composition and configuration overpower and dissolve the understanding: a distinction well seen in the school of Leucippus and Democritus as compared with the other philosophies. For that school is so busied with the particles that it hardly attends to the structure; while the others are so lost in admiration of the structure that they do not penetrate to the simplicity of nature. These kinds of contemplation should therefore be alternated and taken by turns; that so the understanding may be rendered at once penetrating and comprehensive, and the inconveniences above mentioned, with the idols which proceed from them, may be avoided.

LVIII

Let such then be our provision and contemplative prudence for keeping off and dislodging the *Idols of the Cave*, which grow for the most part either out of the predominance of a favourite subject, or out of an excessive tendency to compare or to distinguish, or out of partiality for particular ages, or out of the largeness or minuteness of the objects contemplated. And generally let every student of nature take this as a rule,—that whatever his mind seizes and dwells upon with peculiar satisfaction is to be held in suspicion, and that so much the more care is to be taken in dealing with such questions to keep the understanding even and clear.

LIX

But the *Idols of the Market-place* are the most troublesome of all: idols which have crept into the understanding through the alliances of words and names. For men believe that their reason governs words; but it is also true that words react on the understanding; and this it is that has rendered philosophy and the sciences sophistical and inactive. Now words, being commonly framed and applied according to the capacity of the vulgar, follow those lines of division which are most obvious to the vulgar understanding. And whenever an understanding of greater acuteness or a more diligent observation would alter those lines to suit the true divisions of nature, words stand in the way and resist the change. Whence it comes to pass that the high and formal discussions of learned men end oftentimes in disputes about words and names; with which (according to the use and wisdom of the mathematicians) it would be more prudent to begin, and so by means of definitions reduce them to order. Yet even definitions cannot cure this evil in dealing with natural and material things; since the definitions themselves consist of words, and those words beget others: so that it is necessary to recur to individual instances, and those in due series and order; as I shall say presently when I come to the method and scheme for the formation of notions and axioms.

LX

The idols imposed by words on the understanding are of two kinds. They are either names of things which do not exist (for as there are things left unnamed through lack of observation, so likewise are there names which result from fantastic suppositions and to which nothing in reality corresponds), or they are names of things which exist, but yet confused and ill-defined, and hastily and irregularly derived from realities. Of the former kind are Fortune, the Prime Mover, Planetary Orbits, Element of Fire, and like fictions which owe their origin to false and idle theories. And this class of idols is more easily expelled, because to get rid of them it is only necessary that all theories should be steadily rejected and dismissed as obsolete.

But the other class, which springs out of a faulty and unskilful abstraction, is intricate and deeply rooted. Let us take for example such a word as *humid;* and see how far the several things which the word is used to signify agree with each other; and we shall find the word *humid* to be nothing else than a mark loosely and confusedly applied to denote a variety of actions which will not bear to be reduced to any constant meaning. For it both signifies that which easily spreads itself round any other body; and that which in itself is indeterminate and cannot solidise; and that which readily yields in every direction; and that which easily divides and scatters itself; and that which easily unites and collects itself; and that which readily flows and is put in motion; and that which readily clings to another body and wets it; and that which is easily reduced to a liquid, or being solid easily melts. Accordingly when you come to apply the word,—if you take it in one sense, flame is humid; if in another, air is not humid; if in another, fine dust is humid; if in another, glass is humid. So that it is easy to see that the notion is taken by abstraction only from water and common and ordinary liquids, without any due verification.

There are however in words certain degrees of distortion and error. One of the least faulty kinds is that of names of substances, especially of lowest species and well-deduced (for the notion of *chalk* and of *mud* is good, of *earth* bad); a more faulty kind is that of actions, as *to generate, to corrupt, to alter;* the most faulty is of qualities (except such as are the immediate objects of the sense) as *heavy, light, rare, dense,* and the like. Yet in all these cases some notions are of necessity a little better than others, in proportion to the greater variety of subjects that fall within the range of the human sense.

LXI

But the *Idols of the Theatre* are not innate, nor do they steal into the understanding secretly, but are plainly impressed and received into the mind from the play-books of philosophical systems and the perverted rules of demonstration. To attempt refutations in this case would be merely inconsistent with what I have already said: for since we agree neither upon principles nor upon demonstrations there is no place for argument. And this is so far well, inasmuch as it leaves the honour of the ancients untouched. For they are no wise disparaged—the question between them and me being only as to the way. For as the saying is, the lame man who keeps the right road outstrips the runner who takes a wrong one. Nay it is obvious that when a man runs the wrong way, the more active and swift he is the further he will go astray.

But the course I propose for the discovery of sciences is such as leaves but little to the acuteness and strength of wits, but places all wits and understandings nearly on a level. For as in the drawing of a straight line or a perfect circle, much depends on the steadiness and practice

of the hand, if it be done by aim of hand only, but if with
the aid of rule or compass, little or nothing; so is it exactly with my plan. But though particular confutations
would be of no avail, yet touching the sects and general
divisions of such systems I must say something; something also touching the external signs which show that
they are unsound; and finally something touching the
causes of such great infelicity and of such lasting and
general agreement in error; that so the access to truth
may be made less difficult, and the human understanding
may the more willingly submit to its purgation and dismiss its idols.

LXII

Idols of the Theatre, or of Systems, are many, and
there can be and perhaps will be yet many more. For
were it not that now for many ages men's minds have
been busied with religion and theology; and were it not
that civil governments, especially monarchies, have been
averse to such novelties, even in matters speculative; so
that men labour therein to the peril and harming of their
fortunes,—not only unrewarded, but exposed also to contempt and envy; doubtless there would have arisen many
other philosophical sects like to those which in great
variety flourished once among the Greeks. For as on the
phenomena of the heavens many hypotheses may be con-
structed, so likewise (and more also) many various dogmas may be set up and established on the phenomena of
philosophy. And in the plays of this philosophical theatre
you may observe the same thing which is found in the
theatre of the poets, that stories invented for the stage
are more compact and elegant, and more as one would
wish them to be, than true stories out of history.

In general however there is taken for the material of
philosophy either a great deal out of a few things, or a
very little out of many things; so that on both sides philosophy is based on too narrow a foundation of experiment and natural history, and decides on the authority of

too few cases. For the Rational School of philosophers
snatches from experience a variety of common instances,
neither duly ascertained nor diligently examined and
weighed, and leaves all the rest to meditation and agitation of wit.

There is also another class of philosophers, who having
bestowed much diligent and careful labour on a few experiments, have thence made bold to educe and construct
systems; wresting all other facts in a strange fashion to
conformity therewith.

And there is yet a third class, consisting of those who
out of faith and veneration mix their philosophy with
theology and traditions; among whom the vanity of some
has gone so far aside as to seek the origin of sciences
among spirits and genii. So that this parent stock of errors—this false philosophy—is of three kinds; the Sophistical, the Empirical, and the Superstitious.

LXIII

The most conspicuous example of the first class was
Aristotle, who corrupted natural philosophy by his logic:
fashioning the world out of categories; assigning to the
human soul, the noblest of substances, a genus from words
of the second intention; doing the business of density and
rarity (which is to make bodies of greater or less dimensions, that is, occupy greater or less spaces), by the frigid
distinction of act and power; asserting that single bodies
have each a single and proper motion, and that if they
participate in any other, then this results from an external
cause; and imposing countless other arbitrary restrictions
on the nature of things; being always more solicitous to
provide an answer to the question and affirm something
positive in words, than about the inner truth of things; a
failing best shown when his philosophy is compared with
other systems of note among the Greeks. For the Ho-
mœomera of Anaxagoras; the Atoms of Leucippus and
Democritus; the Heaven and Earth of Parmenides; the
Strife and Friendship of Empedocles; Heraclitus's doctrine how bodies are resolved into the indifferent nature

of fire, and remoulded into solids; have all of them some taste of the natural philosopher,—some savour of the nature of things, and experience, and bodies; whereas in the physics of Aristotle you hear hardly anything but the words of logic; which in his metaphysics also, under a more imposing name, and more forsooth as a realist than a nominalist, he has handled over again. Nor let any weight be given to the fact, that in his books on animals and his problems, and other of his treatises, there is frequent dealing with experiments. For he had come to his conclusion before; he did not consult experience, as he should have done, in order to the framing of his decisions and axioms; but having first determined the question according to his will, he then resorts to experience, and bending her into conformity with his placets leads her about like a captive in a procession; so that even on this count he is more guilty than his modern followers, the schoolmen, who have abandoned experience altogether.

LXIV

But the Empirical school of philosophy gives birth to dogmas more deformed and monstrous than the Sophistical or Rational school. For it has its foundations not in the light of common notions, (which though it be a faint and superficial light, is yet in a manner universal, and has reference to many things,) but in the narrowness and darkness of a few experiments. To those therefore who are daily busied with these experiments, and have infected their imagination with them, such a philosophy seems probable and all but certain; to all men else incredible and vain. Of this there is a notable instance in the alchemists and their dogmas; though it is hardly to be found elsewhere in these times, except perhaps in the philosophy of Gilbert. Nevertheless with regard to philosophies of this kind there is one caution not to be omitted; for I foresee that if ever men are roused by my admonitions to betake themselves seriously to experiment and bid farewell to sophistical doctrines, then indeed

through the premature hurry of the understanding to leap
or fly to universals and principles of things, great danger
may be apprehended from philosophies of this kind;
against which evil we ought even now to prepare.

LXV

But the corruption of philosophy by superstition and
an admixture of theology is far more widely spread, and
does the greatest harm, whether to entire systems or to
their parts. For the human understanding is obnoxious
to the influence of the imagination no less than to the influence of common notions. For the contentious and
sophistical kind of philosophy ensnares the understanding; but this kind, being fanciful and tumid and half
poetical, misleads it more by flattery. For there is in man
an ambition of the understanding, no less than of the
will, especially in high and lofty spirits.

Of this kind we have among the Greeks a striking example in Pythagoras, though he united with it a coarser
and more cumbrous superstition; another in Plato and his
school, more dangerous and subtle. It shows itself likewise in parts of other philosophies, in the introduction of
abstract forms and final causes and first causes, with the
omission in most cases of causes intermediate, and the
like. Upon this point the greatest caution should be used.
For nothing is so mischievous as the apotheosis of error;
and it is a very plague of the understanding for vanity
to become the object of veneration. Yet in this vanity
some of the moderns have with extreme levity indulged
so far as to attempt to found a system of natural philosophy on the first chapter of Genesis, in the book of Job,
and other parts of the sacred writings; seeking for the
dead among the living: which also makes the inhibition
and repression of it the more important, because from
this unwholesome mixture of things human and divine
there arises not only a fantastic philosophy but also an
heretical religion. Very meet it is therefore that we be
sober-minded, and give to faith that only which is faith's.

LXVI

So much then for the mischievous authorities of systems, which are founded either on common notions, or on a few experiments, or on superstition. It remains to speak of the faulty subject-matter of contemplations, especially in natural philosophy. Now the human understanding is infected by the sight of what takes place in the mechanical arts, in which the alteration of bodies proceeds chiefly by composition or separation, and so imagines that something similar goes on in the universal nature of things. From this source has flowed the fiction of elements, and of their concourse for the formation of natural bodies. Again, when man contemplates nature working freely, he meets with different species of things, of animals, of plants, of minerals; whence he readily passes into the opinion that there are in nature certain primary forms which nature intends to educe, and that the remaining variety proceeds from hindrances and aberrations of nature in the fulfilment of her work, or from the collision of different species and the transplanting of one into another. To the first of these speculations we owe our primary qualities of the elements; to the other our occult properties and specific virtues; and both of them belong to those empty *compendia* of thought wherein the mind rests, and whereby it is diverted from more solid pursuits. It is to better purpose that the physicians bestow their labour on the secondary qualities of matter, and the operations of attraction, repulsion, attenuation, conspissation, dilatation, astriction, dissipation, maturation, and the like; and were it not that by those two compendia which I have mentioned (elementary qualities, to wit, and specific virtues) they corrupted their correct observations in these other matters,—either reducing them to first qualities and their subtle and incommensurable mixtures, or not following them out with greater and more diligent observation to third and fourth qualities, but breaking off the scrutiny prematurely,—they had made much greater progress. Nor are powers of this kind (I do not say the same, but similar) to be sought for only in the medicines of the human body, but also in the changes of all other bodies.

But it is a far greater evil that they make the quiescent principles, *wherefrom,* and not the moving principles, *whereby,* things are produced, the object of their contemplation and inquiry. For the former tend to discourse, the latter to works. Nor is there any value in those vulgar distinctions of motion which are observed in the received system of natural philosophy, as generation, corruption, augmentation, diminution, alteration, and local motion. What they mean no doubt is this:—If a body, in other respects not changed, be moved from its place, this is *local motion;* if without change of place or essence, it be changed in quality, this is *alteration;* if by reason of the change the mass and quantity of the body do not remain the same, this is *augmentation* or *diminution;* if they be changed to such a degree that they change their very essence and substance and turn to something else, this is *generation* and *corruption.* But all this is merely popular, and does not at all go deep into nature; for these are only measures and limits, not kinds of motion. What they intimate is *how far,* not *by what means,* or *from what source.* For they do not suggest anything with regard either to the desires of bodies or to the development of their parts: it is only when that motion presents the thing grossly and palpably to the sense as different from what it was, that they begin to mark the division. Even when they wish to suggest something with regard to the causes of motion, and to establish a division with reference to them, they introduce with the greatest negligence a distinction between motion natural and violent; a distinction which is itself drawn entirely from a vulgar notion, since all violent motion is also in fact natural; the external efficient simply setting nature working otherwise than it was before. But if, leaving all this, any one shall observe (for instance) that there is in bodies a desire of mutual contact, so as not to suffer the unity of nature to be quite separated or broken and a vacuum thus made; or if any one say that there is in bodies a desire of resuming their natural dimensions or tension, so that if compressed within or extended beyond them, they immediately strive to recover themselves, and fall back to their old volume and extent; or if any one say that there is in bodies a desire of congregating towards masses of kindred nature,—of dense bodies, for instance, towards the globe of the earth, of thin and rare bodies towards the compass of the sky; all these and the like are truly physical kinds of motion;— but those others are entirely logical and scholastic, as is abundantly manifest from this comparison.

Nor again is it a less evil, that in their philosophies and contemplations their labour is spent in investigating and handling the first principles of things and the highest generalities of nature; whereas utility and the means of working result entirely from things intermediate. Hence it is that men cease not from abstracting nature till they come to potential and uninformed matter, nor on the other hand from dissecting nature till they reach the atom; things which, even if true, can do but little for the welfare of mankind.

LXVII

A caution must also be given to the understanding against the intemperance which systems of philosophy manifest in giving or withholding assent; because intemperance of this kind seems to establish Idols and in some sort to perpetuate them, leaving no way open to reach and dislodge them.

This excess is of two kinds: the first being manifest in those who are ready in deciding, and render sciences dogmatic and magisterial; the other in those who deny that we can know anything, and so introduce a wandering kind of inquiry that leads to nothing; of which kinds the former subdues, the latter weakens the understanding. For the philosophy of Aristotle, after having by hostile confutations destroyed all the rest (as the Ottomans serve their brothers), has laid down the law on all points; which done, he proceeds himself to raise new questions of his own suggestion, and dispose of them likewise; so that nothing may remain that is not certain and decided: a practice which holds and is in use among his successors.

The school of Plato, on the other hand, introduced *Acatalepsia,* at first in jest and irony, and in disdain of the older sophists, Protagoras, Hippias, and the rest, who were of nothing else so much ashamed as of seeming to doubt about anything. But the New Academy made a dogma of it, and held it as a tenet. And though theirs is a fairer seeming way than arbitrary decisions; since they say that they by no means destroy all investigation, like Pyrrho and his Refrainers, but allow of some things to be followed as probable, though of none to be maintained as true; yet still when the human mind has once despaired of finding truth, its interest in all things grows fainter; and the result is that men turn aside to pleasant disputations and discourses and roam as it were from object to object, rather than keep on a course of severe inquisition. But, as I said at the beginning and am ever urging, the human senses and understanding, weak as they are, are not to be deprived of their authority, but to be supplied with helps.

LXVIII

So much concerning the several classes of Idols, and their equipage: all of which must be renounced and put away with a fixed and solemn determination, and the understanding thoroughly freed and cleansed; the entrance into the kingdom of man, founded on the sciences, being not much other than the entrance into the kingdom of heaven, whereinto none may enter except as a little child.

LXIX

But vicious demonstrations are as the strongholds and defences of Idols; and those we have in logic do little else than make the world the bond-slave of human thought, and human thought the bond-slave of words. Demonstrations truly are in effect the philosophies themselves and the sciences. For such as *they* are, well or ill established, such are the systems of philosophy and the contemplations which follow. Now in the whole of the process which leads from the sense and objects to axioms and conclusions, the demonstrations which we use are deceptive and incompetent. This process consists of four parts, and has as many faults. In the first place, the impressions of the sense itself are faulty; for the sense both fails us and deceives us. But its shortcomings are to be supplied, and its deceptions to be corrected. Secondly, notions are ill drawn from the impressions of the senses, and are indefinite and confused, whereas they should be definite and distinctly bounded. Thirdly, the induction is amiss which infers the principles of sciences by simple enumeration, and does not, as it ought, employ exclusions and solutions (or separations) of nature. Lastly, that method of discovery and proof according to which the most general principles are first established, and then intermediate axioms are tried and proved by them, is the parent of error and the curse of all science. Of these things however, which now I do but touch upon, I will speak more largely, when, having performed these expiations and purgings of the mind, I come to set forth the true way for the interpretation of nature.

LXX

But the best demonstration by far is experience, if it go not beyond the actual experiment. For if it be transferred to other cases which are deemed similar, unless such transfer be made by a just and orderly process, it is a fallacious thing. But the manner of making experiments which men now use is blind and stupid. And therefore, wandering and straying as they do with no settled course, and taking counsel only from things as they fall out, they fetch a wide circuit and meet with many matters, but make little progress; and sometimes are full of hope, sometimes are distracted; and always find that there is something beyond to be sought. For it generally happens that men make their trials carelessly, and as it were in play; slightly varying experiments already known, and, if the thing does not answer, growing weary and abandoning the attempt. And even if they apply themselves

to experiments more seriously and earnestly and laboriously, still they spend their labour in working out some
one experiment, as Gilbert with the magnet, and the
chemists with gold; a course of proceeding not less unskilful in the design than small in the attempt. For no
one successfully investigates the nature of a thing in the
thing itself; the inquiry must be enlarged, so as to become more general.

And even when they seek to educe some science or
theory from their experiments, they nevertheless almost
always turn aside with overhasty and unseasonable eagerness to practice; not only for the sake of the uses and
fruits of the practice, but from impatience to obtain in
the shape of some new work an assurance for themselves
that it is worth their while to go on; and also to show
themselves off to the world, and so raise the credit of the
business in which they are engaged. Thus, like Atalanta,
they go aside to pick up the golden apple, but meanwhile
they interrupt their course, and let the victory escape
them. But in the true course of experience, and in carrying it on to the effecting of new works, the divine wisdom
and order must be our pattern. Now God on the first day
of creation created light only, giving to that work an entire day, in which no material substance was created. So
must we likewise from experience of every kind first endeavour to discover true causes and axioms; and seek for
experiments of Light, not for experiments of Fruit. For
axioms rightly discovered and established supply practice with its instruments, not one by one, but in clusters,
and draw after them trains and troops of works. Of the
paths however of experience, which no less than the paths
of judgment are impeded and beset, I will speak hereafter; here I have only mentioned ordinary experimental
research as a bad kind of demonstration. But now the
order of the matter in hand leads me to add something
both as to those *signs* which I lately mentioned,—(signs
that the systems of philosophy and contemplation in use
are in a bad condition)—and also as to the *causes* of what
seems at first so strange and incredible. For a knowledge
of the signs prepares assent; an explanation of the causes

removes the marvel: which two things will do much to render the extirpation of Idols from the understanding more easy and gentle.

LXXI

The sciences which we possess come for the most part from the Greeks. For what has been added by Roman, Arabic, or later writers is not much nor of much importance; and whatever it is, it is built on the foundation of Greek discoveries. Now the wisdom of the Greeks was professorial and much given to disputations; a kind of wisdom most adverse to the inquisition of truth. Thus that name of Sophists, which by those who would be thought philosophers was in contempt cast back upon and so transferred to the ancient rhetoricians, Gorgias, Protagoras, Hippias, Polus, does indeed suit the entire class, Plato, Aristotle, Zeno, Epicurus, Theophrastus, and their successors Chrysippus, Carnades, and the rest. There was this difference only, that the former class was wandering and mercenary, going about from town to town, putting up their wisdom to sale, and taking a price for it; while the latter was more pompous and dignified, as composed of men who had fixed abodes, and who opened schools and taught their philosophy without reward. Still both sorts, though in other respects unequal, were professorial; both turned the matter into disputations, and set up and battled for philosophical sects and heresies; so that their doctrines were for the most part (as Dionysius not unaptly rallied Plato) "the talk of idle old men to ignorant youths." But the elder of the Greek philosophers, Empedocles, Anaxagoras, Leucippus, Democritus, Parmenides, Heraclitus, Xenophanes, Philolaus, and the rest (I omit Pythagoras as a mystic), did not, so far as we know, open schools; but more silently and severely and simply, —that is, with less affectation and parade,—betook themselves to the inquisition of truth. And therefore they were in my judgment more successful; only that their works were in the course of time obscured by those slighter persons who had more which suits and pleases the capacity

and tastes of the vulgar: time, like a river, bringing down
to us things which are light and puffed up, but letting
weighty matters sink. Still even they were not altogether
free from the failing of their nation; but leaned too much
to the ambition and vanity of founding a sect and catching popular applause. But the inquisition of truth must be
despaired of when it turns aside to trifles of this kind. Nor
should we omit that judgment, or rather divination, which
was given concerning the Greeks by the Ægyptian priest,
—that "they were always boys, without antiquity of
knowledge or knowledge of antiquity." Assuredly they
have that which is characteristic of boys; they are prompt
to prattle, but cannot generate; for their wisdom abounds
in words but is barren of works. And therefore the signs
which are taken from the origin and birth-place of the
received philosophy are not good.

LXXII

Nor does the character of the time and age yield much
better signs than the character of the country and nation.
For at that period there was but a narrow and meagre
knowledge either of time or place; which is the worst
thing that can be, especially for those who rest all on experience. For they had no history, worthy to be called
history, that went back a thousand years; but only fables
and rumours of antiquity. And of the regions and districts
of the world they knew but a small portion; giving in-
discriminately the name of Scythians to all in the North,
of Celts to all in the West; knowing nothing of Africa beyond the hither side of Æthiopia, of Asia beyond the
Ganges; much less were they acquainted with the provinces of the New World, even by hearsay or any well-
founded rumour; nay, a multitude of climates and zones,
wherein innumerable nations breathe and live, were pronounced by them to be uninhabitable; and the travels of
Democritus, Plato, and Pythagoras, which were rather
suburban excursions than distant journeys, were talked
of as something great. In our times on the other hand
both many parts of the New World and the limits on

every side of the Old World are known, and our stock of experience has increased to an infinite amount. Wherefore if (like astrologers) we draw signs from the season of their nativity or birth, nothing great can be predicted of those systems of philosophy.

LXXIII

Of all signs there is none more certain or more noble than that taken from fruits. For fruits and works are as it were sponsors and sureties for the truth of philosophies. Now, from all these systems of the Greeks, and their ramifications through particular sciences, there can hardly after the lapse of so many years be adduced a single experiment which tends to relieve and benefit the condition of man, and which can with truth be referred to the speculations and theories of philosophy. And Celsus ingenuously and wisely owns as much, when he tells us that the experimental part of medicine was first discovered, and that afterwards men philosophised about it, and hunted for and assigned causes; and not by an inverse process that philosophy and the knowledge of causes led to the discovery and development of the experimental part. And therefore it was not strange that among the Ægyptians, who rewarded inventors with divine honours and sacred rites, there were more images of brutes than of men; inasmuch as brutes by their natural instinct have produced many discoveries, whereas men by discussion and the conclusions of reason have given birth to few or none.

Some little has indeed been produced by the industry of chemists; but it has been produced accidentally and in passing, or else by a kind of variation of experiments, such as mechanics use; and not by any art or theory; for the theory which they have devised rather confuses the experiments than aids them. They too who have busied themselves with natural magic, as they call it, have but few discoveries to show, and those trifling and imposture-like. Wherefore, as in religion we are warned to show our faith by works, so in philosophy by the same rule the system should be judged of by its fruits, and pronounced frivolous if it be barren, more especially if, in place of fruits of grape and olive, it bear thorns and briars of dispute and contention.

LXXIV

Signs also are to be drawn from the increase and progress of systems and sciences. For what is founded on nature grows and increases; while what is founded on opinion varies but increases not. If therefore those doctrines had not plainly been like a plant torn up from its roots, but had remained attached to the womb of nature and continued to draw nourishment from her, that could never have come to pass which we have seen now for twice a thousand years; namely, that the sciences stand where they did and remain almost in the same condition; receiving no noticeable increase, but on the contrary, thriving most under their first founder, and then declining. Whereas in the mechanical arts, which are founded on nature and the light of experience, we see the contrary happen, for these (as long as they are popular) are continually thriving and growing, as having in them a breath of life; at first rude, then convenient, afterwards adorned, and at all times advancing.

LXXV

There is still another sign remaining (if sign it can be called, when it is rather testimony, nay, of all testimony the most valid); I mean the confession of the very authorities whom men now follow. For even they who lay down the law on all things so confidently, do still in their more sober moods fall to complaints of the subtlety of nature, the obscurity of things, and the weakness of the human mind. Now if this were all they did, some perhaps of a timid disposition might be deterred from further search, while others of a more ardent and hopeful spirit might be whetted and incited to go on farther. But not content to speak for themselves, whatever is beyond their own or their master's knowledge or reach they set down as beyond the bounds of possibility, and pronounce, as if on the authority of their art, that it cannot be known or done; thus most presumptuously and invidiously turning the weakness of their own discoveries into a calumny on nature herself, and the despair of the rest of the world. Hence the school of the New Academy, which held *Acatalepsia* as a tenet and doomed men to perpetual darkness. Hence the opinion that Forms or true differences of things (which are in fact laws of pure act) are past finding out and beyond the reach of man. Hence too those opinions in the department of action and operation; as that the heat of the sun and of fire are quite different in kind,—lest men should imagine that by the operations of fire anything like the works of nature can be educed and formed. Hence the notion that composition only is the work of man, and mixture of none but nature,—lest men should expect from art some power of generating or transforming natural bodies. By this sign, therefore, men will easily take warning not to mix up their fortunes and labours with dogmas not only despaired of but dedicated to despair.

LXXVI

Neither is this other sign to be omitted;—that formerly there existed among philosophers such great disagreement, and such diversities in the schools themselves; a fact which sufficiently shows that the road from the senses to the understanding was not skilfully laid out, when the same groundwork of philosophy (the nature of things to wit) was torn and split up into such vague and multifarious errors. And although in these times disagreements and diversities of opinion on first principles and entire systems are for the most part extinguished, still on parts of philosophy there remain innumerable questions and disputes, so that it plainly appears that neither in the systems themselves nor in the modes of demonstration is there anything certain or sound.

And as for the general opinion that in the philosophy of Aristotle at any rate there is great agreement; since after its publication the systems of older philosophers died away, while in the times which followed nothing better was found; so that it seems to have been so well laid and established as to have drawn both ages in its train; I answer in the first place, that the common notion of the falling off of the old systems upon the publication of Aristotle's works is a false one; for long afterwards, down even to the times of Cicero and subsequent ages, the works of the old philosophers still remained. But in the times which followed, when on the inundation of barbarians into the Roman empire human learning had suffered shipwreck, then the systems of Aristotle and Plato, like planks of lighter and less solid material, floated on the waves of time, and were preserved. Upon the point of consent also men are deceived, if the matter be looked into more keenly. For true consent is that which consists in the coincidence of free judgments, after due examination. But far the greater number of those who have assented to the philosophy of Aristotle have addicted themselves thereto from prejudgment and upon the authority of others; so that it is a following and going along together, rather than consent. But even if it had been a real and widespread consent, still so little ought consent to be deemed a sure and solid confirmation, that it is in fact a strong presumption the other way. For the worst of all auguries is from consent in matters intellectual (divinity excepted, and politics were there is right of vote). For nothing pleases the many unless it strikes the imagination, or binds the understanding with the bands of common notions, as I have already said. We may very well transfer therefore from moral to intellectual matters, the saying of Phocion, that if the multitude assent and applaud men ought immediately to examine themselves as to what blunder or fault they may have committed. This sign therefore is one of the most unfavourable. And so much for this point; namely, that the signs of truth and soundness in the received systems and sciences are not good; whether they be drawn from their origin, or from their fruits, or from their progress, or from the confessions of their founders, or from general consent.

LXXVIII

I now come to the *causes* of these errors, and of so long a continuance in them through so many ages; which are very many and very potent;—that all wonder how these considerations which I bring forward should have escaped men's notice till now, may cease; and the only wonder be, how now at last they should have entered into any man's head and become the subject of his thoughts; which truly I myself esteem as the result of some happy accident, rather than of any excellence of faculty in me; a birth of Time rather than a birth of Wit. Now, in the first place, those so many ages, if you weigh the case truly, shrink into a very small compass. For out of the five and twenty centuries over which the memory and learning of men extends, you can hardly pick out six that were fertile in sciences or favourable to their development. In times no less than in regions there are wastes and deserts. For only three revolutions and periods of learning can properly be reckoned; one among the Greeks, the second among the Romans, and the last among us, that is to say, the nations of Western Europe; and to each of these hardly two centuries can justly be assigned. The intervening ages of the world, in respect of any rich or flourishing growth of the sciences, were unprosperous. For neither the Arabians nor the Schoolmen need be mentioned; who in the intermediate times rather crushed the sciences with a multitude of treatises, than increased their weight. And therefore the first cause of so meagre a progress in the sciences is duly and orderly referred to the narrow limits of the time that has been favourable to them.

LXXIX

In the second place there presents itself a cause of great weight in all ways; namely, that during those very ages in which the wits and learning of men have flourished most, or indeed flourished at all, the least part of their diligence was given to natural philosophy. Yet this very philosophy it is that ought to be esteemed the great mother of the sciences. For all arts and all sciences, if torn from this root, though they may be polished and shaped and made fit for use, yet they will hardly grow. Now it is well known that after the Christian religion was received and grew strong, by far the greater number of the best wits applied themselves to theology; that to this both the highest rewards were offered, and helps of all kinds most abundantly supplied; and that this devotion to theology chiefly occupied that third portion or epoch of time among us Europeans of the West; and the more so because about the same time both literature began to flourish and religious controversies to spring up. In the age before, on the other hand, during the continuance of the second period among the Romans, the meditations and labours of philosophers were principally employed and consumed on moral philosophy, which to the Heathen was as theology to us. Moreover in those times the greatest wits applied themselves very generally to public affairs; the magnitude of the Roman empire requiring the services of a great number of persons. Again, the age in which natural philosophy was seen to flourish most among the Greeks, was but a brief particle of time; for in early ages the Seven Wise Men, as they were called, (all except Thales) applied themselves to morals and politics; and in later times, when Socrates had drawn down philosophy from heaven to earth, moral philosophy became more fashionable than ever, and diverted the minds of men from the philosophy of nature.

Nay, the very period itself in which inquiries concerning nature flourished, was by controversies and the ambitious display of new opinions corrupted and made useless. Seeing therefore that during those three periods natural philosophy was in a great degree either neglected or hindered, it is no wonder if men made but small advance in that to which they were not attending.

LXXX

To this it may be added that natural philosophy, even among those who have attended to it, has scarcely ever possessed, especially in these later times, a disengaged and whole man (unless it were some monk studying in his cell, or some gentleman in his country-house), but that it has been made merely a passage and bridge to something else. And so this great mother of the sciences has with strange indignity been degraded to the offices of a servant; having to attend on the business of medicine or mathematics, and likewise to wash and imbue youthful and unripe wits with a sort of first dye, in order that they may be the fitter to receive another afterwards. Meanwhile let no man look for much progress in the sciences—especially in the practical part of them—unless natural philosophy be carried on and applied to particular sciences, and particular sciences be carried back again to natural philosophy. For want of this, astronomy, optics, music, a number of mechanical arts, medicine itself,—nay, what one might more wonder at, moral and political philosophy, and the logical sciences,—altogether lack profoundness, and merely glide along the surface and variety of things; because after these particular sciences have been once distributed and established, they are no more nourished by natural philosophy; which might have drawn out of the true contemplation of motions, rays, sounds, texture and configuration of bodies, affections, and intellectual perceptions, the means of imparting to them fresh strength and growth. And therefore it is nothing strange if the sciences grow not, seeing they are parted from their roots.

LXXXI

Again there is another great and powerful cause why the sciences have made but little progress; which is this. It is not possible to run a course aright when the goal itself has not been rightly placed. Now the true and lawful goal of the sciences is none other than this: that human life be endowed with new discoveries and powers. But of

this the great majority have no feeling, but are merely
hireling and professorial; except when it occasionally happens that some workman of acuter wit and covetous of
honour applies himself to a new invention; which he
mostly does at the expense of his fortunes. But in general,
so far are men from proposing to themselves to augment
the mass of arts and sciences, that from the mass already
at hand they neither take nor look for anything more than
what they may turn to use in their lectures, or to gain, or
to reputation, or to some similar advantage. And if any
one out of all the multitude court science with honest
affection and for her own sake, yet even with him the
object will be found to be rather the variety of contemplations and doctrines than the severe and rigid search after
truth. And if by chance there be one who seeks after truth
in earnest, yet even he will propose to himself such a kind
of truth as shall yield satisfaction to the mind and understanding in rendering causes for things long since discovered, and not the truth which shall lead to new assurance
of works and new light of axioms. If then the end of the
sciences has not as yet been well placed, it is not strange
that men have erred as to the means.

LXXXII

And as men have misplaced the end and goal of the sciences; so again, even if they had placed it right, yet they
have chosen a way to it which is altogether erroneous and
impassable. And an astonishing thing it is to one who
rightly considers the matter, that no mortal should have
seriously applied himself to the opening and laying out of
a road for the human understanding direct from the sense,
by a course of experiment orderly conducted and well
built up; but that all has been left either to the mist of
tradition, or the whirl and eddy of argument, or the fluctuations and mazes of chance and of vague and ill-digested
experience. Now let any man soberly and diligently consider what the way is by which men have been accustomed to proceed in the investigation and discovery of
things; and in the first place he will no doubt remark a

method of discovery very simple and inartificial; which is the most ordinary method, and is no more than this. When a man addresses himself to discover something, he first seeks out and sets before him all that has been said about it by others; then he begins to meditate for himself; and so by much agitation and working of the wit solicits and as it were evokes his own spirit to give him oracles: which method has no foundation at all, but rests only upon opinions and is carried about with them.

Another may perhaps call in logic to discover it for him; but that has no relation to the matter except in name. For logical invention does not discover principles and chief axioms, of which arts are composed, but only such things as appear to be consistent with them. For if you grow more curious and importunate and busy, and question her of probations and invention of principles or primary axioms, her answer is well known: she refers you to the faith you are bound to give to the principles of each separate art.

There remains simple experience; which, if taken as it comes, is called accident; if sought for, experiment. But this kind of experience is no better than a broom without its band, as the saying is;—a mere groping, as of men in the dark, that feel all around them for the chance of finding their way; when they had much better wait for daylight or light a candle, and then go. But the true method of experience on the contrary first lights the candle, and then by means of the candle shows the way; commencing as it does with experience duly ordered and digested, not bungling or erratic, and from it educing axioms, and from established axioms again new experiments; even as it was not without order and method that the divine word operated on the created mass. Let men therefore cease to wonder that the course of science is not yet wholly run, seeing that they have gone altogether astray; either leaving and abandoning experience entirely, or losing their way in it and wandering round and round as in a labyrinth; whereas a method rightly ordered leads by an unbroken route through the woods of experience to the open ground of axioms.

This evil however has been strangely increased by an opinion or conceit, which though of long standing is vain and hurtful; namely, that the dignity of the human mind is impaired by long and close intercourse with experiments and particulars, subject to sense and bound in matter; especially as they are laborious to search, ignoble to meditate, harsh to deliver, illiberal to practise, infinite in number, and minute in subtlety. So that it has come at length to this, that the true way is not merely deserted, but shut out and stopped up; experience being, I do not say abandoned or badly managed, but rejected with disdain.

LXXXIV

Again, men have been kept back as by a kind of enchantment from progress in the sciences by reverence for antiquity, by the authority of men accounted great in philosophy, and then by general consent. Of the last I have spoken above.

As for antiquity, the opinion touching it which men entertain is quite a negligent one, and scarcely consonant with the word itself. For the old age of the world is to be accounted the true antiquity; and this is the attribute of our own times, not of that earlier age of the world in which the ancients lived; and which, though in respect of us it was the elder, yet in respect of the world it was the younger. And truly as we look for greater knowledge of human things and a riper judgment in the old man than in the young, because of his experience and of the number and variety of the things which he has seen and heard and thought of; so in like manner from our age, if it but knew its own strength and chose to essay and exert it, much more might fairly be expected than from the ancient times, inasmuch as it is a more advanced age of the world, and stored and stocked with infinite experiments and observations.

Nor must it go for nothing that by the distant voyages

and travels which have become frequent in our times, many things in nature have been laid open and discovered which may let in new light upon philosophy. And surely it would be disgraceful if, while the regions of the material globe,—that is, of the earth, of the sea, and of the stars,—have been in our times laid widely open and revealed, the intellectual globe should remain shut up within the narrow limits of old discoveries.

And with regard to authority, it shows a feeble mind to grant so much to authors and yet deny time his rights, who is the author of authors, nay rather of all authority. For rightly is truth called the daughter of time, not of authority. It is no wonder therefore if those enchantments of antiquity and authority and consent have so bound up men's powers that they have been made impotent (like persons bewitched) to accompany with the nature of things.

LXXXV

Nor is it only the admiration of antiquity, authority, and consent, that has forced the industry of man to rest satisfied with the discoveries already made; but also an admiration for the works themselves of which the human race has long been in possession. For when a man looks at the variety and the beauty of the provision which the mechanical arts have brought together for men's use, he will certainly be more inclined to admire the wealth of man than to feel his wants: not considering that the original observations and operations of nature (which are the life and moving principle of all that variety) are not many nor deeply fetched, and that the rest is but patience, and the subtle and ruled motion of the hand and instruments; —as the making of clocks (for instance) is certainly a subtle and exact work: their wheels seem to imitate the celestial orbs, and their alternating and orderly motion, the pulse of animals: and yet all this depends on one or two axioms of nature.

Again, if you observe the refinement of the liberal arts, or even that which relates to the mechanical preparation

of natural substances; and take notice of such things as
the discovery in astronomy of the motions of the heavens,
of harmony in music, of the letters of the alphabet (to this
day not in use among the Chinese) in grammar: or again
in things mechanical, the discovery of the works of
Bacchus and Ceres—that is, of the arts of preparing wine
and beer, and of making bread; the discovery once more
of the delicacies of the table, of distillations and the like;
and if you likewise bear in mind the long periods which
it has taken to bring these things to their present degree
of perfection (for they are all ancient except distillation),
and again (as has been said of clocks) how little they owe
to observations and axioms of nature, and how easily and
obviously and as it were by casual suggestion they may
have been discovered; you will easily cease from wondering, and on the contrary will pity the condition of mankind, seeing that in a course of so many ages there has
been so great a dearth and barrenness of arts and inventions. And yet these very discoveries which we have just
mentioned, are older than philosophy and intellectual
arts. So that, if the truth must be spoken, when the rational and dogmatical sciences began, the discovery of
useful works came to an end.

And again, if a man turn from the workshop to the library, and wonder at the immense variety of books he sees
there, let him but examine and diligently inspect their
matter and contents, and his wonder will assuredly be
turned the other way; for after observing their endless
repetitions, and how men are ever saying and doing what
has been said and done before, he will pass from admiration of the variety to astonishment at the poverty and
scantiness of the subjects which till now have occupied
and possessed the minds of men.

And if again he descend to the consideration of those
arts which are deemed curious rather than safe, and look
more closely into the works of the Alchemists or the Magicians, he will be in doubt perhaps whether he ought
rather to laugh over them or to weep. For the Alchemist
nurses eternal hope, and when the thing fails, lays the
blame upon some error of his own; fearing either that he

has not sufficiently understood the words of his art or of
his authors (whereupon he turns to tradition and auricular whispers), or else that in his manipulations he has
made some slip of a scruple in weight or a moment in
time (whereupon he repeats his trials to infinity); and
when meanwhile among the chances of experiment he
lights upon some conclusions either in aspect new or for
utility not contemptible, he takes these for earnest of
what is to come, and feeds his mind upon them, and mag-
nifies them to the most, and supplies the rest in hope. Not
but that Alchemists have made a good many discoveries,
and presented men with useful inventions. But their case
may be well compared to the fable of the old man, who
bequeathed to his sons gold buried in a vineyard, pretending not to know the exact spot; whereupon the sons
applied themselves diligently to the digging of the vineyard, and though no gold was found there, yet the vintage
by that digging was made more plentiful.

Again the students of natural magic, who explain everything by Sympathies and Antipathies, have in their idle
and most slothful conjectures ascribed to substances wonderful virtues and operations; and if ever they have produced works, they have been such as aim rather at admiration and novelty than at utility and fruit.

In superstitious magic on the other hand (if of this also
we must speak), it is especially to be observed that they
are but subjects of a certain and definite kind wherein the
curious and superstitious arts, in all nations and ages, and
religions also, have worked or played. These therefore we
may pass. Meanwhile it is nowise strange if opinion of
plenty has been the cause of want.

LXXXVI

Further, this admiration of men for knowledges and
arts,—an admiration in itself weak enough, and well-nigh
childish,—has been increased by the craft and artifices of
those who have handled and transmitted sciences. For
they set them forth with such ambition and parade, and
bring them into the view of the world so fashioned and

masked, as if they were complete in all parts and finished. For if you look at the method of them and the divisions, they seem to embrace and comprise everything which can belong to the subject. And although these divisions are ill filled out and are but as empty cases, still to the common mind they present the form and plan of a perfect science. But the first and most ancient seekers after truth were wont, with better faith and better fortune too, to throw the knowledge which they gathered from the contemplation of things, and which they meant to store up for use, into aphorisms; that is, into short and scattered sentences, not linked together by an artificial method; and did not pretend or profess to embrace the entire art. But as the matter now is, it is nothing strange if men do not seek to advance in things delivered to them as long since perfect and complete.

LXXXVII

Moreover the ancient systems have received no slight accession of reputation and credit from the vanity and levity of those who have propounded new ones; especially in the active and practical department of natural philosophy. For there have not been wanting talkers and dreamers who, partly from credulity, partly in imposture, have loaded mankind with promises, offering and announcing the prolongation of life, the retardation of age, the alleviation of pain, the repairing of natural defects, the deceiving of the senses; arts of binding and inciting the affections, of illuminating and exalting the intellectual faculties, of transmuting substances, of strengthening and multiplying motions at will, of making impressions and alterations in the air, of bringing down and procuring celestial influences; arts of divining things future, and bringing things distant near, and revealing things secret; and many more. But with regard to these lavish promisers, this judgment would not be far amiss; that there is as much difference in philosophy between their vanities and true arts, as there is in history between the exploits of Julius Cæsar or Alexander the Great, and the exploits of

Amadis of Gaul or Arthur of Britain. For it is true that those illustrious generals really did greater things than these shadowy heroes are even feigned to have done; but they did them by means and ways of action not fabulous or monstrous. Yet surely it is not fair that the credit of true history should be lessened because it has sometimes been injured and wronged by fables. Meanwhile it is not to be wondered at, if a great prejudice is raised against new propositions, especially when works are also mentioned, because of those impostors who have attempted the like; since their excess of vanity, and the disgust it has bred, have their effect still in the destruction of all greatness of mind in enterprises of this kind.

LXXXVIII

Far more however has knowledge suffered from littleness of spirit and the smallness and slightness of the tasks which human industry has proposed to itself. And what is worst of all, this very littleness of spirit comes with a certain air of arrogance and superiority.

For in the first place there is found in all arts one general device, which has now become familiar,—that the author lays the weakness of his art to the charge of nature: whatever his art cannot attain he sets down on the authority of the same art to be in nature impossible. And truly no art can be condemned if it be judge itself. Moreover the philosophy which is now in vogue embraces and cherishes certain tenets, the purpose of which (if it be diligently examined) is to persuade men that nothing difficult, nothing by which nature may be commanded and subdued, can be expected from art or human labour; as with respect to the doctrine that the heat of the sun and of fire differ in kind, and to that other concerning mixture, has been already observed. Which things, if they be noted accurately, tend wholly to the unfair circumscription of human power, and to a deliberate and factitious despair; which not only disturbs the auguries of hope, but also cuts the sinews and spur of industry, and throws away the chances of experience itself; and all for the sake of having their art thought perfect, and for the miserable vain-glory of making it believed that whatever has not yet been discovered and comprehended can never be discovered or comprehended hereafter.

And even if a man apply himself fairly to facts, and endeavour to find out something new, yet he will confine his aim and intention to the investigation and working out of some one discovery and no more; such as the nature of the magnet, the ebb and flow of the sea, the system of the heavens, and things of this kind, which seem to be in some measure secret, and have hitherto been handled without much success. Whereas it is most unskilful to investigate the nature of anything in the thing itself; seeing that the same nature which appears in some things to be latent and hidden is in others manifest and palpable; wherefore in the former it produces wonder, in the latter excites no attention; as we find it in the nature of consistency, which in wood or stone is not observed, but is passed over under the appellation of solidity, without further inquiry as to why separation or solution of continuity is avoided; while in the case of bubbles, which form themselves into certain pellicles, curiously shaped into hemispheres, so that the solution of continuity is avoided for a moment, it is thought a subtle matter. In fact what in some things is accounted a secret has in others a manifest and well known nature, which will never be recognised as long as the experiments and thoughts of men are engaged on the former only.

But generally speaking, in mechanics old discoveries pass for new, if a man does but refine or embellish them, or unite several in one, or couple them better with their use, or make the work in greater or less volume than it was before, or the like.

Thus then it is no wonder if noble inventions and worthy of mankind have not been brought to light, when men have been contented and delighted with such trifling and puerile tasks, and have even fancied that in them they have been endeavouring after, if not accomplishing, some great matter.

Neither is it to be forgotten that in every age Natural Philosophy has had a troublesome adversary and hard to deal with; namely, superstition, and the blind and immoderate zeal of religion. For we see among the Greeks that those who first proposed to men's then uninitiated ears the natural causes for thunder and for storms, were thereupon found guilty of impiety. Nor was much more forbearance shown by some of the ancient fathers of the Christian church to those who on most convincing grounds (such as no one in his senses would now think of contradicting) maintained that the earth was round, and of consequence asserted the existence of the antipodes.

Moreover, as things now are, to discourse of nature is made harder and more perilous by the summaries and systems of the schoolmen; who having reduced theology into regular order as well as they were able, and fashioned it into the shape of an art, ended in incorporating the contentious and thorny philosophy of Aristotle, more than was fit, with the body of religion.

To the same result, though in a different way, tend the speculations of those who have taken upon them to deduce the truth of the Christian religion from the principles of philosophers, and to confirm it by their authority; pompously solemnising this union of the sense and faith as a lawful marriage, and entertaining men's minds with a pleasing variety of matter, but all the while disparaging things divine by mingling them with things human. Now in such mixtures of theology with philosophy only the received doctrines of philosophy are included; while new ones, albeit changes for the better, are all but expelled and exterminated.

Lastly, you will find that by the simpleness of certain divines, access to any philosophy, however pure, is well nigh closed. Some are weakly afraid lest a deeper search into nature should transgress the permitted limits of sobermindedness; wrongfully wresting and transferring what is said in holy writ against those who pry into sacred mysteries, to the hidden things of nature, which are barred by

no prohibition. Others with more subtlety surmise and reflect that if second causes are unknown everything can
more readily be referred to the divine hand and rod; a
point in which they think religion greatly concerned;
which is in fact nothing else but to seek to gratify God
with a lie. Others fear from past example that movements
and changes in philosophy will end in assaults on religion.
And others again appear apprehensive that in the investigation of nature something may be found to subvert or
at least shake the authority of religion, especially with the
unlearned. But these two last fears seem to me to savour
utterly of carnal wisdom; as if men in the recesses and
secret thoughts of their hearts doubted and distrusted the
strength of religion and the empire of faith over the sense,
and therefore feared that the investigation of truth in
nature might be dangerous to them. But if the matter be
truly considered, natural philosophy is after the word of
God at once the surest medicine against superstition, and
the most approved nourishment for faith, and therefore
she is rightly given to religion as her most faithful hand-
maid, since the one displays the will of God, the other his
power. For he did not err who said "Ye err in that ye
know not the Scriptures and the power of God," thus
coupling and blending in an indissoluble bond information concerning his will and meditation concerning his
power. Meanwhile it is not surprising if the growth of
Natural Philosophy is checked, when religion, the thing
which has most power over men's minds, has by the simpleness and incautious zeal of certain persons been drawn
to take part against her.

XC

Again, in the customs and institutions of schools, acade-
mies, colleges, and similar bodies destined for the abode
of learned men and the cultivation of learning, everything
is found adverse to the progress of science. For the lectures and exercises there are so ordered, that to think or
speculate on anything out of the common way can hardly

occur to any man. And if one or two have the boldness to use any liberty of judgment, they must undertake the task all by themselves; they can have no advantage from the company of others. And if they can endure this also, they will find their industry and largeness of mind no slight hindrance to their fortune. For the studies of men in these places are confined and as it were imprisoned in the writings of certain authors, from whom if any man dissent he is straightway arraigned as a turbulent person and an innovator. But surely there is a great distinction between matters of state and the arts; for the danger from new motion and from new light is not the same. In matters of state a change even for the better is distrusted, because it unsettles what is established; these things resting on authority, consent, fame and opinion, not on demonstration. But arts and sciences should be like mines, where the noise of new works and further advances is heard on every side. But though the matter be so according to right reason, it is not so acted on in practice; and the points above mentioned in the administration and government of learning put a severe restraint upon the advancement of the sciences.

XCI

Nay, even if that jealousy were to cease, still it is enough to check the growth of science, that efforts and labours in this field go unrewarded. For it does not rest with the same persons to cultivate sciences and to reward them. The growth of them comes from great wits; the prizes and rewards of them are in the hands of the people, or of great persons, who are but in very few cases even moderately learned. Moreover this kind of progress is not only unrewarded with prizes and substantial benefits; it has not even the advantage of popular applause. For it is a greater matter than the generality of men can take in, and is apt to be overwhelmed and extinguished by the gales of popular opinions. And it is nothing strange if a thing not held in honour does not prosper.

But by far the greatest obstacle to the progress of science and to the undertaking of new tasks and provinces therein, is found in this—that men despair and think things impossible. For wise and serious men are wont in these matters to be altogether distrustful; considering with themselves the obscurity of nature, the shortness of life, the deceitfulness of the senses, the weakness of the judgment, the difficulty of experiment and the like; and so supposing that in the revolution of time and of the ages of the world the sciences have their ebbs and flows; that at one season they grow and flourish, at another wither and decay, yet in such sort that when they have reached a certain point and condition they can advance no further. If therefore any one believes or promises more, they think this comes of an ungoverned and unripened mind, and that such attempts have prosperous beginnings, become difficult as they go on, and end in confusion. Now since these are thoughts which naturally present themselves to grave men and of great judgment, we must take good heed that we be not led away by our love for a most fair and excellent object to relax or diminish the severity of our judgment; we must observe diligently what encouragement dawns upon us and from what quarter; and, putting aside the lighter breezes of hope, we must thoroughly sift and examine those which promise greater steadiness and constancy. Nay, and we must take stateprudence too into our counsels, whose rule is to distrust, and to take the less favourable view of human affairs. I am now therefore to speak touching Hope; especially as I am not a dealer in promises, and wish neither to force nor to ensnare men's judgments, but to lead them by the hand with their good will. And though the strongest means of inspiring hope will be to bring men to particulars; especially to particulars digested and arranged in my Tables of Discovery (the subject partly of the second, but much more of the fourth part of my Instauration), since this is not merely the promise of the thing but the thing itself; nevertheless that everything may be done with gentleness, I will proceed with my plan of preparing men's minds; of which preparation to give hope is no unimportant part. For without it the rest tends rather to make men sad (by giving them a worse and a meaner opinion of things as they are than they now have, and making them more fully to feel and know the unhappiness of their own condition) than to induce any alacrity or to whet their industry in making trial. And therefore it is fit that I publish and set forth those conjectures of mine which make hope in this matter reasonable; just as Columbus did, before that wonderful voyage of his across the Atlantic, when he gave the reasons for his conviction that new lands and continents might be discovered besides those which were known before; which reasons, though rejected at first, were afterwards made good by experience, and were the causes and beginnings of great events.

XCIII

The beginning is from God: for the business which is in hand, having the character of good so strongly impressed upon it, appears manifestly to proceed from God, who is the author of good, and the Father of Lights. Now in divine operations even the smallest beginnings lead of a certainty to their end. And as it was said of spiritual things, "The kingdom of God cometh not with observation," so is it in all the greater works of Divine Providence; everything glides on smoothly and noiselessly, and the work is fairly going on before men are aware that it has begun. Nor should the prophecy of Daniel be forgotten, touching the last ages of the world:—"Many shall go to and fro, and knowledge shall be increased;" clearly intimating that the thorough passage of the world (which now by so many distant voyages seems to be accomplished, or in course of accomplishment), and the advancement of the sciences, are destined by fate, that is, by Divine Providence, to meet in the same age.

XCIV

Next comes a consideration of the greatest importance

as an argument of hope; I mean that drawn from the errors of past time, and of the ways hitherto trodden. For most excellent was the censure once passed upon a government that had been unwisely administered. "That which is the worst thing in reference to the past, ought to be regarded as best for the future. For if you had done all that your duty demanded, and yet your affairs were no better, you would not have even a hope left you that further improvement is possible. But now, when your misfortunes are owing, not to the force of circumstances, but to your own errors, you may hope that by dismissing or correcting these errors, a great change may be made for the better." In like manner, if during so long a course of years men had kept the true road for discovering and cultivating sciences, and had yet been unable to make further progress therein, bold doubtless and rash would be the opinion that further progress is possible. But if the road itself has been mistaken, and men's labour spent on unfit objects, it follows that the difficulty has its rise not in things themselves, which are not in our power, but in the human understanding, and the use and application thereof, which admits of remedy and medicine. It will be of great use therefore to set forth what these errors are; for as many impediments as there have been in times past from this cause, so many arguments are there of hope for the time to come. And although they have been partly touched before, I think fit here also, in plain and simple words, to represent them.

XCV

Those who have handled sciences have been either men of experiment or men of dogmas. The men of experiment are like the ant; they only collect and use: the reasoners resemble spiders, who make cobwebs out of their own substance. But the bee takes a middle course; it gathers its material from the flowers of the garden and of the field, but transforms and digests it by a power of its own. Not unlike this is the true business of philosophy; for it neither relies solely or chiefly on the powers of the mind, nor does it take the matter which it gathers from natural history and mechanical experiments and lay it up in the memory whole, as it finds it; but lays it up in the understanding altered and digested. Therefore from a closer and purer league between these two faculties, the experimental and the rational, (such as has never yet been made) much may be hoped.

XCVI

We have as yet no natural philosophy that is pure; all is tainted and corrupted; in Aristotle's school by logic; in Plato's by natural theology; in the second school of Platonists, such as Proclus and others, by mathematics, which ought only to give definiteness to natural philosophy, not to generate or give it birth. From a natural philosophy pure and unmixed, better things are to be expected.

XCVII

No one has yet been found so firm of mind and purpose as resolutely to compel himself to sweep away all theories and common notions, and to apply the understanding, thus made fair and even, to a fresh examination of particulars. Thus it happens that human knowledge, as we have it, is a mere medley and ill-digested mass, made up of much credulity and much accident, and also of the childish notions which we at first imbibed.

Now if any one of ripe age, unimpaired senses, and well-purged mind, apply himself anew to experience and particulars, better hopes may be entertained of that man. In which point I promise to myself a like fortune to that of Alexander the Great; and let no man tax me with vanity till we have heard the end; for the thing which I mean tends to the putting off of all vanity. For of Alexander and his deeds Æschines spake thus: "Assuredly we do not live the life of mortal men; but to this end were we born, that in after ages wonders might be told of us;" as if what Alexander had done seemed to him miraculous. But in the next age Titus Livius took a better and a deeper view of the matter, saying in effect, that Alexander "had done no more than take courage to despise vain apprehensions." And a like judgment I suppose may be passed on myself in future ages: that I did no great things, but simply made less account of things that were accounted great. In the meanwhile, as I have already said, there is no hope except in a new birth of science; that is, in raising it regularly up from experience and building it afresh; which no one (I think) will say has yet been done or thought of.

XCVIII

Now for grounds of experience—since to experience we must come—we have as yet had either none or very weak ones; no search has been made to collect a store of particular observations sufficient either in number, or in kind, or in certainty, to inform the understanding, or in any way adequate. On the contrary, men of learning, but easy withal and idle, have taken for the construction or for the confirmation of their philosophy certain rumours and vague fames or airs of experience, and allowed to these the weight of lawful evidence. And just as if some kingdom or state were to direct its counsels and affairs, not by letters and reports from ambassadors and trustworthy messengers, but by the gossip of the streets; such exactly is the system of management introduced into philosophy with relation to experience. Nothing duly investigated, nothing verified, nothing counted, weighed, or measured, is to be found in natural history: and what in observation is loose and vague, is in information deceptive and treacherous. And if any one thinks that this is a strange thing to say, and something like an unjust complaint, seeing that Aristotle, himself so great a man, and supported by the wealth of so great a king, has composed so accurate a history of animals; and that others with greater diligence, though less pretence, have made many additions; while others, again, have compiled copious histories and descriptions of metals, plants, and fossils; it seems that he does not rightly apprehend what it is that we are now about. For a natural history which is composed for its own sake is not like one that is collected to supply the understanding with information for the building up of philosophy. They differ in many ways, but especially in this; that the former contains the variety of natural species only, and not experiments of the mechanical arts. For even as in the business of life a man's disposition and the secret workings of his mind and affections are better discovered when he is in trouble than at other times; so likewise the secrets of nature reveal themselves more readily under the vexations of art than when they go their own way. Good hopes may therefore be conceived of natural philosophy, when natural history, which is the basis and foundation of it, has been drawn up on a better plan; but not till then.

XCIX

Again, even in the great plenty of mechanical experiments, there is yet a great scarcity of those which are of most use for the information of the understanding. For the mechanic, not troubling himself with the investigation of truth, confines his attention to those things which bear upon his particular work, and will not either raise his mind or stretch out his hand for anything else. But then only will there be good ground of hope for the further advance of knowledge, when there shall be received and gathered together into natural history a variety of experiments, which are of no use in themselves, but simply serve to discover causes and axioms; which I call "*Experimenta lucifera*," experiments of *light*, to distinguish them from those which I call "*fructifera*," experiments of *fruit*.

Now experiments of this kind have one admirable property and condition; they never miss or fail. For since they are applied, not for the purpose of producing any particular effect, but only of discovering the natural cause of some effect, they answer the end equally well whichever way they turn out; for they settle the question.

C

But not only is a greater abundance of experiments to be sought for and procured, and that too of a different kind from those hitherto tried; an entirely different method, order, and process for carrying on and advancing experience must also be introduced. For experience, when it wanders in its own track, is, as I have already remarked, mere groping in the dark, and confounds men rather than instructs them. But when it shall proceed in accordance with a fixed law, in regular order, and without interruption, then may better things be hoped of knowledge.

CI

But even after such a store of natural history and experience as is required for the work of the understanding, or of philosophy, shall be ready at hand, still the understanding is by no means competent to deal with it off hand and by memory alone; no more than if a man should hope by force of memory to retain and make himself master of the computation of an ephemeris. And yet hitherto more has been done in matter of invention by thinking than by writing; and experience has not yet learned her letters. Now no course of invention can be satisfactory unless it be carried on in writing. But when this is brought into use, and experience has been taught to read and write, better things may be hoped.

CII

Moreover, since there is so great a number and army of particulars, and that army so scattered and dispersed as to distract and confound the understanding, little is to be hoped for from the skirmishings and slight attacks and desultory movements of the intellect, unless all the particulars which pertain to the subject of inquiry shall, by means of Tables of Discovery, apt, well arranged, and as it were animate, be drawn up and marshalled; and the mind be set to work upon the helps duly prepared and digested which these tables supply.

But after this store of particulars has been set out duly and in order before our eyes, we are not to pass at once to the investigation and discovery of new particulars or works; or at any rate if we do so we must not stop there. For although I do not deny that when all the experiments of all the arts shall have been collected and digested, and brought within one man's knowledge and judgment, the mere transferring of the experiments of one art to others may lead, by means of that experience which I term *literate*, to the discovery of many new things of service to the life and state of man, yet it is no great matter that can be hoped from that; but from the new light of axioms, which having been educed from those particulars by a certain method and rule, shall in their turn point out the way again to new particulars, greater things may be looked for. For our road does not lie on a level, but ascends and descends; first ascending to axioms, then descending to works.

The understanding must not however be allowed to jump and fly from particulars to remote axioms and of almost the highest generality (such as the first principles, as they are called, of arts and things), and taking stand upon them as truths that cannot be shaken, proceed to prove and frame the middle axioms by reference to them; which has been the practice hitherto; the understanding being not only carried that way by a natural impulse, but also by the use of syllogistic demonstration trained and inured to it. But then, and then only, may we hope well of the sciences, when in a just scale of ascent, and by successive steps not interrupted or broken, we rise from particulars to lesser axioms; and then to middle axioms, one above the other; and last of all to the most general. For the lowest axioms differ but slightly from bare experience, while the highest and most general (which we now have) are notional and abstract and without solidity. But the middle are the true and solid and living axioms, on which depend the affairs and fortunes of men; and above them again, last of all those which are indeed the most general; such I mean as are not abstract, but of which those intermediate axioms are really limitations.

The understanding must not therefore be supplied with wings, but rather hung with weights, to keep it from leaping and flying. Now this has never yet been done; when it is done, we may entertain better hopes of the sciences.

CV

In establishing axioms, another form of induction must be devised than has hitherto been employed; and it must be used for proving and discovering not first principles (as they are called) only, but also the lesser axioms, and the middle, and indeed all. For the induction which proceeds by simple enumeration is childish; its conclusions are precarious, and exposed to peril from a contradictory instance; and it generally decides on too small a number of facts, and on those only which are at hand. But the induction which is to be available for the discovery and demonstration of sciences and arts, must analyse nature by proper rejections and exclusions; and then, after a sufficient number of negatives, come to a conclusion on the affirmative instances: which has not yet been done or even attempted, save only by Plato, who does indeed employ this form of induction to a certain extent for the purpose of discussing definitions and ideas. But in order to furnish this induction or demonstration well and duly for its work, very many things are to be provided which no mortal has yet thought of; insomuch that greater labour will have to be spent in it than has hitherto been spent on the syllogism. And this induction must be used not only to discover axioms, but also in the formation of notions. And it is in this induction that our chief hope lies.

CVI

But in establishing axioms by this kind of induction, we must also examine and try whether the axiom so established be framed to the measure of those particulars only from which it is derived, or whether it be larger and wider. And if it be larger and wider, we must observe whether by indicating to us new particulars it confirm that wideness and largeness as by a collateral security; that we may not either stick fast in things already known, or loosely grasp at shadows and abstract forms; not at things solid and realised in matter. And when this process shall have come into use, then at last shall we see the dawn of a solid hope.

CVII

And here also should be remembered what was said above concerning the extending of the range of natural philosophy to take in the particular sciences, and the referring or bringing back of the particular sciences to natural philosophy; that the branches of knowledge may not be severed and cut off from the stem. For without this the hope of progress will not be so good.

CVIII

So much then for the removing of despair and the raising of hope through the dismissal or rectification of the errors of past time. We must now see what else there is to ground hope upon. And this consideration occurs at once—that if many useful discoveries have been made by accident or upon occasion, when men were not seeking for them but were busy about other things; no one can doubt but that when they apply themselves to seek and make this their business, and that too by method and in order and not by desultory impulses, they will discover far more. For although it may happen once or twice that a man shall stumble on a thing by accident which, when taking great pains to search for it, he could not find; yet upon the whole it unquestionably falls out the other way.

And therefore far better things, and more of them, and at shorter intervals, are to be expected from man's reason and industry and direction and fixed application, than from accident and animal instinct and the like, in which inventions have hitherto had their origin.

CIX

Another argument of hope may be drawn from this,—that some of the inventions already known are such as before they were discovered it could hardly have entered any man's head to think of; they would have been simply set aside as impossible. For in conjecturing what may be men set before them the example of what has been, and divine of the new with an imagination preoccupied and coloured by the old; which way of forming opinions is very fallacious; for streams that are drawn from the springheads of nature do not always run in the old channels.

If, for instance, before the invention of ordnance, a man had described the thing by its effects, and said that there was a new invention, by means of which the strongest towers and walls could be shaken and thrown down at a great distance; men would doubtless have begun to think over all the ways of multiplying the force of catapults and mechanical engines by weights and wheels and such machinery for ramming and projecting; but the notion of a fiery blast suddenly and violently expanding and exploding would hardly have entered into any man's imagination or fancy; being a thing to which nothing immediately analogous had been seen, except perhaps in an earthquake or in lightning, which as *magnalia* or marvels of nature, and by man not imitable, would have been immediately rejected.

In the same way, if before the discovery of silk, any one had said that there was a kind of thread discovered for the purposes of dress and furniture, which far surpassed the thread of linen or of wool in fineness and at the same time in strength, and also in beauty and softness; men would have begun immediately to think of some silky

kind of vegetable, or of the finer hair of some animal, or
of the feathers and down of birds; but of a web woven
by a tiny worm, and that in such abundance, and renewing itself yearly, they would assuredly never have thought.
Nay, if any one had said anything about a worm, he
would no doubt have been laughed at as dreaming of a
new kind of cobwebs.

So again, if before the discovery of the magnet, any
one had said that a certain instrument had been invented
by means of which the quarters and points of the heavens
could be taken and distinguished with exactness; men
would have been carried by their imagination to a variety
of conjectures concerning the more exquisite construction of astronomical instruments; but that anything could
be discovered agreeing so well in its movements with the
heavenly bodies, and yet not a heavenly body itself, but
simply a substance of metal or stone, would have been
judged altogether incredible. Yet these things and others
like them lay for so many ages of the world concealed
from men, nor was it by philosophy or the rational arts
that they were found out at last, but by accident and
occasion; being indeed, as I said, altogether different in
kind and as remote as possible from anything that was
known before; so that no preconceived notion could possibly have led to the discovery of them.

There is therefore much ground for hoping that there
are still laid up in the womb of nature many secrets of excellent use, having no affinity or parallelism with any
thing that is now known, but lying entirely out of the
beat of the imagination, which have not yet been found
out. They too no doubt will some time or other, in the
course and revolution of many ages, come to light of
themselves, just as the others did; only by the method of
which we are now treating they can be speedily and suddenly and simultaneously presented and anticipated.

CX

But we have also discoveries to show of another kind,
which prove that noble inventions may be lying at our

very feet, and yet mankind may step over without seeing them. For however the discovery of gunpowder, of silk, of the magnet, of sugar, of paper, or the like, may seem to depend on certain properties of things themselves and nature, there is at any rate nothing in the art of printing which is not plain and obvious. Nevertheless for want of observing that although it is more difficult to arrange types of letters than to write letters by the motion of the hand, there is yet this difference between the two, that types once arranged serve for innumerable impressions, but letters written with the hand for a single copy only; or perhaps again for want of observing that ink can be so thickened as to colour without running (particularly when the letters face upwards and the impression is made from above)—for want, I say, of observing these things, men went for so many ages without this most beautiful discovery, which is of so much service in the propagation of knowledge.

But such is the infelicity and unhappy disposition of the human mind in this course of invention, that it first distrusts and then despises itself: first will not believe that any such thing can be found out; and when it is found out, cannot understand how the world should have missed it so long. And this very thing may be justly taken as an argument of hope; namely, that there is a great mass of inventions still remaining, which not only by means of operations that are yet to be discovered, but also through the transferring, comparing, and applying of those already known, by the help of that Learned Experience of which I spoke, may be deduced and brought to light.

CXI

There is another ground of hope that must not be omitted. Let men but think over their infinite expenditure of understanding, time, and means on matters and pursuits of far less use and value; whereof if but a small part were directed to sound and solid studies, there is no difficulty that might not be overcome. This I thought good to add, because I plainly confess that a collection of history natural and experimental, such as I conceive it and as it ought to be, is a great, I may say a royal work, and of much labour and expense.

CXII

Meantime, let no man be alarmed at the multitude of particulars, but let this rather encourage him to hope. For the particular phenomena of art and nature are but a handful to the inventions of the wit, when disjoined and separated from the evidence of things. Moreover this road has an issue in the open ground and not far off; the other has no issue at all, but endless entanglement. For men hitherto have made but short stay with experience, but passing her lightly by, have wasted an infinity of time on meditations and glosses of the wit. But if some one were by that could answer our questions and tell us in each case what the fact in nature is, the discovery of all causes and sciences would be but the work of a few years.

CXIII

Moreover I think that men may take some hope from my own example. And this I say not by way of boasting, but because it is useful to say it. If there be any that despond, let them look at me, that being of all men of my time the most busied in affairs of state, and a man of health not very strong (whereby much time is lost), and in this course altogether a pioneer, following in no man's track, nor sharing these counsels with any one, have nevertheless by resolutely entering on the true road, and submitting my mind to Things, advanced these matters, as I suppose, some little way. And then let them consider what may be expected (after the way has been thus indicated) from men abounding in leisure, and from association of labours, and from successions of ages: the rather because it is not a way over which only one man can pass at a time (as is the case with that of reasoning), but one in which the labours and industries of men (especially as regards the collecting of experience) may with the best effect be first distributed and then combined. For then only will men begin to know their strength, when instead of great numbers doing all the same things, one shall take charge of one thing and another of another.

CXIV

Lastly, even if the breath of hope which blows on us from that New Continent were fainter than it is and harder to perceive; yet the trial (if we would not bear a spirit altogether abject) must by all means be made. For there is no comparison between that which we may lose by not trying and by not succeeding; since by not trying we throw away the chance of an immense good; by not succeeding we only incur the loss of a little human labour. But as it is, it appears to me from what has been said, and also from what has been left unsaid, that there is hope enough and to spare not only to make a bold man try, but also to make a sober-minded and wise man believe.

CXV

Concerning the grounds then for putting away despair, which has been one of the most powerful causes of delay and hindrance to the progress of knowledge, I have now spoken. And this also concludes what I had to say touching the *signs* and *causes* of the errors, sluggishness, and ignorance which have prevailed; especially since the more subtle causes, which do not fall under popular judgment and observation, must be referred to what has been said on the Idols of the human mind.

And here likewise should close that part of my Instauration, which is devoted to pulling down; which part is performed by three refutations; first, by the refutation of the *natural human reason,* left to itself; secondly, by the refutation of the *demonstrations;* and thirdly, by refutation of the *theories,* or the received systems of philosophy and doctrine. And the refutation of these has been such, as alone it could be: that is to say, by signs and the evidence of causes; since no other kind of confutation was open to me, differing as I do from others both on first principles and on rules of demonstration.

It is time therefore to proceed to the art itself and rule

of interpreting nature; still however there remains something to be premised. For whereas in this first book of aphorisms I proposed to prepare men's minds as well for understanding as for receiving what is to follow; now that I have purged and swept and levelled the floor of the mind, it remains that I place the mind in a good position and as it were in a favourable aspect towards what I have to lay before it. For in a new matter, it is not only the strong preoccupation of some old opinion that tends to create a prejudice, but also a false preconception or prefiguration of the new thing which is presented. I will endeavour therefore to impart sound and true opinions as to the things I propose, although they are to serve only for the time, and by way of interest (so to speak), till the thing itself, which is the principal, be fully known.

CXVI

First, then, I must request men not to suppose that after the fashion of ancient Greeks, and of certain moderns, as Telesius, Patricius, Severinus, I wish to found a new sect in philosophy. For this is not what I am about; nor do I think that it matters much to the fortunes of men what abstract notions one may entertain concerning nature and the principles of things; and no doubt many old theories of this kind can be revived and many new ones introduced; just as many theories of the heavens may be supposed, which agree well enough with the phenomena and yet differ with each other.

But for my part I do not trouble myself with any such speculative and withal unprofitable matters. My purpose, on the contrary, is to try whether I cannot in very fact lay more firmly the foundations, and extend more widely the limits, of the power and greatness of man. And although on some special subjects and in an incomplete form I am in possession of results which I take to be far more true and more certain and withal more fruitful than those now received, (and these I have collected into the fifth part of my Instauration,) yet I have no entire or universal theory to propound. For it does not seem that the time is come for such an attempt. Neither can I hope to live to complete the sixth part of the Instauration (which is destined for the philosophy discovered by the legitimate interpretation of nature), but hold it enough if in the intermediate business I bear myself soberly and profitably, sowing in the meantime for future ages the seeds of a purer truth, and performing my part towards the commencement of the great undertaking.

CXVII

And as I do not seek to found a school, so neither do I hold out offers or promises of particular works. It may be thought indeed, that I who make such frequent mention of works and refer everything to that end, should produce some myself by way of earnest. But my course and method, as I have often clearly stated and would wish to state again, is this,—not to extract works from works or experiments from experiments (as an empiric), but from works and experiments to extract causes and axioms, and again from those causes and axioms new works and experiments, as a legitimate interpreter of nature. And although in my tables of discovery (which compose the fourth part of the Instauration), and also in the examples of particulars (which I have adduced in the second part), and moreover in my observations on the history (which I have drawn out in the third part), any reader of even moderate sagacity and intelligence will everywhere observe indications and outlines of many noble works; still I candidly confess that the natural history which I now have, whether collected from books or from my own investigations, is neither sufficiently copious nor verified with sufficient accuracy to serve the purposes of legitimate interpretation.

Accordingly, if there be any one more apt and better prepared for mechanical pursuits, and sagacious in hunting out works by the mere dealing with experiment, let him by all means use his industry to gather from my history and tables many things by the way, and apply them to the production of works, which may serve as interest until the principal be forthcoming. But for myself, aiming as I do at greater things, I condemn all unseasonable and premature tarrying over such things as these; being (as I often say) like Atalanta's balls. For I do not run off like a child after golden apples, but stake all on the victory of art over nature in the race; nor do I make haste to mow down the moss or the corn in blade, but wait for the harvest in its due season.

CXVIII

There will be found no doubt, when my history and tables of discovery are read, some things in the experiments themselves that are not quite certain, or perhaps that are quite false; which may make a man think that the foundations and principles upon which my discoveries rest are false and doubtful. But this is of no consequence; for such things must needs happen at first. It is only like the occurrence in a written or printed page of a letter or two mistaken or misplaced; which does not much hinder the reader, because such errors are easily corrected by the sense. So likewise may there occur in my natural history many experiments which are mistaken and falsely set down, and yet they will presently by the discovery of causes and axioms be easily expunged and rejected. It is nevertheless true that if the mistakes in natural history and experiments are important, frequent, and continual, they cannot possibly be corrected or amended by any felicity of wit or art. And therefore, if in my natural history, which has been collected and tested with so much diligence, severity, and I may say religious care, there still lurk at intervals certain falsities or errors in the particulars,—what is to be said of common natural history, which in comparison with mine is so negligent and inexact? and what of the philosophy and sciences built on such a sand (or rather quicksand)? Let no man therefore trouble himself for this.

CXIX

There will be met with also in my history and experiments many things which are trivial and commonly known; many which are mean and low; many, lastly, which are too subtle and merely speculative, and that seem to be of no use; which kind of things may possibly avert and alienate men's interest.

And first for those things which seem common; let men bear in mind that hitherto they have been accustomed to do no more than refer and adapt the causes of things which rarely happen to such as happen frequently; while of those which happen frequently they never ask the cause, but take them as they are for granted. And therefore they do not investigate the causes of weight, of the rotation of heavenly bodies, of heat, cold, light, hardness, softness, rarity, density, liquidity, solidity, animation, inanimation, similarity, dissimilarity, organisation, and the like; but admitting these as self-evident and obvious, they dispute and decide on other things of less frequent and familiar occurrence.

But I, who am well aware that no judgment can be passed on uncommon or remarkable things, much less anything new brought to light, unless the causes of common things, and the causes of those causes, be first duly examined and found out, am of necessity compelled to admit the commonest things into my history. Nay, in my judgment philosophy has been hindered by nothing more than this,—that things of familiar and frequent occurrence do not arrest and detain the thoughts of men, but are received in passing without any inquiry into their causes; insomuch that information concerning things which are not known is not oftener wanted than attention concerning things which are.

CXX

And for things that are mean or even filthy,—things which (as Pliny says) must be introduced with an apology,—such things, no less than the most splendid and costly, must be admitted into natural history. Nor is natural history polluted thereby; for the sun enters the sewer no less than the palace, yet takes no pollution. And for myself, I am not raising a capitol or pyramid to the pride of man, but laying a foundation in the human understanding for a holy temple after the model of the world. That model therefore I follow. For whatever deserves to exist deserves also to be known, for knowledge is the image of existence; and things mean and splendid exist alike. Moreover as from certain putrid substances—musk, for instance, and civet—the sweetest odours are sometimes generated, so too from mean and sordid instances there sometimes emanates excellent light and information. But enough and more than enough of this; such fastidiousness being merely childish and effeminate.

CXXI

But there is another objection which must be more carefully looked to: namely, that there are many things in this History which to common apprehension, or indeed to any understanding accustomed to the present system, will seem to be curiously and unprofitably subtle. Upon this point therefore above all I must say again what I have said already,—that at first and for a time I am seeking for experiments of light, not for experiments of fruit; following therein, as I have often said, the example of the divine creation; which on the first day produced light only, and assigned to it alone one entire day, nor mixed up with it on that day any material work.

To suppose therefore that things like these are of no use is the same as to suppose that light is of no use, because it is not a thing solid or material. And the truth is that the knowledge of simple natures well examined and defined is as light; it gives entrance to all the secrets of nature's workshop, and virtually includes and draws after it whole bands and troops of works, and opens to us the sources of the noblest axioms; and yet in itself it is of no great use. So also the letters of the alphabet in themselves and apart have no use or meaning, yet they are the subject-matter for the composition and apparatus of all discourse. So again the seeds of things are of much latent virtue, and yet of no use except in their development. And the scattered rays of light itself, until they are made to converge, can impart none of their benefit.

But if objection be taken to speculative subtleties, what is to be said of the schoolmen, who have indulged in subtleties to such excess? in subtleties too that were spent on words, or at any rate on popular notions (which is much the same thing), not on facts or nature; and such as were useless not only in their origin but also in their consequences; and not like those I speak of, useless indeed for the present, but promising infinite utility hereafter. But let men be assured of this, that all subtlety of disputation and discourse, if not applied till after axioms are discovered, is out of season and preposterous; and that the true and proper or at any rate the chief time for subtlety is in weighing experience and in founding axioms thereon; for that other subtlety, though it grasps and snatches at nature, yet can never take hold of her. Certainly what is said of opportunity or fortune is most true of nature; she has a lock in front, but is bald behind.

Lastly, concerning the disdain to receive into natural history things either common, or mean, or over-subtle and in their original condition useless, the answer of the poor woman to the haughty prince, who had rejected her petition as an unworthy thing and beneath his dignity, may be taken for an oracle,—"Then leave off being king." For most certain it is that he who will not attend to things like these, as being too paltry and minute, can neither win the kingdom of nature nor govern it.

CXXII

It may be thought also a strange and a harsh thing that we should at once and with one blow set aside all sciences and all authors; and that too without calling in any of the ancients to our aid and support, but relying on our own strength.

And I know that if I had chosen to deal less sincerely, I might easily have found authority for my suggestions by referring them either to the old times before the Greeks (when natural science was perhaps more flourishing, though it made less noise, not having yet having passed into the pipes and trumpets of the Greeks), or even, in part at least, to some of the Greeks themselves; and so gained for them both support and honour; as men of no family devise for themselves by the good help of genealogies the nobility of a descent from some ancient stock. But for my part, relying on the evidence and truth of things, I reject all forms of fiction and imposture; nor do I think that it matters any more to the business in hand, whether the discoveries that shall now be made were long ago known to the ancients, and have their settings and their risings according to the vicissitude of things and course of ages, than it matters to mankind whether the new world be that island of Atlantis with which the ancients were acquainted, or now discovered for the first time. For new discoveries must be sought from the light of nature, not fetched back out of the darkness of antiquity.

And as for the universality of the censure, certainly if the matter be truly considered, such a censure is not only more probable but more modest too, than a partial one would be. For if the errors had not been rooted in primary notions, there must have been some true discoveries to correct the false. But the errors being fundamental, and not so much of false judgment as of inattention and oversight, it is no wonder that men have not obtained what they have not tried for, nor reached a mark which they never set up, nor finished a course which they never entered on or kept.

And as for the presumption implied in it; certainly if a man undertakes by steadiness of hand and power of eye to describe a straighter line or more perfect circle than any one else, he challenges a comparison of abilities; but if he only says that he with the help of a rule or a pair of compasses can draw a straighter line or a more perfect circle than any one else can by eye and hand alone, he makes no great boast. And this remark, be it observed, applies not merely to this first and inceptive attempt of mine, but to all that shall take the work in hand hereafter. For my way of discovering sciences goes far to level men's wits, and leaves but little to individual excellence; because it performs everything by the surest rules and demonstrations. And therefore I attribute my part in all this, as I have often said, rather to good luck than to ability, and account it a birth of time rather than of wit. For certainly chance has something to do with men's thoughts, as well as with their works and deeds.

CXXIII

I may say then of myself that which one said in jest (since it marks the distinction so truly), "It cannot be that we should think alike, when one drinks water and the other drinks wine." Now other men, as well in ancient as in modern times, have in the matter of sciences drunk a crude liquor like water, either flowing spontaneously from the understanding, or drawn up by logic, as by wheels from a well. Whereas I pledge mankind in a liquor strained from countless grapes, from grapes ripe and fully seasoned, collected in clusters, and gathered, and then squeezed in the press, and finally purified and clarified in the vat. And therefore it is no wonder if they and I do not think alike.

CXXIV

Again, it will be thought, no doubt, that the goal and mark of knowledge which I myself set up (the very point which I object to in others) is not the true or the best; for that the contemplation of truth is a thing worthier and loftier than all utility and magnitude of works; and that this long and anxious dwelling with experience and matter and the fluctuations of individual things, drags down the mind to earth, or rather sinks it to a very Tartarus of turmoil and confusion; removing and withdrawing it from the serene tranquillity of abstract wisdom, a condition far more heavenly. Now to this I readily assent; and indeed this which they point at as so much to be preferred, is the very thing of all others which I am about. For I am building in the human understanding a true model of the world, such as it is in fact, not such as a man's own reason would have it to be; a thing which cannot be done without a very diligent dissection and anatomy of the world. But I say that those foolish and apish images of worlds which the fancies of men have created in philosophical systems, must be utterly scattered to the winds. Be it known then how vast a difference there is (as I said above) between the Idols of the human mind and the Ideas of the divine. The former are nothing more than arbitrary abstractions; the latter are the creator's own stamp upon creation, impressed and defined in matter by true and exquisite lines. Truth therefore and utility are here the very same things: and works themselves are of greater value as pledges of truth than as contributing to the comforts of life.

CXXV

It may be thought again that I am but doing what has been done before; that the ancients themselves took the same course which I am now taking; and that it is likely therefore that I too, after all this stir and striving, shall come at last to some one of those systems which prevailed in ancient times. For the ancients too, it will be said, provided at the outset of their speculations a great store and abundance of examples and particulars, digested the same into notebooks under heads and titles, from them completed their systems and arts, and afterwards, when they understood the matter, published them to the world,—adding a few examples here and there for proof and illustration; but thought it superfluous and inconvenient to publish their notes and minutes and digests of particulars; and therefore did as builders do,—after the house was built they removed the scaffolding and ladders out of sight. And so no doubt they did. But this objection (or scruple rather) will be easily answered by any one who has not quite forgotten what I have said above. For the form of inquiry and discovery that was in use among the ancients is by themselves professed, and appears on the very face of their writings. And that form was simply this. From a few examples and particulars (with the addition of common notions and perhaps of some portion of the received opinions which have been most popular) they flew at once to the most general conclusions, or first principles of science: taking the truth of these as fixed and immoveable, they proceeded by means of intermediate propositions to educe and prove from them the inferior conclusions; and out of these they framed the art. After that, if any new particulars and examples repugnant to their dogmas were mooted and adduced, either they subtly moulded them into their system by distinctions or explanations of their rules, or else coarsely got rid of them by exceptions; while to such particulars as were not repugnant they laboured to assign causes in conformity with those their principles. But this was not the natural history and experience that was wanted; far from it; and besides, that flying off to the highest generalities ruined all.

CXXVI

It will also be thought that by forbidding men to pronounce and to set down principles as established until they have duly arrived through the intermediate steps at the highest generalities, I maintain a sort of suspension of the judgment, and bring it to what the Greeks call *Acatalepsia,*—a denial of the capacity of the mind to comprehend truth. But in reality that which I meditate and propound is not *Acatalepsia,* but *Eucatalepsia;* not denial of the capacity to understand, but provision for understanding truly; for I do not take away authority from the senses, but supply them with helps: I do not slight the understanding, but govern it. And better surely it is that we should know all we need to know, and yet think our knowledge imperfect, than that we should think our knowledge perfect, and yet not know anything we need to know.

CXXVII

It may also be asked (in the way of doubt rather than objection) whether I speak of natural philosophy only, or whether I mean that the other sciences, logic, ethics, and politics, should be carried on by this method. Now I certainly mean what I have said to be understood of them all; and as the common logic, which governs by the syllogism, extends not only to natural but to all sciences; so does mine also, which proceeds by induction, embrace everything. For I form a history and tables of discovery for anger, fear, shame, and the like; for matters political; and again for the mental operations of memory, composition and division, judgment and the rest; not less than for heat and cold, or light, or vegetation, or the like. But nevertheless since my method of interpretation, after the history has been prepared and duly arranged, regards not the working and discourse of the mind only (as the common logic does) but the nature of things also, I supply the mind with such rules and guidance that it may in every case apply itself aptly to the nature of things. And therefore I deliver many and diverse precepts in the doctrine of Interpretation, which in some measure modify the method of invention according to the quality and condition of the subject of the inquiry.

CXXVIII

On one point not even a doubt ought to be entertained; namely, whether I desire to pull down and destroy the philosophy and arts and sciences which are at present in use. So far from that, I am most glad to see them used, cultivated, and honoured. There is no reason why the arts which are now in fashion should not continue to supply matter for disputation and ornaments for discourse, to be employed for the convenience of professors and men of business; to be in short like current coin, which passes among men by consent. Nay I frankly declare that what I am introducing will be but little fitted for such purposes as these, since it cannot be brought down to common apprehension, save by effects and works only. But how sincere I am in my professions of affection and good will towards the received sciences, my published writings, especially the books on the Advancement of Learning, sufficiently show; and therefore I will not attempt to prove it further by words. Meanwhile I give constant and distinct warning that by the methods now in use neither can any great progress be made in the doctrines and contemplative part of sciences, nor can they be carried out to any magnitude of works.

CXXIX

It remains for me to say a few words touching the excellency of the end in view. Had they been uttered earlier, they might have seemed like idle wishes; but now that hopes have been raised and unfair prejudices removed, they may perhaps have greater weight. Also if I had finished all myself, and had no occasion to call in others to help and take part in the work, I should even now have abstained from such language, lest it might be taken as a proclamation of my own deserts. But since I want to quicken the industry and rouse and kindle the zeal of others, it is fitting that I put men in mind of some things.

In the first place then, the introduction of famous discoveries appears to hold by far the first place among human actions; and this was the judgment of the former ages. For to the authors of inventions they awarded divine honours; while to those who did good service in the state (such as founders of cities and empires, legislators, saviours of their country from long endured evils, quellers of tyrannies, and the like) they decreed no higher honours than heroic. And certainly if a man rightly compare the two, he will find that this judgment of antiquity was just. For the benefits of discoveries may extend to the whole race of man, civil benefits only to particular places; the latter last not beyond a few ages, the former through all time. Moreover the reformation of a state in civil matters is seldom brought in without violence and confusion; but discoveries carry blessings with them, and confer benefits without causing harm or sorrow to any.

Again, discoveries are as it were new creations, and imitations of God's works; as well sang the poet:—

"To man's frail race great Athens long ago
   First gave the seed whence waving harvests grow,
And *re-created* all our life below."

And it appears worthy of remark in Solomon, that though mighty in empire and in gold; in the magnificence of his works, his court, his household, and his fleet; in the lustre of his name and the worship of mankind; yet he took none of these to glory in, but pronounced that "The glory of God is to conceal a thing; the glory of the king to search it out."

Again, let a man only consider what a difference there is between the life of men in the most civilised province of Europe, and in the wildest and most barbarous districts of New India; he will feel it be great enough to justify the saying that "man is a god to man," not only in regard of aid and benefit, but also by a comparison of condition. And this difference comes not from soil, not from climate, not from race, but from the arts.

Again, it is well to observe the force and virtue and consequences of discoveries; and these are to be seen nowhere more conspicuously than in those three which were unknown to the ancients, and of which the origin, though recent, is obscure and inglorious; namely, printing, gunpowder, and the magnet. For these three have changed the whole face and state of things throughout the world; the first in literature, the second in warfare, the third in navigation; whence have followed innumerable changes; insomuch that no empire, no sect, no star seems to have exerted greater power and influence in human affairs than these mechanical discoveries.

Further, it will not be amiss to distinguish the three kinds and as it were grades of ambition in mankind. The first is of those who desire to extend their own power in their native country; which kind is vulgar and degenerate. The second is of those who labour to extend the power of their country and its dominion among men. This certainly has more dignity, though not less covetousness. But if a man endeavour to establish and extend the power and dominion of the human race itself over the universe, his ambition (if ambition it can be called) is without doubt both a more wholesome thing and a more noble than the other two. Now the empire of man over things depends wholly on the arts and sciences. For we cannot command nature except by obeying her.

Again, if men have thought so much of some one particular discovery as to regard him as more than man who has been able by some benefit to make the whole human race his debtor, how much higher a thing to discover that by means of which all things else shall be discovered with ease! And yet (to speak the whole truth), as the uses of light are infinite, in enabling us to walk, to ply our arts, to read, to recognise one another; and nevertheless the very beholding of the light is itself a more excellent and a fairer thing than all the uses of it;—so assuredly the very contemplation of things, as they are, without superstition or imposture, error or confusion, is in itself more worthy than all the fruit of inventions.

Lastly, if the debasement of arts and sciences to purposes of wickedness, luxury, and the like, be made a ground of objection, let no one be moved thereby. For the same may be said of all earthly goods; of wit, courage, strength, beauty, wealth, light itself, and the rest. Only let the human race recover that right over nature which belongs to it by divine bequest, and let power be given it; the exercise thereof will be governed by sound reason and true religion.

CXXX

And now it is time for me to propound the art itself of interpreting nature; in which, although I conceive that I have given true and most useful precepts, yet I do not say either that it is absolutely necessary (as if nothing could be done without it) or that it is perfect. For I am of opinion that if men had ready at hand a just history of nature and experience, and laboured diligently thereon; and if they could bind themselves to two rules,—the first, to lay aside received opinions and notions; and the second, to refrain the mind for a time from the highest generalisations, and those next to them,—they would be able by the native and genuine force of the mind, without any other art, to fall into my form of interpretation. For interpretation is the true and natural work of the mind when freed from impediments. It is true however that by my precepts everything will be in more readiness, and much more sure.

Nor again do I mean to say that no improvement can be made upon these. On the contrary, I that regard the mind not only in its own faculties, but in its connection with things, must needs hold that the art of discovery may advance as discoveries advance.

A PRAYER

OR

PSALM

[1621]

MOST gracious Lord God, my merciful Father, from my youth up, my Creator, my Redeemer, my Comforter. Thou (O Lord) soundest and searchest the depths and secrets of all hearts; thou knowledgest the upright of heart, thou judgest the hypocrite, thou ponderest men's thought and doings as in a balance, thou measurest their intentions as with a line, vanity and crooked ways cannot be hid from thee.

Remember (O Lord) how thy servant walked before thee: remember what I have first sought, and what hath been principal in mine intentions. I have loved thy assemblies, I have mourned for the divisions of thy Church, I have delighted in the brightness of thy sanctuary. This vine which thy right hand hath planted in this nation, I have ever prayed unto thee that it might have the first and the latter rain; and that it might stretch her branches to the seas and to the floods. The state and bread of the poor and oppressed have been precious in mine eyes: I have hated all cruelty and hardness of heart: I have (though in a despised weed) procured the good of all men. If any have been mine enemies, I thought not of them; neither hath the sun almost set upon my displeasure; but I have been as a dove, free from superfluity of maliciousness. Thy creatures have been my books, but thy Scriptures much more. I have sought thee in the courts, fields, and gardens, but I have found thee in thy temples.

Thousand have been my sins, and ten thousand my transgressions; but thy sanctifications have remained with me, and my heart, through thy grace, hath been an unquenched coal upon thy altar. O Lord, my strength, I have since my youth met with thee in all my ways, by thy fatherly compassions, by thy comfortable chastisements, and by thy most visible providence. As thy favours have increased upon me, so have thy corrections; so as thou hast been alway near me, O Lord; and ever as my worldly blessings were exalted, so secret darts from thee have pierced me; and when I ascended before men, I have descended in humiliation before thee.

And now when I thought most of peace and honour, thy hand is heavy upon me, and hath humbled me, according to thy former loving-kindness, keeping me still in thy fatherly school, not as a bastard, but as a child. Just are thy judgments upon me for my sins, which are more in number than the sands of the sea, but have no proportion to thy mercies; for what are the sands of the sea, to the sea, earth, heavens? and all these are nothing to thy mercies.

Besides my innumerable sins, I confess before thee, that I am debtor to thee for the gracious talent of thy gifts and graces, which I have neither put into a napkin, nor put it (as I ought) to exchanges, where it might have been made best profit; but misspent it in things for which I was least fit; so as I may truly say, my soul hath been a stranger in the course of my pilgrimage. Be merciful unto me (O Lord) for my Saviour's sake, and receive me into thy bosom, or guide me in thy ways.

NEW ATLANTIS
A WORK UNFINISHED

WRITTEN BY

THE RIGHT HONOURABLE

FRANCIS LORD VERULAM,

VISCOUNT ST. ALBAN

[1624]

TO THE READER

THIS fable my Lord devised, to the end that he might exhibit therein a model or description of a college instituted for the interpreting of nature and the producing of great and marvellous works for the benefit of men, under the name of Salomon's House, or the College of the Six Days' Works. And even so far his Lordship hath proceeded, as to finish that part. Certainly the model is more vast and high than can possibly be imitated in all things; notwithstanding most things therein are within men's power to effect. His Lordship thought also in this present fable to have composed a frame of Laws, or of the best state or mould of a commonwealth; but foreseeing it would be a long work, his desire of collecting the Natural History diverted him, which he preferred many degrees before it.

This work of the *New Atlantis* (as much as concerneth the English edition) his Lordship designed for this place; in regard it hath so near affinity (in one part of it) with the preceding Natural History.

W. RAWLEY

NEW ATLANTIS

WE sailed from Peru, (where we had continued by the space of one whole year,) for China and Japan, by the South Sea; taking with us victuals for twelve months; and had good winds from the east, though soft and weak, for five months' space and more. But then the wind came about, and settled in the west for many days, so as we could make little or no way, and were sometimes in purpose to turn back. But then again there arose strong and great winds from the south, with a point east; which carried us up (for all that we could do) towards the north: by which time our victuals failed us, though we had made good spare of them. So that finding ourselves in the midst of the greatest wilderness of waters in the world, without victual, we gave ourselves for lost men, and prepared for death. Yet we did lift up our hearts and voices to God above, who *showeth his wonders in the deep;* beseeching him of his mercy, that as in the beginning he discovered the face of the deep, and brought forth dry land, so he would now discover land to us, that we might not perish. And it came to pass that the next day about evening, we saw within a kenning before us, towards the north, as it were thick clouds, which did put us in some hope of land; knowing how that part of the South Sea was utterly unknown; and might have islands or continents, that hitherto were not come to light. Wherefore we bent our course thither, where we saw the appearance of land, all that night; and in the dawning of the next day, we might plainly discern that it was a land; flat to our sight, and full of boscage; which made it shew the more dark. And after an hour and a half's sailing, we entered into a good haven, being the port of a fair city; not great indeed, but well built, and that gave a pleasant view from the sea: and we thinking every minute long till we were on land, came close to the shore, and offered to land. But straightways we saw divers of the people, with bastons in their hands, as it were forbidding us to land; yet without any cries or fierceness, but only as warning us off by signs that they made. Whereupon being not a little discomforted, we were advising with ourselves what we should do. During which time there made forth to us a small boat, with about eight persons in it; whereof one of them had in his hand a tipstaff of a yellow cane, tipped at both ends with blue, who came aboard our ship, without any show of distrust at all. And when he saw one of our number present himself somewhat afore the rest, he drew forth a little scroll of parchment, (somewhat yellower than our parchment, and shining like the leaves of writing tables, but otherwise soft and flexible,) and delivered it to our foremost man. In which scroll were written in ancient Hebrew, and in ancient Greek, and in good Latin of the School, and in Spanish, these words; "Land ye not, none of you; and provide to be gone from this coast within sixteen days, except you have further time given you. Meanwhile, if you want fresh water, or victual, or help for your sick, or that your ship needeth repair, write down your wants, and you shall have that which belongeth to mercy." This scroll was signed with a stamp of cherubins' wings, not spread but hanging downwards, and by them a cross. This being delivered, the officer returned, and left only a servant with us to receive our answer. Consulting hereupon amongst ourselves, we were much perplexed. The denial of landing and hasty warning us away troubled us much; on the other side, to find that the people had languages and were so full of humanity, did comfort us not a little. And above all, the sign of the cross to that instrument was to us a great rejoicing, and as it were a certain presage of good. Our answer was in the Spanish tongue; "That for our ship, it was well; for we had rather met with calms and contrary winds than any tempests. For our sick, they were many, and in very ill case; so that if they were not permitted to land, they ran danger of their lives." Our other wants we set down in particular; adding, "that we had some little store of merchandise, which if it pleased them to deal for, it might supply our wants without being chargeable unto them." We offered some reward in pistolets unto the servant, and a piece of crimson velvet to be presented to the officer; but the servant took them not, nor would scarce look upon them; and so left us, and went back in another little boat which was sent for him.

About three hours after we had dispatched our answer, there came towards us a person (as it seemed) of place. He had on him a gown with wide sleeves, of a kind of water chamolet, of an excellent azure colour, far more glossy than ours; his under apparel was green; and so was his hat, being in the form of a turban, daintily made, and not so huge as the Turkish turbans; and the locks of his hair came down below the brims of it. A reverend man was he to behold. He came in a boat, gilt in some part of it, with four persons more only in that boat; and was followed by another boat, wherein were some twenty. When he was come within a flight-shot of our ship, signs were made to us that we should send forth some to meet him upon the water; which we presently did in our ship-boat, sending the principal man amongst us save one, and four of our number with him. When we were come within six yards of their boat, they called to us to stay, and not to approach farther; which we did. And thereupon the man whom I before described stood up, and with a loud voice in Spanish, asked, "Are ye Christians?" We answered, "We were;" fearing the less, because of the cross we had seen in the subscription. At which answer the said person lifted up his right hand towards heaven, and drew it softly to his mouth, (which is the gesture they use when they thank God,) and then said: "If ye will swear (all of you) by the merits of the Saviour that ye are no pirates, nor have shed blood lawfully nor unlawfully within forty days past, you may have licence to come on land." We said, "We were all ready to take that oath." Whereupon one of those that were with him, being (as it seemed) a notary, made an entry of this act. Which done, another of the attendants of the great person, which was with him in the same boat, after his lord had spoken a little to him, said aloud; "My lord would have you know, that it is not of pride or greatness that he cometh not aboard your ship; but for that in your answer you declare that you have many sick amongst you, he was warned by the Conservator of Health of the city that he should keep a distance." We bowed ourselves towards him, and answered, "We were his humble servants; and accounted for great honour and singular humanity towards us that which was already done; but hoped well that the nature of the sickness of our men was not infectious." So he returned; and a while after came the notary to us aboard our ship; holding in his hand a fruit of that country, like an orange, but of colour between orange-tawney and scarlet, which cast a most excellent odour. He used it (as it seemeth) for a preservative against infection. He gave us our oath; "By the name of Jesus and his merits:" and after told us that the next day by six of the clock in the morning we should be sent to, and brought to the Strangers' House, (so he called it,) where we should be accommodated of things both for our whole and for our sick. So he left us; and when we offered him some pistolets, he smiling said, "He must not be twice paid for one labour": meaning (as I take it) that he had salary sufficient of the state for his service. For (as I after learned) they call an officer that taketh rewards, *twice paid*.

The next morning early, there came to us the same officer that came to us at first with his cane, and told us, he came to conduct us to the Strangers' House; and that he had prevented the hour, because we might have the whole day before us for our business. "For," said he, "if you will follow my advice, there shall first go with me some few of you, and see the place, and how it may be made convenient for you; and then you may send for your sick, and the rest of your number which ye will bring on land." We thanked him, and said, "That this care which he took of desolate strangers God would reward." And so six of us went on land with him: and when we were on land, he went before us, and turned to us, and said, "He was but our servant, and our guide." He led us through three fair streets; and all the way we went there were gathered some people on both sides standing in a row; but in so civil a fashion, as if it had been not to wonder at us but to welcome us; and divers of them, as we passed by them, put their arms a little abroad; which is their gesture when they bid any welcome. The Strangers' House is a fair and spacious house, built of brick, of somewhat a bluer colour than our brick; and with handsome windows, some of glass, some of a kind of cambric oiled. He brought us first into a fair parlour above stairs, and then asked us, "What number of persons we were? And how many sick?" We answered "We were in all (sick and whole) one and fifty persons, whereof our sick were seventeen." He desired us to have patience a little, and to stay till he came back to us; which was about an hour after; and then he led us to see the chambers which were provided for us, being in number nineteen: they having cast it (as it seemeth) that four of those chambers, which were better than the rest, might receive four of the principal men of our company, and lodge them alone by themselves; and the other fifteen chambers were to lodge us two and two together. The chambers were handsome and cheerful chambers, and furnished civilly. Then he led us to a long gallery, like a dorture, where he showed us all along the one side (for the other side was but wall and window) seventeen cells, very neat ones, having partitions of cedar wood. Which gallery and cells, being in all forty, (many more than we needed,) were instituted as an infirmary for sick persons. And he told us withal, that as any of our sick waxed well, he might be removed from his cell to a chamber; for which purpose there were set forth ten spare chambers, besides the number we spake of before. This done, he brought us back to the parlour, and lifting up his cane a little, (as they do when they give any charge or command,) said to us, "Ye are to know that the custom of the land requireth, that after this day and to-morrow, (which we give you for removing of your people from your ship,) you are to keep within doors for three days. But let it not trouble you, nor do not think yourselves restrained, but rather left to your rest and ease. You shall want nothing, and there are six of our people appointed to attend you, for any business you may have abroad." We gave him thanks with all affection and respect, and said, "God surely is manifested in this land." We offered him also twenty pistolets; but he smiled, and only said; "What? twice paid!" And so he left us. Soon after our dinner was served in; which was right good viands, both for bread and meat; better than any collegiate diet that I have known in Europe. We had also drink of three sorts, all wholesome and good; wine of the grape; a drink of grain, such as is with us our ale, but more clear; and a kind of cider made of a fruit of that country; a wonderful pleasing and refreshing drink. Besides, there were brought in to us great store of those scarlet oranges for our sick; which (they said) were an assured remedy for sickness taken at sea. There was given us also a box of small grey or whitish pills, which they wished our sick should take, one of the pills every night before sleep; which (they said) would hasten their recovery. The next day, after that our trouble of carriage and removing of our men and goods out of our ship was somewhat settled and quiet, I thought good to call our company together; and when they were assembled said unto them; "My dear friends, let us know ourselves, and how it standeth with us. We are men cast on land, as Jonas was out of the whale's belly, when we were as buried in the deep: and now we are on land, we are but between death and life; for we are beyond both the old world and the new; and whether ever we shall see Europe, God only knoweth. It is a kind of miracle hath brought us hither: and it must be little less that shall bring us hence. Therefore in regard of our deliverance past, and our danger present and to come, let us look up to God, and every man reform his own ways. Besides we are come here amongst a Christian people, full of piety and humanity: let us not bring that confusion of face upon ourselves, as to show our vices or unworthiness before them. Yet there is more. For they have by commandment (though in form of courtesy) cloistered us within these walls for three days: who knoweth whether it be not to take some taste of our manners and conditions? and if they find them bad, to banish us straightways; if good, to give us further time.

For these men that they have given us for attendance may withal have an eye upon us. Therefore for God's love, and as we love the weal of our souls and bodies, let us so behave ourselves as we may be at peace with God, and may find grace in the eyes of this people." Our company with one voice thanked me for my good admonition, and promised me to live soberly and civilly, and without giving any the least occasion of offence. So we spent our three days joyfully and without care, in expectation what would be done with us when they were expired. During which time, we had every hour joy of the amendment of our sick; who thought themselves cast into some divine pool of healing, they mended so kindly and so fast.

The morrow after our three days were past, there came to us a new man that we had not seen before, clothed in blue as the former was, save that his turban was white, with a small red cross on the top. He had also a tippet of fine linen. At his coming in, he did bend to us a little, and put his arms abroad. We of our parts saluted him in a very lowly and submissive manner; as looking that from him we should receive sentence of life or death. He desired to speak with some few of us: whereupon six of us only stayed and the rest avoided the room. He said, "I am by office governor of this House of Strangers, and by vocation I am a Christian priest; and therefore am come to you to offer you my service, both as strangers and chiefly as Christians. Some things I may tell you, which I think you will not be unwilling to hear. The state hath given you licence to stay on land for the space of six weeks: and let it not trouble you if your occasions ask further time, for the law in this point is not precise; and I do not doubt but myself shall be able to obtain for you such further time as may be convenient. Ye shall also understand, that the Strangers' House is at this time rich, and much aforehand; for it hath laid up revenue these thirty-seven years; for so long it is since any stranger arrived in this part: and therefore take ye no care; the state will defray you all the time you stay; neither shall you stay one day the less for that. As for any merchandise ye have brought, ye shall be well used, and have your return either in merchandise or in gold and silver: for to us it is all one. And if you have any other request to make, hide it not. For ye shall find we will not make your countenance to fall by the answer ye shall receive. Only this I must tell you, that none of you must go above a *karan*" (that is with them a mile and a half) "from the walls of the city, without especial leave." We answered, after we had looked awhile one upon another admiring this gracious and parent-like usage; "That we could not tell what to say: for we wanted words to express our thanks; and his noble free offers left us nothing to ask. It seemed to us that we had before us a picture of our salvation in heaven; for we that were awhile since in the jaws of death, were now brought into a place where we found nothing but consolations. For the commandment laid upon us, we would not fail to obey it, though it was impossible but our hearts should be inflamed to tread further upon this happy and holy ground." We added; "That our tongues should first cleave to the roofs of our mouths, ere we should forget either his reverend person or this whole nation in our prayers." We also most humbly besought him to accept of us as his true servants, by as just a right as ever men on earth were bounden; laying and presenting both our persons and all we had at his feet. He said; "He was a priest, and looked for a priest's reward: which was our brotherly love and the good of our souls and bodies." So he went from us, not without tears of tenderness in his eyes; and left us also confused with joy and kindness, saying amongst ourselves, "That we were come into a land of angels, which did appear to us daily and prevent us with comforts, which we thought not of, much less expected."

The next day, about ten of the clock, the governor came to us again, and after salutations said familiarly, "That he was come to visit us"; and called for a chair, and sat him down: and we, being some ten of us, (the rest were of the meaner sort, or else gone abroad,) sat down with him. And when we were set, he began thus: "We of this island of Bensalem," (for so they call it in their language,) "have this; that by means of our solitary situation, and of the laws of secrecy which we have for our travellers, and our rare admission of strangers, we know well most part of the habitable world, and are ourselves unknown. Therefore because he that knoweth least is fittest to ask questions, it is more reason, for the entertainment of the time, that ye ask me questions, than that I ask you." We answered; "That we humbly thanked him that he would give us leave so to do: and that we conceived by the taste we had already, that there was no worldly thing on earth more worthy to be known than the state of that happy land. But above all," (we said,) "since that we were met from the several ends of the world, and hoped assuredly that we should meet one day in the kingdom of heaven, (for that we were both parts Christians,) we desired to know (in respect that land was so remote, and so divided by vast and unknown seas, from the land where our Saviour walked on earth,) who was the apostle of that nation, and how it was converted to the faith?" It appeared in his face that he took great contentment in this our question: he said, "Ye knit my heart to you, by asking this question in the first place; for it sheweth that you *first seek the kingdom of heaven;* and I shall gladly and briefly satisfy your demand.

"About twenty years after the ascension of our Saviour, it came to pass that there was seen by the people of Renfusa, (a city upon the eastern coast of our island,) within night, (the night was cloudy and calm,) as it might be some mile into the sea, a great pillar of light; not sharp, but in form of a column or cylinder, rising from the sea a great way up towards heaven: and on the top of it was seen a large cross of light, more bright and resplendent than the body of the pillar. Upon which so strange a spectacle, the people of the city gathered apace together upon the sands, to wonder; and so after put themselves into a number of small boats, to go nearer to this marvellous sight. But when the boats were come within about sixty yards of the pillar, they found themselves all bound, and could go no further; yet so as they might move to go about, but might not approach nearer: so as the boats stood all as in a theatre, beholding this light as an heavenly sign. It so fell out, that there was in one of the boats one of the wise men of the society of Salomon's House; which house or college (my good brethren) is the very eye of this kingdom; who having awhile attentively and devoutly viewed and contemplated this pillar and cross, fell down upon his face; and then raised himself upon his knees, and lifting up his hands to heaven, made his prayers in this manner:

"'Lord God of heaven and earth, thou hast vouchsafed of thy grace to those of our order, to know thy works of creation, and the secrets of them; and to discern (as far as appertaineth to the generations of men) between divine miracles, works of nature, works of art, and impostures and illusions of all sorts. I do here acknowledge and testify before this people, that the thing which we now see before our eyes is thy Finger and a true Miracle; and forasmuch as we learn in our books that thou never workest miracles but to a divine and excellent end, (for the laws of nature are thine own laws, and thou exceedest them not but upon great cause,) we most humbly beseech thee to prosper this great sign, and to give us the interpretation and use of it in mercy; which thou dost in some part secretly promise by sending it unto us.'

"When he had made his prayer, he presently found the boat he was in moveable and unbound; whereas all the rest remained still fast; and taking that for an assurance of leave to approach, he caused the boat to be softly and with silence rowed towards the pillar. But ere he came near it, the pillar and cross of light brake up, and cast itself abroad, as it were, into a firmament of many stars; which also vanished soon after, and there was nothing left to be seen but a small ark or chest of cedar, dry, and not wet at all with water, though it swam. And in the fore-end of it, which was towards him, grew a small green branch of palm; and when the wise man had take it with all reverence into his boat, it opened of itself, and there were found in it a Book and a Letter; both written in fine parchment, and wrapped in sindons of linen. The Book contained all the canonical books of the Old and New Testament, according as you have them, (for we know well what the Churches with you receive); and the

Apocalypse itself, and some other books of the New Testament which were not at that time written, were nevertheless in the Book. And for the Letter, it was in these words:

"'I Bartholomew, a servant of the Highest, and Apostle of Jesus Christ, was warned by an angel that appeared to me in a vision of glory, that I should commit this ark to the floods of the sea. Therefore I do testify and declare unto that people where God shall ordain this ark to come to land, that in the same day is come unto them salvation and peace and good-will, from the Father, and from the Lord Jesus.'

"There was also in both these writings, as well the Book as the Letter, wrought a great miracle, conform to that of the Apostles in the original Gift of Tongues. For there being at that time in this land Hebrews, Persians, and Indians, besides the natives, every one read upon the Book and Letter, as if they had been written in his own language. And thus was this land saved from infidelity (as the remain of the old world was from water) by an ark, through the apostolical and miraculous evangelism of St. Bartholomew." And here he paused, and a messenger came, and called him from us. So this was all that passed in that conference.

The next day, the same governor came again to us immediately after dinner and excused himself, saying, "That the day before he was called from us somewhat abruptly, but now he would make us amends, and spend time with us, if we held his company and conference agreeable." We answered, "That we held it so agreeable and pleasing to us, as we forgot both dangers past and fears to come, for the time we heard him speak; and that we thought an hour spent with him, was worth years of our former life." He bowed himself a little to us, and after we were set again, he said; "Well, the questions are on your part." One of our number said, after a little pause; "That there was a matter we were no less desirous to know, than fearful to ask, lest we might presume too far. But encouraged by his rare humanity towards us, (that could scarce think ourselves strangers, being his vowed and professed servants,) we would take the hardiness to propound it: humbly beseeching him, if he thought it not fit to be answered, that he would pardon it, though he rejected it." We said; "We well observed those his words, which he formerly spake, that this happy island where we now stood was known to few, and yet knew most of the nations of the world; which we found to be true, considering they had the languages of Europe, and knew much of our state and business; and yet we in Europe (notwithstanding all the remote discoveries and navigations of this last age,) never heard any of the least inkling or glimpse of this island. This we found wonderful strange; for that all nations have inter-knowledge one of another either by voyage into foreign parts, or by strangers that come to them: and though the traveller into a foreign country doth commonly know more by the eye, than he that stayeth at home can by relation of the traveller; yet both ways suffice to make a mutual knowledge, in some degree, on both parts. But for this island, we never heard tell of any ship of theirs that had been seen to arrive upon any shore of Europe; no, nor of either the East or West Indies; nor yet of any ship of any other part of the world that had made return from them. And yet the marvel rested not in this. For the situation of it (as his lordship said) in the secret conclave of such a vast sea might cause it. But then that they should have knowledge of the languages, books, affairs, of those that lie such a distance from them, it was a thing we could not tell what to make of; for that it seemed to us a condition and propriety of divine powers and beings, to be hidden and unseen to others, and yet to have others open and as in a light to them." At this speech the governor gave a gracious smile, and said; "That we did well to ask pardon for this question we now asked; for that it imported as if we thought this land a land of magicians, that sent forth spirits of the air into all parts, to bring them news and intelligence of other countries." It was answered by us all, in all possible humbleness, but yet with a countenance taking knowledge that we knew that he spake it but merrily, "That we were apt enough to think there was somewhat supernatural in this island; but yet rather as angelical than magical. But to let his lordship know truly what it was that made us tender and doubtful to ask this question, it was not any such conceit, but because we remembered he had given a touch in his former speech, that this land had laws of secrecy touching strangers." To this he said; "You remember it aright; and therefore in that I shall say to you I must reserve some particulars, which it is not lawful for me to reveal; but there will be enough left to give you satisfaction.

"You shall understand (that which perhaps you will scarce think credible) that about three thousand years ago, or somewhat more, the navigation of the world, (specially for remote voyages,) was greater than at this day. Do not think with yourselves that I know not how much it is increased with you within these six-score years: I know it well: and yet I say greater then than now; whether it was, that the example of the ark, that saved the remnant of men from the universal deluge, gave men confidence to adventure upon the waters; or what it was; but such is the truth. The Phœnicians, and especially the Tyrians, had great fleets. So had the Carthaginians, their colony, which is yet further west. Toward the east, the shipping of Egypt and of Palestina was likewise great. China also, and the great Atlantis (that you call America), which have now but junks and canoes, abounded then in tall ships. This island (as appeareth by faithful registers of those times) had then fifteen hundred strong ships, of great content. Of all this there is with you sparing memory, or none; but we have large knowledge thereof.

"At that time, this land was known and frequented by the ships and vessels of all the nations before named. And (as it cometh to pass) they had many times men of other countries, that were no sailors, that came with them; as Persians, Caldeans, Arabians; so as almost all nations of might and fame resorted hither; of whom we have some stirps and little tribes with us at this day. And for our own ships, they went sundry voyages, as well to your Straits, which you call the Pillars of Hercules, as to other parts in the Atlantic and Mediterrane Seas; as to Paquin (which is the same with Cambaline) and Quinzy, upon the Oriental Seas, as far as to the borders of the East Tartary.

"At the same time, and an age after, or more, the inhabitants of the great Atlantis did flourish. For though the narration and description which is made by a great man with you, that the descendants of Neptune planted there; and of the magnificent temple, palace, city, and hill; and the manifold streams of goodly navigable rivers, (which, as so many chains, environed the same site and temple); and the several degrees of ascent whereby men did climb up to the same, as if it had been a *scala cœli* [ladder to heaven]; be all poetical and fabulous: yet so much is true, that the said country of Atlantis, as well that of Peru, then called Coya, as that of Mexico, then named Tyrambel, were mighty and proud kingdoms in arms, shipping, and riches: so mighty, as at one time, (or at least within the space of ten years) they both made two great expeditions; they of Tyrambel through the Atlantic to the Mediterrane Sea; and they of Coya through the South Sea upon this our island. And for the former of these, which was into Europe, the same author amongst you (as it seemeth) had some relation from the Egyptian priest whom he citeth. For assuredly such a thing there was. But whether it were the ancient Athenians that had the glory of the repulse and resistance of those forces, I can say nothing: but certain it is, there never came back either ship or man from that voyage. Neither had the other voyage of those of Coya upon us had better fortune, if they had not met with enemies of greater clemency. For the king of this island (by name Altabin) a wise man and a great warrior, knowing well both his own strength and that of his enemies, handled the matter so, as he cut off their land-forces from their ships; and entoiled both their navy and their camp with a greater power than theirs, both by sea and land; and compelled them to render themselves without striking stroke: and after they were at his mercy, contenting himself only with their oath that they should no more bear arms against him, dismissed them all in safety. But the Divine

Revenge overtook not long after those proud enterprises. For within less than the space of one hundred years, the great Atlantis was utterly lost and destroyed: not by a great earthquake, as your man saith, (for that whole tract is little subject to earthquakes,) but by a particular deluge or inundation; those countries having, at this day, far greater rivers and far higher mountains to pour down waters, than any part of the old world. But it is true that the same inundation was not deep; not past forty foot, in most places, from the ground: so that although it destroyed man and beast generally, yet some few wild inhabitants of the wood escaped. Birds also were saved by flying to the high trees and woods. For as for men, although they had buildings in many places higher than the depth of the water, yet that inundation, though it were shallow, had a long continuance; whereby they of the vale that were not drowned, perished for want of food and other things necessary. So as marvel you not at the thin population of America, nor at the rudeness and ignorance of the people; for you must account your inhabitants of America as a young people; younger a thousand years, at the least, than the rest of the world; for that there was so much time between the universal flood and their particular inundation. For the poor remnant of human seed which remained in their mountains peopled the country again slowly, by little and little; and being simple and savage people, (not like Noah and his sons, which was the chief family of the earth,) they were not able to leave letters, arts, and civility to their posterity; and having likewise in their mountainous habitations been used (in respect of the extreme cold of those regions) to clothe themselves with the skins of tigers, bears, and great hairy goats, that they have in those parts; when after they came down into the valley, and found the intolerable heats which are there, and knew no means of lighter apparel, they were forced to begin the custom of going naked, which continueth at this day. Only they take great pride and delight in the feathers of birds, and this also they took from those their ancestors of the mountains, who were invited unto it by the infinite flights of birds that came up to the high grounds, while the waters stood below. So you see, by this main accident of time, we lost our traffic with the Americans, with whom of all others, in regard they lay nearest to us, we had most commerce. As for the other parts of the world, it is most manifest that in the ages following (whether it were in respect of wars, or by a natural revolution of time,) navigation did every where greatly decay; and specially far voyages (the rather by the use of galleys, and such vessels as could hardly brook the ocean,) were altogether left and omitted. So then, that part of intercourse which could be from other nations to sail to us, you see how it hath long since ceased; except it were by some rare accident, as this of yours. But now of the cessation of that other part of intercourse, which might be by our sailing to other nations, I must yield you some other cause. For I cannot say (if I shall say truly,) but our shipping, for number, strength, mariners, pilots, and all things that appertain to navigation, is as great as ever: and therefore why we should sit at home, I shall now give you an account by itself: and it will draw nearer to give you satisfaction to your principal question.

"There reigned in this island, about nineteen hundred years ago, a King, whose memory of all others we most adore; not superstitiously, but as a divine instrument, though a mortal man; his name was Solamona: and we esteem him as the lawgiver of our nation. This king had a *large heart*, inscrutable for good; and was wholly bent to make his kingdom and people happy. He therefore, taking into consideration how sufficient and substantive this land was to maintain itself without any aid at all of the foreigner; being five thousand six hundred miles in circuit, and of rare fertility of soil in the greatest part thereof; and finding also the shipping of this country might be plentifully set on work, both fishing and by transportations from port to port, and likewise by sailing unto some small islands that are not far from us, and are under the crown and laws of this state; and recalling into his memory the happy and flourishing estate wherein this land then was, so as it might be a thousand ways altered to the worse, but scarce any one way to the better; thought nothing wanted to his noble and heroical intentions, but only (as far as human foresight might reach) to give perpetuity to that which was in his time so happily established. Therefore amongst his other fundamental laws of this kingdom, he did ordain the interdicts and prohibitions which we have touching entrance of strangers; which at that time (though it was after the calamity of America) was frequent; doubting novelties, and commixture of manners. It is true, the like law against the admission of strangers without licence is an ancient law in the kingdom of China, and yet continued in use. But there it is a poor thing; and hath made them a curious, ignorant, fearful, foolish nation. But our lawgiver made his law of another temper. For first, he hath preserved all points of humanity, in taking order and making provision for the relief of strangers distressed; whereof you have tasted." At which speech (as reason was) we all rose up, and bowed ourselves. He went on. "That king also, still desiring to join humanity and policy together; and thinking it against humanity to detain strangers here against their wills, and against policy that they should return and discover their knowledge of this estate, he took this course: he did ordain that of the strangers that should be permitted to land, as many (at all times) might depart as would; but as many as would stay should have very good conditions and means to live from the state. Wherein he saw so far, that now in so many ages since the prohibition, we have memory not of one ship that ever returned; and but of thirteen persons only, at several times, that chose to return in our bottoms. What those few that returned may have reported abroad I know not. But you must think, whatsoever they have said could be taken where they came but for a dream. Now for our travelling from hence into parts abroad, our Lawgiver thought fit altogether to restrain it. So is it not in China. For the Chinese sail where they will or can; which sheweth that their law of keeping out strangers is a law of pusillanimity and fear. But this restraint of ours hath one only exception, which is admirable; preserving the good which cometh by communicating with strangers, and avoiding the hurt; and I will now open it to you. And here I shall seem a little to digress, but you will by and by find it pertinent. Ye shall understand (my dear friends) that amongst the excellent acts of that king, one above all hath the pre-eminence. It was the erection and institution of an Order or Society which we call *Salomon's House;* the noblest foundation (as we think) that ever was upon the earth; and the lanthorn of this kingdom. It is dedicated to the study of the Works and Creatures of God. Some think it beareth the founder's name a little corrupted, as if it should be Solamona's House. But the records write it as it is spoken. So as I take it to be denominate of the King of the Hebrews, which is famous with you, and no stranger to us. For we have some parts of his works which with you are lost; namely, that Natural History which he wrote, of all plants, from the *cedar of Libanus* to the *moss that groweth out of the wall,* and of all *things that have life and motion.* This maketh me think that our king, finding himself to symbolize in many things with that king of the Hebrews (which lived many years before him), honoured him with the title of this foundation. And I am the rather induced to be of this opinion, for that I find in ancient records this Order or Society is sometimes called Salomon's House, and sometimes the College of the Six Days Works; whereby I am satisfied that our excellent king had learned from the Hebrews that God had created the world and all that therein is within six days; and therefore he instituting that House for the finding out of the true nature of all things, (whereby God might have the more glory in the workmanship of them, and men the more fruit in the use of them,) did give it also that second name. But now to come to our present purpose. When the king had forbidden to all his people navigation into any part that was not under his crown, he made nevertheless this ordinance; That every twelve years there should be set forth out of this kingdom two ships, appointed to several voyages; That in either of these ships there should be a mission of three of the Fellows or Brethren of Salomon's

House; whose errand was only to give us knowledge of the affairs and state of those countries to which they were designed, and especially of the sciences, arts, manufactures, and inventions of all the world; and withal to bring unto us books, instruments, and patterns in every kind; That the ships, after they had landed the brethren, should return; and that the brethren should stay abroad till the new mission. These ships are not otherwise fraught, than with store of victuals, and good quantity of treasure to remain with the brethren, for the buying of such things and rewarding of such persons as they should think fit. Now for me to tell you how the vulgar sort of mariners are contained from being discovered at land; and how they that must be put on shore for any time, colour themselves under the names of other nations; and to what places these voyages have been designed; and what places of *rendez-vous* are appointed for the new missions; and the like circumstances of the practique; I may not do it: neither is it much to your desire. But thus you see we maintain a trade, not for gold, silver, or jewels; nor for silks; nor for spices; nor any other commodity of matter; but only for God's first creature, which was *Light:* to have *light* (I say) of the growth of all parts of the world." And when he had said this, he was silent; and so were we all. For indeed we were all astonished to hear so strange things so probably told. And he, perceiving that we were willing to say somewhat but had it not ready, in great courtesy took us off, and descended to ask us questions of our voyage and fortunes; and in the end concluded, that we might do well to think with ourselves what time of stay we would demand of the state; and bade us not to scant ourselves; for he would procure such time as we desired. Whereupon we all rose up, and presented ourselves to kiss the skirt of his tippet; but he would not suffer us; and so took his leave. But when it came once amongst our people that the state used to offer conditions to strangers that would stay, we had work enough to get any of our men to look to our ship, and to keep them from going presently to the governor to crave conditions.

But with much ado we refrained them, till we might agree what course to take.

We took ourselves now for free men, seeing there was no danger of our utter perdition; and lived most joyfully, going abroad and seeing what was to be seen in the city and places adjacent within our tedder; and obtaining acquaintance with many of the city, not of the meanest quality; at whose hands we found such humanity, and such a freedom and desire to take strangers as it were into their bosom, as was enough to make us forget all that was dear to us in our own countries: and continually we met with many things right worthy of observation and relation; as indeed, if there be a mirror in the world worthy to hold men's eyes, it is that country. One day there were two of our company bidden to a Feast of the Family, as they call it. A most natural, pious, and reverend custom it is, showing that nation to be compounded of all goodness. This is the manner of it. It is granted to any man that shall live to see thirty persons descended of his body alive together, and all above three years old, to make this feast; which is done at the cost of the state. The Father of the Family, whom they call the *Tirsan*, two days before the feast, taketh to him three of such friends as he liketh to choose; and is assisted also by the governor of the city or place where the feast is celebrated; and all the persons of the family, of both sexes, are summoned to attend him. These two days the Tirsan sitteth in consultation concerning the good estate of the family. There, if there be any discord or suits between any of the family, they are compounded and appeased. There, if any of the family be distressed or decayed, order is taken for their relief and competent means to live. There, if any be subject to vice, or take ill courses, they are reproved and censured. So likewise direction is given touching marriages, and the courses of life which any of them should take, with divers other the like orders and advices. The governor assisteth, to the end to put in execution by his public authority the decrees and orders of the Tirsan, if they should be disobeyed; though that seldom needeth; such reverence and obedience they give to the order of nature. The Tirsan doth also then ever choose one man from amongst his sons, to live in house with him: who is called ever after the Son of the Vine. The reason will hereafter appear. On the feast-day, the Father or Tirsan cometh forth after divine service into a large room where the feast is celebrated; which room hath an half-pace at the upper end. Against the wall, in the middle of the half-pace is a chair placed for him, with a table and carpet before it. Over the chair is a state, made round or oval, and it is of ivy; an ivy somewhat whiter than ours, like the leaf of a silver asp, but more shining; for it is green all winter. And the state is curiously wrought with silver and silk of divers colours, broiding or binding in the ivy; and is ever of the work of some of the daughters of the family; and veiled over at the top with a fine net of silk and silver. But the substance of it is true ivy; whereof, after it is taken down, the friends of the family are desirous to have some leaf or sprig to keep. The Tirsan cometh forth with all his generation or lineage, the males before him, and the females following him; and if there be a mother from whose body the whole lineage is descended, there is a traverse placed in a loft above on the right hand of the chair, with a privy door, and a carved window of glass, leaded with gold and blue; where she sitteth, but is not seen. When the Tirsan is come forth, he sitteth down in the chair; and all the lineage place themselves against the wall, both at his back and upon the return of the half-pace, in order of their years without difference of sex; and stand upon their feet. When he is set; the room being always full of company, but well kept and without disorder; after some pause there cometh in from the lower end of the room a *Taratan* (which is as much as an herald) and on either side of him two young lads; whereof one carrieth a scroll of their shining yellow parchment; and the other a cluster of grapes of gold, with a long foot or stalk. The herald and children are clothed with mantles of sea-water green satin; but the herald's mantle is streamed with gold, and hath a train. Then the herald with three curtesies, or rather inclinations, cometh up as far as the half-pace; and there first taketh into his hand the scroll. This scroll is the King's Charter, containing gift of revenew, and many privileges, exemptions, and points of honour, granted to the Father of the Family; and is ever styled and directed, *To such an one our well-beloved friend and creditor:* which is a title proper only to this case. For they say the king is debtor to no man, but for propagation of his subjects. The seal set to the king's charter is the king's image, imbossed or moulded in gold; and though such charters be expedited of course, and as of right, yet they are varied by discretion, according to the number and dignity of the family. This charter the herald readeth aloud; and while it is read, the father or Tirsan standeth up, supported by two of his sons, such as he chooseth. Then the herald mounteth the half-pace, and delivereth the charter into his hand: and with that there is an acclamation by all that are present in their language, which is thus much: *Happy are the people of Bensalem.* Then the herald taketh into his hand from the other child the cluster of grapes, which is of gold, both the stalk and the grapes. But the grapes are daintily enamelled; and if the males of the family be the greater number, the grapes are enamelled purple, with a little sun set on the top; if the females, then they are enamelled into a greenish yellow, with a crescent on the top. The grapes are in number as many as there are descendants of the family. This golden cluster the herald delivereth also to the Tirsan; who presently delivereth it over to that son that he had formerly chosen to be in house with him: who beareth it before his father as an ensign of honour when he goeth in public, ever after; and is thereupon called the Son of the Vine. After this ceremony ended, the father or Tirsan retireth; and after some time cometh forth again to dinner, where he sitteth alone under the state, as before; and none of his descendants sit with him, of what degree or dignity soever, except he hap to be of Salomon's House. He is served only by his own children, such as are male; who perform unto him all service of the table upon the knee; and the women only stand about him, leaning against the wall. The room below the half-pace hath tables on the sides for the guests that are bidden; who are served with great and comely order; and towards the end of dinner (which in the greatest feasts with them lasteth never above an hour and an half) there is an hymn sung, varied according to the invention of him that composeth it, (for they have excellent poesy,) but the subject of it is (always) the praises of Adam and Noah and Abraham; whereof the former two peopled the world, and the last was the Father of the Faithful: concluding ever with a thanksgiving for the nativity of our Saviour, in whose birth the births of all are only blessed. Dinner being done, the Tirsan retireth again; and having withdrawn himself alone into a place where he maketh some private prayers, he cometh forth the third time, to give the blessing; with all his descendants, who stand about him as at the first. Then he calleth them forth by one and by one, by name, as he pleaseth, though seldom the order of age be inverted. The person that is called (the table being before removed) kneeleth down before the chair, and the father layeth his hand upon his head, or her head, and giveth the blessing in these words: *Son of Bensalem, (or Daughter of Bensalem,) thy father saith it; the man by whom thou hast breath and life speaketh the word; The blessing of the everlasting Father, the Prince of Peace, and the Holy Dove be upon thee, and make the days of thy pilgrimage good and many.* This he saith to every of them; and that done, if there be any of his sons of eminent merit and virtue, (so they be not above two,) he calleth for them again; and saith, laying his arm over their shoulders, they standing; *Sons, it is well ye are born, give God the praise, and persevere to the end.* And withal delivereth to either of them a jewel, made in the figure of an ear of wheat, which they ever after wear in the front of their turban or hat. This done, they fall to music and dances, and other recreations, after their manner, for the rest of the day. This is the full order of that feast.

By that time six or seven days were spent, I was fallen into strait acquaintance with a merchant of that city, whose name was Joabin. He was a Jew, and circumcised: for they have some few stirps of Jews yet remaining among them, whom they leave to their own religion. Which they may the better do, because they are of a far differing disposition from the Jews in other parts. For whereas they hate the name of Christ, and have a secret inbred rancour against the people amongst whom they live: these (contrariwise) give unto our Saviour many high attributes, and love the nation of Bensalem extremely. Surely this man of whom I speak would ever acknowledge that Christ was born of a Virgin, and that he was more than a man; and he would tell how God made him ruler of the Seraphims which guard his throne; and they call him also the *Milken Way*, and the *Eliah* of the *Messiah*; and many other high names; which though they be inferior to his divine Majesty, yet they are far from the language of other Jews. And for the country of Bensalem, this man would make no end of commending it: being desirous, by tradition among the Jews there, to have it believed that the people thereof were of the generations of Abraham, by another son, whom they call Nachoran; and that Moses by a secret cabala ordained the laws of Bensalem which they now use; and that when the Messiah should come, and sit in his throne at Hierusalem, the king of Bensalem should sit at his feet, whereas other kings should keep a great distance. But yet setting aside these Jewish dreams, the man was a wise man, and learned, and of great policy, and excellently seen in the laws and customs of that nation. Amongst other discourses, one day I told him I was much affected with the relation I had from some of the company, of their custom in holding the Feast of the Family; for that (methought) I had never heard of a solemnity wherein nature did so much preside. And because propagation of families proceedeth from the nuptial copulation, I desired to know of him what laws and customs they had concerning marriage; and whether they kept marriage well; and whether they were tied to one wife? For that where population is so much affected, and such as with them it seemed to be, there is commonly permission of plurality of wives. To this he said, "You have reason for to commend that excellent institution of the Feast of the Family. And indeed we have experience, that those families that are partakers of the blessing of that feast do flourish and prosper ever after in an extraordinary manner. But hear me now, and I will tell you what I know. You shall understand that there is not under the heavens so chaste a nation as this of Bensalem; nor so free from all pollution or foulness. It is the virgin of the world. I remember I have read in one of your European books, of an holy hermit amongst you that desired to see the Spirit of Fornication; and there appeared to him a little foul ugly Æthiop. But if he had desired to see the Spirit of Chastity of Bensalem, it would have appeared to him in the likeness of a fair beautiful Cherubin. For there is nothing amongst mortal men more fair and admirable, than the chaste minds of this people. Know therefore, that with them there are no stews, no dissolute houses, no courtesans, nor any thing of that kind. Nay they wonder (with detestation) at you in Europe, which permit such things. They say ye have put marriage out of office: for marriage is ordained a remedy for unlawful concupiscence; and natural concupiscence seemeth as a spur to marriage. But when men have at hand a remedy more agreeable to their corrupt will, marriage is almost expulsed. And therefore there are with you seen infinite men that marry not, but chuse rather a libertine and impure single life, than to be yoked in marriage; and many that do marry, marry late, when the prime and strength of their years is past. And when they do marry, what is marriage to them but a very bargain; wherein is sought alliance, or portion, or reputation, with some desire (almost indifferent) of issue; and not the faithful nuptial union of man and wife, that was first instituted. Neither is it possible that those that have cast away so basely so much of their strength, should greatly esteem children, (being of the same matter,) as chaste men do. So likewise during marriage, is the case much amended, as it ought to be if those things were tolerated only for necessity? No, but they remain still as a very affront to marriage. The haunting of those dissolute places, or resort to courtesans, are no more punished in married men than in bachelors. And the depraved custom of change, and the delight in meretricious embracements, (where sin is turned into art,) maketh marriage a dull thing, and a kind of imposition or tax. They hear you defend these things, as done to avoid greater evils; as advoutries, deflouring of virgins, unnatural lust, and the like. But they say this is a preposterous wisdom; and they call it *Lot's offer*, who to save his guests from abusing, offered his daughters: nay they say farther that there is little gained in this; for that the same vices and appetites do still remain and abound; unlawful lust being like a furnace, that if you stop the flames altogether, it will quench; but if you give it any vent, it will rage. As for masculine love, they have no touch of it; and yet there are not so faithful and inviolate friendships in the world again as are there; and to speak generally, (as I said before,) I have not read of any such chastity in any people as theirs. And their usual saying is, *That whosoever is unchaste cannot reverence himself*; and they say, *That the reverence of a man's self is, next religion, the chiefest bridle of all vices.*" And when he had said this, the good Jew paused a little; whereupon I, far more willing to hear him speak on than to speak myself, yet thinking it decent that upon his pause of speech I should not be altogether silent, said only this; "That I would say to him, as the widow of Sarepta said to Elias; that he was come to bring to memory our sins; and that I confess the righteousness of Bensalem was greater than the righteousness of Europe." At which speech he bowed his head, and went on in this manner: "They have also many wise and excellent laws touching marriage. They allow no polygamy. They have ordained that none do intermarry or contract, until a month be passed from their first interview. Marriage without consent of parents they do not make void, but they mulct it in the inheritors: for the children of such marriages are not admitted to inherit above a third part of their parents' inheritance. I have read in a book of one of your men, of a Feigned Commonwealth, where the married couple are permitted, before they contract, to see one another naked. This they dislike; for they think it a scorn to give a refusal after so familiar knowledge: but because of many hidden defects in men and women's bodies, they have a more civil way; for they have near every town a couple of pools, (which they call *Adam and Eve's pools*,) where it is permitted to one of the friends of the man, and another of the friends of the woman, to see them severally bathe naked."

And as we were thus in conference, there came one that seemed to be a messenger, in a rich huke, that spake with the Jew: whereupon he turned to me and said; "You will pardon me, for I am commanded away in haste." The next morning he came to me again, joyful as it seemed, and said, "There is word come to the governor of the city, that one of the Fathers of Salomon's House will be here this day seven-night: we have seen none of them this dozen years. His coming is in state; but the cause of his coming is secret. I will provide you and your fellows of a good standing to see his entry." I thanked him, and told him, "I was most glad of the news." The day being come, he made his entry. He was a man of middle stature and age, comely of person, and had an aspect as if he pitied men. He was clothed in a robe of fine black cloth, with wide sleeves and a cape. His under garment was of excellent white linen down to the foot, girt with a girdle of the same; and a sindon or tippet of the same about his neck. He had gloves that were curious, and set with stone; and shoes of peach-coloured velvet. His neck was bare to the shoulders. His hat was like a helmet, or Spanish Montera; and his locks curled below it decently: they were of colour brown. His beard was cut round, and of the same colour with his hair, somewhat lighter. He was carried in a rich chariot without wheels, litter-wise; with two horses at either end, richly trapped in blue velvet embroidered; and two footmen on each side in the like attire. The chariot was all of cedar, gilt, and adorned with crystal; save that the fore-end had pannels of sapphires, set in borders of gold, and the hinder-end the like of emeralds of the Peru colour. There was also a sun of gold, radiant, upon the top, in the midst; and on the top before, a small cherub of gold, with wings displayed. The chariot was covered with cloth of gold tissued upon blue. He had before him fifty attendants, young men all, in white satin loose coats to the mid-leg; and stockings of white silk; and shoes of blue velvet; and hats of blue velvet; with fine plumes of divers colours, set round like hat-bands. Next before the chariot went two men, bare-headed, in linen garments down to the foot, girt, and shoes of blue velvet; who carried the one a crosier, the other a pastoral staff like a sheep-hook; neither of them of metal, but the crosier of balm-wood, the pastoral staff of cedar. Horsemen he had none, neither before nor behind his chariot: as it seemeth, to avoid all tumult and trouble. Behind his chariot went all the officers and principals of the Companies of the City. He sat alone, upon cushions of a kind of excellent plush, blue; and under his foot curious carpets of silk of divers colours, like the Persian, but far finer. He held up his bare hand as he went, as blessing the people, but in silence. The street was wonderfully well kept: so that there was never any army had their men stand in better battle-array, than the people stood. The windows likewise were not crowded, but every one stood in them as if they had been placed. When the shew was past, the Jew said to me; "I shall not be able to attend you as I would, in regard of some charge the city hath laid upon me, for the entertaining of this great person." Three days after, the Jew came to me again, and said; "Ye are happy men; for the Father of Salomon's House taketh knowledge of your being here, and commanded me to tell you that he will admit all your company to his presence, and have private conference with one of you that ye shall choose: and for this hath appointed the next day after to-morrow. And because he meaneth to give you his blessing he hath appointed it in the forenoon." We came at our day and hour, and I was chosen by my fellows for the private access. We found him in a fair chamber, richly hanged, and carpeted under foot, without any degrees to the state. He was set upon a low throne richly adorned, and a rich cloth of state over his head, of blue satin embroidered. He was alone, save that he had two pages of honour, on either hand one, finely attired in white. His under-garments were the like that we saw him wear in the chariot; but instead of his gown, he had on him a mantle with a cape, of the same fine black, fastened about him. When we came in, as we were taught, we bowed low at our first entrance; and when we were come near his chair, he stood up, holding forth his hand ungloved, and in posture of blessing; and we every one of us stooped down, and kissed the hem of his tippet. That done, the rest departed, and I remained. Then he warned the pages forth of the room, and caused me to sit down beside him, and spake to me thus in the Spanish tongue:

"God bless thee, my son; I will give thee the greatest jewel I have. For I will impart unto thee, for the love of God and men, a relation of the true state of Salomon's House. Son, to make you know the true state of Salomon's House, I will keep this order. First, I will set forth unto you the end of our foundation. Secondly, the preparations and instruments we have for our works. Thirdly, the several employments and functions whereto our fellows are assigned. And fourthly, the ordinances and rites which we observe.

"The End of our Foundation is the knowledge of Causes, and secret motions of things; and the enlarging of the bounds of Human Empire, to the effecting of all things possible.

"The Preparations and Instruments are these. We have large and deep caves of several depths: the deepest are sunk six hundred fathom; and some of them are digged and made under great hills and mountains: so that if you reckon together the depth of the hill and the depth of the cave, they are (some of them) above three miles deep. For we find that the depth of a hill, and the depth of a cave from the flat, is the same thing; both remote alike from the sun and heaven's beams, and from the open air. These caves we call the Lower Region. And we use them for all coagulations, indurations, refrigerations, and conservations of bodies. We use them likewise for the imitation of natural mines; and the producing also of new artificial metals, by compositions and materials which we use, and lay there for many years. We use them also sometimes, (which may seem strange,) for curing of some diseases, and for prolongation of life in some hermits that choose to live there, well accommodated of all things necessary; and indeed live very long; by whom also we learn many things.

"We have burials in several earths, where we put divers cements, as the Chineses do their porcellain. But we have them in greater variety, and some of them more fine. We have also great variety of composts, and soils, for the making of the earth fruitful.

"We have high towers; the highest about half a mile in height; and some of them likewise set upon high mountains; so that the vantage of the hill with the tower is in the highest of them three miles at least. And these places we call the Upper Region: accounting the air between the high places and the low, as a Middle Region. We use these towers, according to their several heights and situations, for insolation, refrigeration, conservation; and for the view of divers meteors; as winds, rain, snow, hail; and some of the fiery meteors also. And upon them, in some places, are dwellings of hermits, whom we visit sometimes, and instruct what to observe.

"We have great lakes both salt and fresh, whereof we have use for the fish and fowl. We use them also for burials of some natural bodies: for we find a difference in things buried in earth or in air below the earth, and things buried in water. We have also pools, of which some do strain fresh water out of salt; and others by art do turn fresh water into salt. We have also some rocks in the midst of the sea, and some bays upon the shore, for some works wherein is required the air and vapour of the sea. We have likewise violent streams and cataracts, which serve us for many motions: and likewise engines for multiplying and enforcing of winds, to set also on going divers motions.

"We have also a number of artificial wells and fountains, made in imitation of the natural sources and baths; as tincted upon vitriol, sulphur, steel, brass, lead, nitre, and other minerals. And again we have little wells for infusions of many things, where the waters take the virtue quicker and better than in vessels or basons. And amongst them we have a water which we call Water of Paradise, being, by that we do to it, made very sovereign for health, and prolongation of life.

"We have also great and spacious houses, where we imitate and demonstrate meteors; as snow, hail, rain, some artificial rains of bodies and not of water, thunders, lightnings; also generations of bodies in air; as frogs, flies, and divers others.

"We have also certain chambers, which we call Chambers of Health, where we qualify the air as we think good and proper for the cure of divers diseases, and preservation of health.

"We have also fair and large baths, of several mixtures, for the cure of diseases, and the restoring of man's body from arefaction: and others for the confirming of it in strength of sinews, vital parts, and the very juice and substance of the body.

"We have also large and various orchards and gardens, wherein we do not so much respect beauty, as variety of ground and soil, proper for divers trees and herbs: and some very spacious, where trees and berries are set whereof we make divers kinds of drinks, besides the vineyards. In these we practise likewise all conclusions of grafting and inoculating, as well of wild-trees as fruit-trees, which produceth many effects. And we make (by art) in the same orchards and gardens, trees and flowers to come earlier or later than their seasons; and to come up and bear more speedily than by their natural course they do. We make them also by art greater much than their nature; and their fruit greater and sweeter and of differing taste, smell, colour, and figure, from their nature. And many of them we so order, as they become of medicinal use.

"We have also means to make divers plants rise by mixtures of earths without seeds; and likewise to make divers new plants, differing from the vulgar; and to make one tree or plant turn into another.

"We have also parks and inclosures of all sorts of beasts and birds, which we use not only for view or rareness, but likewise for dissections and trials; that thereby we may take light what may be wrought upon the body of man. Wherein we find many strange effects; as continuing life in them, though divers parts, which you account vital, be perished and taken forth; resuscitating of some that seem dead in appearance; and the like. We try also all poisons and other medicines upon them, as well of chirurgery as physic. By art likewise, we make them greater or taller than their kind is; and contrariwise dwarf them, and stay their growth: we make them more fruitful and bearing than their kind is; and contrariwise barren and not generative. Also we make them differ in colour, shape, activity, many ways. We find means to make commixtures and copulations of different kinds; which have produced many new kinds, and them not barren, as the general opinion is. We make a number of kinds of serpents, worms, flies, fishes, of putrefaction; whereof some are advanced (in effect) to be perfect creatures, like beasts or birds; and have sexes, and do propagate. Neither do we this by chance, but we know beforehand of what matter and commixture what kind of those creatures will arise.

"We have also particular pools, where we make trials upon fishes, as we have said before of beasts and birds.

"We have also places for breed and generation of those kinds of worms and flies which are of special use; such as are with you your silk-worms and bees.

"I will not hold you long with recounting of our brewhouses, bake-houses, and kitchens, where are made divers drinks, breads, and meats, rare and of special effects. Wines we have of grapes; and drinks of other juice of fruits, of grains, and of roots: and of mixtures with honey, sugar, manna, and fruits dried and decocted. Also of the tears or woundings of trees, and of the pulp of canes. And these drinks are of several ages, some to the age or last of forty years. We have drinks also brewed with several herbs, and roots, and spices; yea with several fleshes, and white meats; whereof some of the drinks are such, as they are in effect meat and drink both: so that divers, especially in age, do desire to live with them, with little or no meat or bread. And above all, we strive to have drinks of extreme thin parts, to insinuate into the body, and yet without all biting, sharpness, or fretting; insomuch as some of them put upon the back of your hand will, with a little stay, pass through to the palm, and yet taste mild to the mouth. We have also waters which we ripen in that fashion, as they become nourishing; so that they are indeed excellent drink; and many will use no other. Breads we have of several grains, roots, and kernels: yea and some of flesh and fish dried; with divers kinds of leavenings and seasonings: so that some do extremely move appetites; some do nourish so, as divers do live of them, without any other meat; who live very long. So for meats, we have some of them so beaten and made tender and mortified, yet without all corrupting, as a weak heat of the stomach will turn them into good chylus, as well as a strong heat would meat otherwise prepared. We have some meats also and breads and drinks, which taken by men enable them to fast long after; and some other, that used make the very flesh of men's bodies sensibly more hard and tough, and their strength far greater than otherwise it would be.

"We have dispensatories, or shops of medicines. Wherein you may easily think, if we have such variety of plants and living creatures more than you have in Europe, (for we know what you have,) the simples, drugs, and ingredients of medicines, must likewise be in so much the greater variety. We have them likewise of divers ages, and long fermentations. And for their preparations, we have not only all manner of exquisite distillations and separations, and especially by gentle heats and percolations through divers strainers, yea and substances; but also exact forms of composition, whereby they incorporate almost, as they were natural simples.

"We have also divers mechanical arts, which you have not; and stuffs made by them; as papers, linen, silks, tissues; dainty works of feathers of wonderful lustre; excel-

lent dyes, and many others; and shops likewise, as well
for such as are not brought into vulgar use amongst us as
for those that are. For you must know that of the things
before recited, many of them are grown into use throughout the kingdom; but yet if they did flow from our invention, we have of them also for patterns and principals.

"We have also furnaces of great diversities, and that
keep great diversity of heats; fierce and quick; strong and
constant; soft and mild; blown, quiet; dry, moist; and the
like. But above all, we have heats in imitation of the sun's
and heavenly bodies' heats, that pass divers inequalities
and (as it were) orbs, progresses, and returns, whereby
we produce admirable effects. Besides, we have heats of
dungs, and of bellies and maws of living creatures, and of
their bloods and bodies; and of hays and herbs laid up
moist; of lime unquenched; and such like. Instruments also which generate heat only by motion. And farther,
places for strong insolations; and again, places under the
earth, which by nature or art yield heat. These divers
heats we use, as the nature of the operation which we
intend requireth.

"We have also perspective-houses, where we make
demonstrations of all lights and radiations; and of all
colours; and out of things uncoloured and transparent,
we can represent unto you all several colours; not in rainbows, as it is in gems and prisms, but of themselves single.
We represent also all multiplications of light, which we
carry to great distance, and make so sharp as to discern
small points and lines; also all colorations of light: all de-
lusions and deceits of the sight in figures, magnitudes,
motions, colours: all demonstrations of shadows. We find
also divers means, yet unknown to you, of producing of
light originally from divers bodies. We procure means of
seeing objects afar off; as in the heaven and remote
places; and represent things near as afar off, and things
afar off as near; making feigned distances. We have also
helps for the sight, far above spectacles and glasses in use.
We have also glasses and means to see small and minute
bodies perfectly and distinctly; as the shapes and colours
of small flies and worms, grains and flaws in gems, which

cannot otherwise be seen; observations in urine and blood, not otherwise to be seen. We make artificial rainbows, halos, and circles about light. We represent also all manner of reflexions, refractions and multiplications of visual beams of objects.

"We have also precious stones of all kinds, many of them of great beauty, and to you unknown; crystals likewise; and glasses of divers kinds; and amongst them some of metals vitrificated, and other materials besides those of which you make glass. Also a number of fossils, and imperfect minerals, which you have not. Likewise loadstones of prodigious virtue; and other rare stones, both natural and artificial.

"We have also sound-houses, where we practise and demonstrate all sounds, and their generation. We have harmonies which you have not, of quarter-sounds, and lesser slides of sounds. Divers instruments of music likewise to you unknown, some sweeter than any you have; together with bells and rings that are dainty and sweet. We represent small sounds as great and deep; likewise great sounds extenuate and sharp; we make divers tremblings and warblings of sounds, which in their original are entire. We represent and imitate all articulate sounds and letters, and the voices and notes of beasts and birds. We have certain helps which set to the ear do further the hearing greatly. We have also divers strange and artificial echoes, reflecting the voice many times, and as it were tossing it: and some that give back the voice louder than it came; some shriller, and some deeper; yea, some rendering the voice differing in the letters or articulate sound from that they receive. We have also means to convey sounds in trunks and pipes, in strange lines and distances.

"We have also perfume-houses; wherewith we join also practices of taste. We multiply smells, which may seem strange. We imitate smells, making all smells to breathe out of other mixtures than those that give them. We make divers imitations of taste likewise, so that they will deceive any man's taste. And in this house we contain also a confiture house; where we make all sweet-meats, dry and moist, and divers pleasant wines, milks, broths, and sallets, far in greater variety than you have.

"We have also engine-houses, where are prepared engines and instruments for all sorts of motions. There we imitate and practise to make swifter motions than any you have, either out of your muskets or any engine that you have; and to make them and multiply them more easily, and with small force, by wheels and other means: and to make them stronger, and more violent than yours are; exceeding your greatest cannons and basilisks. We represent also ordnance and instruments of war, and engines of all kinds: and likewise new mixtures and compositions of gun-powder, wildfires burning in water, and unquenchable. Also fireworks of all variety both for pleasure and use. We imitate also flights of birds; we have some degrees of flying in the air; we have ships and boats for going under water, and brooking of seas; also swimming-girdles and supporters. We have divers curious clocks, and other like motions of return, and some perpetual motions. We imitate also motions of living creatures, by images of men, beasts, birds, fishes, and serpents. We have also a great number of other various motions, strange for equality, fineness, and subtilty.

"We have also a mathematical house, where are represented all instruments, as well of geometry as astronomy, exquisitely made.

"We have also houses of deceits of the senses; where we represent all manner of feats of juggling, false apparitions, impostures, and illusions; and their fallacies. And surely you will easily believe that we that have so many things truly natural which induce admiration, could in a world of particulars deceive the senses, if we would disguise those things and labour to make them seem more miraculous. But we do hate all impostures and lies: insomuch as we have severely forbidden it to all our fellows, under pain of ignominy and fines, that they do not shew any natural work or thing, adorned or swelling; but only pure as it is, and without all affectation of strangeness.

"These are (my son) the riches of Salomon's House.

"For the several employments and offices of our fellows; we have twelve that sail into foreign countries, under the names of other nations, (for our own we conceal;) who bring us the books, and abstracts, and patterns of experiments of all other parts. These we call Merchants of Light.

"We have three that collect the experiments which are in all books. These we call Depredators.

"We have three that collect the experiments of all mechanical arts; and also of liberal sciences; and also of practices which are not brought into arts. These we call Mystery-men.

"We have three that try new experiments, such as themselves think good. These we call Pioners or Miners.

"We have three that draw the experiments of the former four into titles and tables, to give the better light for the drawing of observations and axioms out of them. These we call Compilers.

"We have three that bend themselves, looking into the experiments of their fellows, and cast about how to draw out of them things of use and practice for man's life, and knowledge as well for works as for plain demonstration of causes, means of natural divinations, and the easy and clear discovery of the virtues and parts of bodies. These we call Dowry-men or Benefactors.

"Then after divers meetings and consults of our whole number, to consider of the former labours and collections, we have three that take care, out of them, to direct new experiments, of a higher light, more penetrating into nature than the former. These we call Lamps.

"We have three others that do execute the experiments so directed, and report them. These we call Inoculators.

"Lastly, we have three that raise the former discoveries by experiments into greater observations, axioms, and aphorisms. These we call Interpreters of Nature.

"We have also, as you must think, novices and apprentices, that the succession of the former employed men do not fail; besides a great number of servants and attendants, men and women. And this we do also: we have consultations, which of the inventions and experiences which we have discovered shall be published, and which not: and take all an oath of secrecy, for the concealing of those which we think fit to keep secret: though some of those we do reveal sometimes to the state, and some not.

"For our ordinances and rites: we have two very long and fair galleries: in one of these we place patterns and samples of all manner of the more rare and excellent inventions: in the other we place the statua's of all principal inventors. There we have the statua of your Columbus, that discovered the West Indies: also the inventor of ships: your monk that was the inventor of ordnance and of gunpowder: the inventor of music: the inventor of letters: the inventor of printing: the inventor of observations of astronomy: the inventor of works in metal: the inventor of glass: the inventor of silk of the worm: the inventor of wine: the inventor of corn and bread: the inventor of sugars: and all these by more certain tradition than you have. Then have we divers inventors of our own, of excellent works; which since you have not seen, it were too long to make descriptions of them; and besides, in the right understanding of those descriptions you might easily err. For upon every invention of value, we erect a statua to the inventor, and give him a liberal and honourable reward. These statua's are some of brass; some of marble and touch-stone; some of cedar and other special woods gilt and adorned: some of iron; some of silver; some of gold.

"We have certain hymns and services, which we say daily of laud and thanks to God for his marvellous works: and forms of prayers, imploring his aid and blessing for the illumination of our labours, and the turning of them into good and holy uses.

"Lastly, we have circuits or visits of divers principal cities of the kingdom; where, as it cometh to pass, we do publish such new profitable inventions as we think good. And we do also declare natural divinations of diseases, plagues, swarms of hurtful creatures, scarcity, tempests, earthquakes, great inundations, comets, temperature of the year, and divers other things; and we give counsel thereupon what the people shall do for the prevention and remedy of them."

And when he had said this, he stood up; and I, as I had been taught, kneeled down; and he laid his right hand upon my head, and said; "God bless thee, my son, and God bless this relation which I have made. I give thee leave to publish it for the good of other nations; for we here are in God's bosom, a land unknown." And so he left me; having assigned a value of about two thousand ducats, for a bounty to me and my fellows. For they give great largesses where they come upon all occasions.

[THE REST WAS NOT PERFECTED.]

Washington Square Press

A new and growing series presenting distinguished literary works in an inexpensive, well-designed format

• • • • • • • • • • • • • • • •

NOVELS

HAWTHORNE, NATHANIEL, *The House of the Seven Gables*. W 215 (45¢)

HAWTHORNE, NATHANIEL, *The Scarlet Letter*. Afterword by Maxwell Geismar. W 226 (45¢)

READE, CHARLES, *The Cloister and the Hearth*. Introduction by Morris Gall. W 1003 (90¢)

SCOTT, SIR WALTER, *Ivanhoe*. W 219 (45¢)

STEVENSON, ROBERT LOUIS, *Kidnapped*. Introduction and Glossary by Hardy R. Finch. Illustrated. W 234 (45¢)

STEVENSON, ROBERT LOUIS, *Treasure Island*. Introduction by Max J. Herzberg. Illustrated. W 249 (45¢)

TWAIN, MARK, *The Adventures of Huckleberry Finn*. Illustrated. W 242 (45¢)

TWAIN, MARK, *The Adventures of Tom Sawyer*. Illustrated. W 239 (45¢)

TWAIN, MARK, *A Connecticut Yankee in King Arthur's Court*. W 150 (45¢)

WILDER, THORNTON, *The Bridge of San Luis Rey*. W 236 (45¢)

OTHER TITLES NOW IN
WASHINGTON SQUARE PRESS EDITIONS

CRANE, STEPHEN, *Maggie and Other Stories*. Selected and with an Introduction by Austin McC. Fox. W 133 (45¢)

FRANKLIN, BENJAMIN, *Autobiography*. Postscript by Richard B. Morris. W 218 (45¢)

SAINT AUGUSTINE, *Confessions*. Translated by Edward B. Pusey, D.D., Introduction by Harold C. Gardiner, S.J. W 245 (45¢)

SOPHOCLES, *Oedipus the King*. Translated and with an Introduction by Bernard M. W. Knox. W 99 (45¢)

• • • • • • • • • • • • • • •

If your bookseller does not have the titles you want, you may order them by sending retail price, plus 10¢ per book for postage and handling, to: Mail Service Department, Washington Square Press, Inc., 1 West 39th Street, New York 18, N.Y. Please enclose check or money order—not responsible for orders containing cash.

The Folger Library

GENERAL READER'S SHAKESPEARE

Edited by Louis B. Wright, Director,
and Virginia A. LaMar, Executive Secretary, The Folger Shakespeare Library

PUBLISHED BY WASHINGTON SQUARE PRESS, INC.
AVAILABLE IN THIS SERIES:

*Price will be changed to 45¢ on future editions.

FOL-5